CHURCH, WORLD, MISSION

ALEXANDER SCHMEMANN

CHURCH, WORLD, MISSION
Reflections on Orthodoxy
In the West

ST. VLADIMIR'S SEMINARY PRESS
CRESTWOOD, NY 10707
1979

By the Same Author:

For the Life of the World: Sacraments and Orthodoxy
(1963)
The Historical Road of Eastern Orthodoxy
(1963)
Ultimate Questions: An Anthology of Russian Religious Thought
(1965)
Introduction to Liturgical Theology
(1966)
Great Lent
(1969)
Of Water and the Spirit: A Liturgical Study of Baptism
(1974)
Liturgy and Life
(1974)

Library of Congress Cataloging in Publication Data

Schmemann, Alexander, 1921-
  Church, world, mission.

  1. Orthodox Eastern Church—Doctrinal and controversial works—Orthodox Eastern authors—Collected works.
2. Orthodox Eastern Church—Collected works. I. Title.
BX320.2.S29   281.9   79-27597
ISBN 0-913836-49-4

© Copyright 1979
by
ST. VLADIMIR'S SEMINARY PRESS

ISBN 0-913836-49-4

PRINTED IN THE UNITED STATES OF AMERICA
BY
ATHENS PRINTING COMPANY
NEW YORK, NY

CONTENTS

I

THE UNDERLYING QUESTION

> "The time has come for the *crisis*
> (judgment) to begin with the house
> of God."   1 Peter 4:17

1.

The articles and essays collected in this volume were written over a period of more than twenty years, for a great variety of readers, Orthodox as well as non-Orthodox, and more often than not as an *ad hoc* response to, or reflection upon, some event, some development that I considered to be of vital significance for the Orthodox Church. If today, in spite of the somewhat accidental and dated character of these *membra disjecta*, I dare to give them "another chance," it is not so much because of answers they contain or suggest, and which may appear now as then tentative and incomplete, but because of questions I tried to formulate and which, I am convinced, remain as essential and urgent today as they were one or two decades ago.

These questions, as the reader will see, pertain to a wide range of subjects: history, theology, liturgy, canonical order, the ecumenical movement, mission ... What gives them, I hope, a certain inner unity and common perspective is the one underlying question from which, in one way or another, they all stem and to which ultimately they all refer: the question of the destiny of the Orthodox Church in this second half of the twentieth century, in a world radically different from that which shaped our mentality, our thought-forms, indeed our whole life as Orthodox, in a world moreover deeply marked by a

7

spiritual crisis which acquires with each passing year truly
universal dimensions.

I am convinced that this "underlying question," its essence
and its urgency, are rooted primarily in two developments
which, because both are new and unprecedented in the history
of the Orthodox Church, form the focus of a deep crisis permeating today the whole life of our Church. The first development is the tragically spectacular collapse, one after another,
of the old and organic "Orthodox worlds" which only a few
decades ago appeared as the self-evident, natural and permanent "home" and environment of the Orthodox Church —
and not merely their collapse but also their transformation
into the stage for a violent attack launched by an extreme and
totalitarian secularism against religion, against the spiritual
nature and vocation of man. The second is the rapid and
massive growth in the West of the Orthodox diaspora which,
however "accidental" it may have been in its origins, signifies
the end of the isolation of Orthodoxy in, and its total identification with, the "East," and thus the beginning of a new
destiny, in the West and within the context of Western
culture.

It seems to me that even a superficial analysis of these
developments would reveal their exceptional, truly crucial
importance for the Orthodox Church, as the end of one era
and the beginning of another. Indeed, what these two developments bring to an end is not something "accidental," something
marginal to the life of the Church, but that organic correlation
and mutual integration of the Church and a society, a culture,
a way of life shaped and nurtured by the Church, which until
quite recently was the essential and, in fact, the only mode of
the Orthodox Church's relationship to the "world." There
exists, to be sure, a profound difference between the tragic
fate of the Church under the totalitarian and militantly atheistic
regimes of the East and her apparent "success" in the free and
democratic West. This difference, however, ought not to conceal from us a deeper meaning common to both developments,
which makes them into two dimensions, two "expresions" of
the same, radically new and unprecedented situation — a
situation characterized by Orthodoxy's loss of her historical

home, the "Orthodox world"; by her forced divorce from "culture," i.e. from the entire texture of national and social life; and, last but not least, by an imposed encounter with the "West." Indeed, the ideologies in whose name Orthodoxy is persecuted in the "East" and those which in a very subtle yet equally powerful manner challenge her in the "West" not only are Western by their origin but also are, in spite of their differences and their clash with one another, the result — the "crisis" — of Western spiritual and intellectual development and thus fruits of the same, unmistakably Western tree.

Thus the ultimate meaning of our present crisis is that the world in which the Orthodox Church must live today, be it in the East or in the West, is not her world, not even a "neutral" one, but a world challenging her in her very essence and being, a world trying consciously or unconsciously to reduce her to values, philosophies of life and world-views profoundly differently from, if not totally opposed to, her vision and experience of God, man and life. This makes today's crisis infinitely more radical and decisive than the one brought about by the fall of Byzantium in 1453. The Turkish conquest was a political and national catastrophy; it was not the end, not even an "interruption," of the "Orthodox world," i.e. of a culture, a way of life, a world-view integrating religion and life and making them, however imperfectly, into "symphony." For centuries the Orthodox lived under the Turks, yet in their own world, by their own way of life, rooted in their own religious vision. Today that world is gone and that way of life is being swept away by a culture which is not only alien to Orthodoxy but estranged more and more from its own Christian roots.

I have used the word *crisis*, which, as everyone knows, is much abused today. If, however, we use it in its original, and Christian, meaning — as judgment, as a situation calling for choice and decision, for discerning the will of God and for the courage to obey it — then the situation of the Orthodox Church today is truly *critical*. This book is made up of reflections upon and reactions to this crisis and its various aspects and dimensions. It is an attempt, however tentative and incomplete, not only to discern the true meaning of the crisis but also the will of God which it reveals to us.

2.

What worries me, and therefore constitutes the prime motivation behind virtually every article printed here, is not so much the crisis itself, which for reasons explained elsewhere in this book I consider as potentially beneficial for Orthodoxy. It is always good for the Church to be reminded by God that "this world," even when it calls itself Christian, is in fact at odds with the Gospel of Christ, and that "crisis" and the tension created by it are, after all, the only "normal" mode of the Church's relationship with the world, with *any* world. What worries me is the *absence* of such a tension from today's Orthodox consciousness, our seeming inability to understand the real meaning of the crisis, to face it and to seek ways of dealing with it.

We see, it is true, the reappearance within the Church of that apocalyptic fringe which regularly emerges at each major "turn" in the Church's earthly pilgrimage with an announcement of the end of the world. But this attitude has never been accepted by the Orthodox Church as expressing her faith, her understanding of the Church's mission in the world. For if the Christian faith is indeed eschatological, it is precisely not apocalyptic. Eschatological means that by her very nature the Church belongs to the *end:* to the ultimate reality of the "world to come," the Kingdom of God. This means that from her very beginning, since the "last and great" day of Pentecost, she has lived in the "last days," in the light of the Kingdom, and that her real life is always "hidden with Christ in God." This means also that it is precisely her knowledge and constant partaking of the "end" that *relates* the Church to the world, creates that correlation between the *now* and the *not yet* which is the very essence of her message to the world and also the only source of the "victory that overcomes the world." Apocalypticism, on the other hand, is truly a heresy, for it is the rejection of Christian eschatology, its replacement with

Manichean dualism, the abandonment of that tension between being "in the world" and yet "not of the world" which is constitutive of the Church and of her life. What our neo-apocalyptics do not know is that, in spite of their self-proclaimed exclusive faithfulness to "true Orthodoxy," they are spiritually much closer to certain fringe movements and sects typical of the Western religious landscape than to the catholicity of the Orthodox tradition, with its sobriety and its freedom from emotionalism, fear and reductionism of any kind. Theirs is the typical attitude of "defeatists" who, unable to face the crisis, to discern its true meaning, have been simply crushed by it and, like all their predecessors, seek refuge in the neurotic pseudo-security of the "holy remnant."

But then, what about the "majority"? What about the Orthodox "establishment" — hierarchical, ecclesiastical, theological? Here, precisely because we deal not with some sectarian deviation but with the Church herself, the situation seems to me to be even more serious. The attitude of this "establishment" is that of a simple denial, conscious or unconscious, of any significant crisis. Someone has once half-jokingly remarked that our Greek brothers still do not know that in 1453 Constantinople was taken by the Turks and since then has been called Istanbul. *Mutatis mutandis* this remark can be extended today to an overwhelming majority of the Orthodox people everywhere. It is as if the radical changes mentioned above were but passing "accidents" with no special significance for, or impact upon, the Church's "business as usual."

This attitude is best expressed and illustrated by the rhetoric which has become virtually the only "official" language of the Orthodox establishment, rhetoric made up of a mixture of unshakeable optimism, obligatory triumphalism and amazing self-righteousness. Those who do not use that language, who dare to raise questions and to express doubts about the state of the Church in a rapidly changing world, are accused of disturbing the peace of the Church, of provoking troubles and, in a word, of undermining Orthodoxy. The very function of that rhetoric lies in its remarkable power to conceal reality by replacing it with a wishful "pseudo-reality," and therefore simply to wipe away the questions which the "real" reality would unavoidably have raised.

Thus, if we take the first of the two major developments mentioned earlier — the collapse of the organic "Orthodox worlds" and the persecution of religion by militant atheism — it becomes, in the "official" interpretation, a temporary victory of "dark forces" after whose imminent defeat the inherently good, faithful and innocent Orthodox nations, purified by sufferings and adorned by their martyrs, shall enthusiastically *return* to the eternal Orthodox ideals and way of life that have once and for all shaped their "souls." As decisive proofs of this forthcoming resurrection, several facts are noted: the survival under totalitarian regimes of the Church as institution, the renewed zeal of the faithful "crowding the churches as never before," the growing interest in religion among the youth and the intelligentsia. . . . Now, each of these facts is in itself true, important and promising. But do they justify the interpretation which so easily transforms an ineffable tragedy into a potential triumph? What is missing here is not only a more sober evalution of the facts themselves: the acknowledgement, for example, that the survival of the Church is paid for by her unprecedented surrender to the state, the ugly servility of her leadership, and the almost total control of her life by the KGB and its many equivalents; the explanation, at least a partial one, of the overcrowded churches by their radical decrease in number (e.g. in Moscow there are some fifty "operating" churches for a population of nearly five million) ; the recognition that the religious awakening among the young and the intelligentsia leads them not only to Orthodoxy but, in even greater numbers, to sects, to Zen, to astrology and to virtually every form of the dubious and confused "religiosity" typical nowadays of the West. . . . What is missing in the "official" interpretation is, above all, the preliminary question, encompassing within itself all other questions: *Why and how did all this happen?* Why is it that the "dark forces" of secularism, materialism and atheism, whose roots are ascribed, and not without justification, to the West, have triumphed in fact in the East? Why did the "Orthodox worlds" prove themselves to be so fragile and so vulnerable? Why, for example, is religious resistance so strong in Catholic Poland and by comparison so weak in Orthodox lands? But these questions are not raised because all of them in some way or another imply and presuppose *questioning the past*, i.e. that mythical "golden age" of Orthodoxy which not only in today's official rhetoric, but on a much deeper level of Orthodox mentality, constitutes the only term of reference, the final destination of all "returns," the unique treasure of the heart's desire. To raise these questions is to face that past, to probe and reevaluate it and, above all, to ask whether the seeds of corruption and decay, of indeed a tragic betrayal of something essential in Orthodoxy, were not at work for a long time in those "Orthodox worlds," making inevitable their spectacular and almost instantaneous collapse.

Even worse — in its blindness, in its insensitivity — is the reaction of our "establishment" to the Orthodox diaspora in the West. Here also the very existence of any serious problem stemming from the implantation of Orthodox churches in a different, and in many ways alien, culture is more often than not simply ignored. The existence, in the first place, of a basic canonical, ecclesiological problem. That ecclesiastically the diaspora has resulted in the coexistence on the same territories, within the same cities, of a dozen of "national" or "ethnic" jurisdictions, is considered by an overwhelming majority of the Orthodox people as something perfectly normal, as expressive of the very essence of that diaspora whose main vocation, as everyone knows and proudly proclaims, is the preservation of the various "cultural heritages" proper to each "Orthodox world." The existence, in the second place, of a much deeper and more threatening problem: that of the progressive, although often unconscious, surrender of the Orthodox "consciousness" to the secularistic world-view and way of life. For, paradoxical as this may seem, what makes this surrender unconscious and undetected is precisely that very faithfulness to the "heritage" by which one thinks to preserve and to assure the Orthodox "identity." The Orthodox "establishment" and the vast majority of the Orthodox living in the West do not realize that the "heritage" which they claim to preserve is *not* that only heritage which is worth being preserved and lived by: the vision of God, man and life revealed in the Orthodox faith.

It is not even the rich and in many ways deeply Christian culture which grew up from that vision and which would force
us to discern and to face the challenge of the West, but a
miserable reduction of that heritage to a few superficial
"symbols" which, by creating the illusion of faithfulness to
the "faith of our fathers," masks the progressive surrender of
"real life" to the great, and indeed "Western" heresy of our
age: secularism; the surrender not only of "secular" life, but
of the Church's life as well, of her approach be it to faith and
liturgy, to parish administration and pastoral ministry, or to
education and mission.

Our "official rhetoric" ignores all this, and the reason for
this is, once more, the inability of today's Orthodox consciousness to come to terms with the *past*, a fundamental confusion about the true content and meaning of our "heritage"
and thus of Tradition itself. If the Orthodox Church seems
unable to discern the radically new situation in which she
lives, if she is unaware of the new world surrounding and
challenging her, it is because she herself continues to live in
a "world" which, although it no longer exists, still shapes and
determines the Orthodox consciousness. Hence the tragic
nominalism which permeates the entire life of the Church and
prevents her from fulfilling her essential mission, her task of
judging, evaluating, inspiring, changing, transforming the
whole life of man, of generating that creative *tension* between
herself and the world which makes her into "the salt of the
earth." It is with this problem of the past, of its impact on,
and meaning for us today that I deal, however tentatively and
incompletely, in several essays in this book.

3.

In the Orthodox perspective, however, the problem of the
"past" can never be merely a "historical" one, left to the exclusive care of historians. It of necessity implies theology
because it is precisely for theology that the past presents
itself — and not only today but always — as a *problem*. Why?
Because for Orthodoxy the past is the essential channel and

carrier of Tradition, of that continuity and identity of the Church in time and space which establishes her catholicity, reveals her always as the same church, the same faith, the same life. Tradition and past are by no means identical, yet the former comes to us from the latter, so that the true knowledge, i.e. understanding, of Tradition is impossible without the knowledge, i.e. understanding, of the past; just as the true knowledge, i.e. understanding, of the past is impossible without obedience to Tradition. But here two dangers always threaten the Church. The first consists in a simple reduction of Tradition to the past, in such an identification of one with the other that the past as such becomes the content as well as the criterion of Tradition. As for the second danger, it consists in an artificial separation of Tradition from the past by means of their common evaluation in terms of the "present." Here one accepts from the past — and thus makes into "tradition" — only that which is arbitrarily considered to be "acceptable," "valid" and "relevant" today.

To seek the ways of avoiding and overcoming these dangers, of assuring the correct "reading" of Tradition and therefore the proper understanding by the Church of her own past, has always been one of the essential tasks of theology, of the theological calling within the Church. Hence a second question, implied in a second group of articles collected in this volume: How is this task performed by our theology today? My answer to this question also needs a few words of introduction.

The present state of Orthodox theology seems to me to be ambiguous. On the one hand it is impossible to deny that a real theological renaissance has been taking place in the Orthodox Church, which is expressed primarily in the return of our theology to its essential source: the patristic tradition. This "return to the Fathers" has greatly contributed to the progressive liberation of Orthodox theology from the "Western captivity" which for centuries imposed on it intellectual categories and thought forms alien to the Orthodox Tradition. Entire strata of that tradition, such as Palamism, have been literally rediscovered, so that today hardly a study in Orthodoxy would not refer to hesychasm, the philocalic tradition, and the patristic vision in general. The importance of this "renaissance" is self-evident.

On the other hand, I have the strange impression that seldom in the past has our theology been more isolated from the Church. Seldom has it had less impact on her life, has it been so exclusively a "theology for theologians" as today in the Orthodox Church. It was often said that the "westernized" theology taught in Orthodox seminaries in the nineteenth century — for a long time in Latin! — was *divorced* from the Church. This is certainly true if by this we mean its inner alienation from the sources and indeed from the entire "ethos" of the Eastern Tradition. But this is not true of its influence. Its alienation did not prevent that theology from having a profound impact on the Church, on her life, piety, spirituality, etc.— so much so that even today it is that impact which determines for an overwhelming majority of the Orthodox their very approach to the Church and to her religious demands, discipline, worship and sacraments. The best, although ironic, proof of this can be seen in the defense of that "westernized" theology by our ultra-conservatives.

By comparison our present theology, with all its patristic references and inspiration, with all its faithfulness to the Tradition of the Fathers and the Councils, seems to have very little influence even when it is accepted and given proper respect. It is as if the "real" Church did not know what to do with it, how to apply it to her "real" life. Whatever aspect of that life we consider — ecclesiastical government, parish structure, worship, spirituality and even theological education—, they all seem to operate by a "logics," a tradition, a routine having little if anything to do with the tradition rediscovered, studied and exposed in theological books.

Why is this so? The theologians themselves tend to explain this "discrepancy," this generalized indifference towards their work, by the lack of education among the clergy, by the alleged "anti-intellectualism" of the Orthodox laity and by other similar factors, all extrinsic to theology itself. But this explanation, even if it was true in the past, is no longer tenable today. On the one hand, the divorce between theology and life is typical not only of the older generation of clergy but also of bishops and priests who received their theological education in this new (or old) patristic key and who usually are personally involved in promoting Orthodox education. As to the laity, on the other hand, an ever growing number of them have a lively interest in the teachings of the Church, in a more conscious approach to their religion.

The inevitable conclusion is that something must be wrong with theology itself. What is it? It is, I am convinced, its failure to reveal the true meaning and therefore the power, the *saving* and *transforming* power, of the genuine Orthodox Tradition within the context of our present situation, to make it into a consistent critique of, but also an answer to, the values, the world-view and the way of life which stem from today's spiritual and intellectual crisis. It is one thing to "rediscover" the Fathers, their teachings and their "vision." But it is quite another thing, and a much more difficult one indeed, to relate that vision to the real, concrete life, shaped and conditioned as it is now by a totally different vision. Such, however, has always been and still ought to be the proper task of theology. If, by definition, it deals with the "past," this is in order to *transform* the past, to reveal Tradition as being always alive, always operating, "contemporary" in the deepest sense of this word. And of this the Fathers themselves are the best example for by their "theologizing" they exorcized, transformed and Christianized a world and a culture which were as opposed to the "foolishness" of the Gospel as is our world and culture today.

In this task our theology seems to fail. And my suspicion is that it fails because in a very subtle and unconscious way it remains conditioned by a double reduction, *historical* and *intellectual*, inherited from that very "West" which it claims to oppose and to denounce. By "historical" reduction I mean here the limitation of theology — or rather of its sources — to *texts*, to "conceptual" evidence to the exclusion of the living *experience* of the Church, from which the theology of the Fathers stems, to which it refers and bears testimony, without which it cannot be understood in its total and precisely "existential" meaning and significance. Hence the "intellectual" reduction, which consists in dealing with the Fathers as if they were "thinkers" working with concepts and ideas at the

elaboration of a self-contained and a self-explanatory "system."
Hence the transformation of the Fathers into "authorities"
simply to be quoted for a formal justification of ideas, affirmations and even "theologies" whose roots and presuppositions
may have very little, if anything, to do with the Orthodox
faith. There exist today manuals of Orthodox systematic theology with patristic references and quotations on virtually
every page and which, in spite of this, contain the most
"Western" and "scholastic" type of theology I can think of.
The same can be said of the treatment by our theology of other
aspects and dimensions of Tradition: the ecclesiological, the
spiritual, etc. Here also a formal "re-discovery" seems to lead
nowhere, to remain an idea whose "applications" are not even
to be discussed. It is as if, having found something essential
and precious, we do not know what to do with it except analyze
it in scholarly books and periodicals, from inside an academic
ivory tower standing in the midst of general, although re-
spectful, indifference.

No wonder then that the "real" Church, while paying lip
service to theology — indeed, it has become quite fashionable
today to quote the Fathers and the Philocalia and to have books
on Byzantium in one's library—, virtually ignores it in her
"real" life. And the first to ignore it are the clergy whose very
place and function in the Church make them especially "real-
istic." It is not uncommon for a priest who wrote his seminary
graduation thesis on St. Maximus the Confessor or the
"created" versus "uncreated" grace controversy to seek help
and guidance in his pastoral work in theories of psychotherapy
and in clinical techniques derived from a vision of man totally
different from the one implied in St. Maximus and in the
Orthodox doctrine of grace. What is even more remarkable
is that usually he does not see any incompatibility or conflict
between those two approaches, between the *dogma* one finds
in theological books and the *practice* one learns from the
scientifically proven wisdom of "this world."

The situation is complicated but in reality not significantly
altered by the new wave of religiosity, of passionate interest
in "spirituality" and "mysticism," which seems to succeed today
those obviously exhausted movements of the "death of God,"

"secular Christianity" and "social involvement." Many welcome it as a sign of a genuine religious revival, of a decisive breakdown of secularism. And in terms of *quest*, of "hunger and thirst" for an authentic religious experience, this may be true. Yet how can one fail to see that on a deeper level that wave and that experience remain hopelessly conditioned by the individualism, the narcissism and self-centeredness which constitute the "religious" epiphenomena of secularism itself, of the anthropocentrism inherent to it. The priest who yesterday measured himself against the great idol of our society: the therapist, would now gladly accept the role of the "staretz," but without noticing that this change of titles and "symbols" in fact changes nothing in the religious situation itself.

This situation will last as long as our theology does not overcome its own historical and intellectual "reduction" and recover its pastoral and *soteriological* dimension and motivation. As it operates today it is, in the words of a friend of mine, better and better equipped to fight heresies defeated some fifteen centuries ago, but apparently unable not only to fight but even to detect and to name the real and truly destructive heresies permeating our modern secularistic culture. Strangely enough it supplies them with an "alibi" by covering them up with Christian terminology and—*vice versa*— by introducing concepts and entire categories proper to them into its own terminology and, above all, by assuring that they are not "heresies" but scientifically proven *methods* and *techniques,* which as such cannot contradict any dogma of the Church.

Let there be no mistake: it is not a conversion of our theology to a cheap and superficial "relevance" that is being advocated here, not a transposition of the "Christian message" into terms and concepts supposedly understandable to the "modern man." The disastrous effects of that obsession with "relevance" and the mythical "modern man" in the West need not even be mentioned here. When I speak of the soteriological motivation of theology I have in mind that unique quality proper to patristic theology which makes it an eternal "model" of all true theology: its constant preoccupation with Truth as *saving* and *transforming* Truth, with Truth as a matter truly of life and death, and therefore its awareness of error as a truly demonic lie which distorts and mutilates life itself, leading man to spiritual suicide, literally to hell. This "existentialism" of the Fathers, which is not to be confused or identified with modern philosophical existentialism, stems from the fact that Christianity for them was not primarily an idea or a doctrine, as it would seem from some patrological studies dealing with the "patristic idea" of this and the "patristic doctrine" of that. For the Fathers, Christianity was above all an *experience*, the totally unique and *sui generis* experience of the Church, or even more precisely: *the Church as experience.*

I know that the word "experience" has, especially in the West, strong psychological, individualistic and subjectivistic connotations which in the eyes of many theologians disqualify it as a theological term, relegate it to the always ambiguous area of "religious experience," of *le sentiment religieux*. This is why, when using this word to denote the essential, although more often than not implicit, source and term of reference of all patristic theology as distinct from the "post-patristic," I define that experience as unique and *sui generis*, i.e. as experience which precisely cannot be reduced to the categories of the "subjective" and "objective," "individual" and "corporate." This is the experience of the Church as new reality, new creation, new life — as a reality, in other terms, not of some "other world" but of creation and life renewed and transformed in Christ, made into the knowledge of and the communion with God and His eternal Kingdom. It is this experience — radically new because it is not of "this world," but whose gift and presence, continuity and fulfillment in "this world" is the Church — that for the Fathers constitutes the self-evident source of theology, the source of its very possibility as precisely *theology*, i.e. words adequate to God and adequate therefore to all reality. This experience is the source, but also the "end," the *beyond* to which theology bears witness, whose reality, whose saving and transforming power it proclaims, announces, reveals and defends, and without which the theology of the Fathers cannot be *heard* in its true significance and is "alienated" either into an extrinsic and formal authority to be quoted, or into ideas to be "discussed."

This essential connection and interdependence between patristic theology and the experience of the Church is often ignored because, as has been said more than once, the Fathers do not "theologize" about the Church. They do not seem to be interested in "ecclesiology" as we understand it today: a theological discipline having the Church as the object of its study and investigation, aiming at the elaboration of a full and consistent doctrine of the Church. But the reason for this is that the Church for the Fathers is precisely not the "object" but always the "subject" of theology, the reality which makes it possible to know God and, in Him, man and the world, to know the Way, the Truth, the Life and, therefore, truth about all reality. The appearance of ecclesiology as a separate theological discipline is the fruit of *doubt*, of that need for justification which is inevitable, indeed "normal," in a theology which is itself conceived as "justification" — rational, or philosophical, legal or practical — of the Christian faith and which, as we know only too well today, always leads to (because, in fact, it is rooted in) an evaluation of the "Church" and of her faith and life in terms of the world, of its philosophies, of its trends and of its needs, and thus, ultimately to a surrender to the world. But the Fathers' theological *demarche* is exactly an opposite one. For them it is only in and from the experience of the Church that the world, i.e. man, society, nature, life, can be truly known in its ultimate meaning and "needs" and therefore be "acted upon." They too use the philosophical and cultural categories of the world in which they live, of which they are an integral part. In fact for the most part they speak the "language of their time" better and more consistently than we today speak the language of our time. But when they use it, its meaning changes, its very "semantics" are transformed, it is made into a tool of Christian thought and action, whereas modern theology succeeds at times in forcing even biblical and patristic language to carry ideas hopelessly alien, if not opposed, to the Christian faith and vision.

Thus I am convinced that the "alienation" of theology from the *real* Church and her *real* life always begins with its divorce from the experience of the Church, the Church as experience. By this, as the reader will see, I mean primarily, although not exclusively, the liturgical experience, that *lex orandi* which is the very gift and expression of the Church's experience and which alone therefore transcends the past, the present and the future, which alone actualizes Tradition into life, fulness and power. This does not mean, as some may think, that I advocate a liturgical reduction of theology. Just as they do not theologize about the Church, the Fathers do not theologize about the liturgy. Liturgy as the life, as the "sacrament" of the Church is not the "object" but the source of their theology because it is the epiphany of the Truth, of that fulness from which the "mouth speaks." Rooted in the experience of the Church as *heaven on earth*, the theology of the Fathers is free from "this world" and therefore capable of facing it, of "discerning" and changing it. Divorced from that experience, today's theology appears to live in a permanent identity-crisis, always in search of its own foundations, presuppositions and methods, of its "legitimacy," and therefore with no effect be it in the Church or in the world.

What the "world" needs today — as, indeed, it always needs — is not mere ideas, not even mere "religion." Of both it has plenty, for strange as it may seem *secularism*, the great heresy of our time, is a powerful generator not only of ideas and ideologies but also of "religiosity." It is a widely acknowledged fact that the most "secularized" society of our time — the American — is at the same time the most "religious" one, is truly obsessed with religion in a way in which no other society has ever been. But this "religiosity," like the various "ideologies" clashing with one another, remains wholly conditioned and determined by the secularistic experience and vision of the world, and this even when it preaches and offers an escape into "spirituality" or "utopia." What the world needs, therefore, is above all a new *experience* of the world itself, of life itself in its personal and social, cosmical and eschatological dimensions. Of this experience the Church, in her Orthodox understanding and "experience," is the revelation, the gift and the source. This experience our theology must "rediscover" at its own source, so as to become its witness, its *language* in the Church and in the world.

4.

Such, then, is the thesis underlying explicitly or implicitly the writings collected in this volume, giving it its inner unity. If, however, in an apparent contradiction with that thesis, I often deal with problems pertaining to "external" ecclesiology: councils, canonical order, liturgical practices, etc., it is because of my profound conviction that every attempt to recover the true *experience* of the Church requires, as its very condition, the removal of the one main obstacle which is in fact blocking, and thus obscuring and mutilating that experience. This obstacle is *nominalism*, to which the Orthodox seem so accustomed that for all practical reasons it itself has become a part of our "tradition."

By nominalism I mean here the peculiar divorce of the *forms* of the Church's life from their content, from that reality whose presence, power and meaning they are meant to express and, as a consequence, the transformation of those forms into an end in itself so that the very task of the Church is seen as the preservation of the "ancient," "venerable" and "beautiful" forms, regardless of the "reality" to which they refer. Such divorce, such nominalism indeed permeates the entire life of the Church. In the canonical area it can be seen, for example, in the nominalism of the episcopal *titles*, which in the early Church had a great significance in that they expressed the Church's relation to, and place within the concrete, "real" world into which she is sent. But to what concrete reality correspond the sonorous words adorning the titles of our Patriarchs, primates and bishops: "New Rome," "All the East," "Pope and Judge of the Universe," or the names of the mythical, non-existing cities and lands to whose equally non-existing episcopal sees one can be elected, consecrated and occasionally even transferred? Or, conversely, what does a "real" title referring to a real location — e.g. "bishop of New York" — mean when in fact the jurisdiction claimed is jurisdiction over a particular ethnic group or, even better, people "in exile," i.e. people precisely not identifying themselves with any location? Of the similar, and even greater, nominalism evident in liturgical life (where, for example, the very idea that an

evening service was originally related to the real evening and
thus, together with the entire *liturgy of time*, to real time,
appears to be a totally "irrelevant" one) I have written elsewhere and need not speak here.

What is tragic is the acceptance of that nominalism as
normal, as "expressive" of Orthodoxy itself. We are told
that all this — titles, rites, customs, ceremonies — are *symbolic,*
that together they constitute the "rich symbolism" of which the
Orthodox are to be proud. But the only important question
seems to have been forgotten and ignored: symbolic of *what?*
For what it questions is not the Orthodox attachment to forms,
which is by no means "accidental" for it is rooted in a very
deep, and essentially Orthodox, experience of the Church as
truly an *epiphany:* the revelation of, the participation in, a
reality which because it is not "of this world" is given to us —
in "this world" — in symbols. What it questions is the radical
"deterioration" of the symbol, its progressive disconnection
from that reality, as in fact from all reality. And it is precisely
because *symbolic realism* is so essential to the Christian faith
that there can be no room for any symbolic nominalism in the
Church. Once accepted in any area, however minor, the latter
sooner or later begins to affect the whole life of the Church,
making it, horrible as it may sound, into a *game.* Thus there
is no more urgent task for Orthodox theology than that of
denouncing the nominalism that threatens us from all sides,
and of defending the *true* experience of the Church.

II

THE "ORTHODOX WORLD,"
PAST AND PRESENT

1.

In spite of the ecumenical encounter between the Christian East and the Christian West, an encounter that has lasted now for more than half a century, in spite of an officially acknowledged state of "dialogue," in my opinion it is still very difficult for a Western Christian fully to understand Orthodoxy, and not so much the officially formulated dogmas and doctrines of the Orthodox Church as the fundamental world view, the experience that lies beneath these formulations and constitutes their living and "existential" context. This, of course, is also often true of the Eastern Christian in regard to Western "experience." The difference here, however, is that whereas the West — its intellectual categories, its ethos and culture — has in some form or another permeated the whole world, has truly become universal, the experience of the Christian East is no longer a self-evident component of Western civilization and to a Western man remains extrinsic and even exotic. For us Orthodox one of the most agonizing aspects of the ecumenical encounter lies very often precisely in this inability of the "West" to grasp anything "Orthodox" unless it is reduced to Western categories, expressed in Western terms and more often than not, altered in its true meaning.

I begin with this somewhat harsh observation not only because frankness and sincerity are the *conditio sine qua non* of any genuine ecumenical conversation, but also because this

---

* Originally a lecture given at Villanova University, Villanova, Pennsylvania, in 1968.

fundamental difficulty is nowhere more obvious than in matters pertaining to the immediate and burning issues of Church-world, Church-state and Church-society relationship. Even many Orthodox following the Western dichotomy between "Faith and Order" on the one hand, "Life and Work" on the other, naively think that, the "real" ecumenical difficulties being concentrated in the area of dogma, the area of life or "practical" Christianity presents no major problems. This, I am convinced, is a very naive and superficial assumption, although I concede that it is not easy to show why the recent pronouncements on these issues by the Second Vatican Council, the Uppsala Assembly of the World Council of Churches, and the theologians of "secular Christianity," different as they may be from one another and in spite of some perfectly acceptable points, on the whole are representative of an orientation which is deeply alien to the Orthodox mind and from which the Orthodox "experience" is almost totally absent.

The difficulty is further increased by what to a Western Christian may appear as a rather poor record of Eastern Orthodoxy in the area under consideration. He may ask, and not without justification: Is it a mere "accident" that today some ninety percent of Orthodox people live in totalitarian, atheistic and militantly anti-Christian states? Does this not indicate a failure of the Eastern approach to the problems of the world? And, given that failure, what can the Orthodox contribute to the present passionate search for new or renewed guidelines of Christian action and involvement in and for the world?

To explain the Orthodox "experience," to answer these questions is not easy. They must be answered however, and not for the sake of an "apology" of Orthodoxy, but because in answering them a different perspective, a different set of values may be be disclosed, which is not, it is hoped, totally irrelevant to the problems faced today by Christians everywhere. Now that the crisis of all Christian "establishments" has reached unprecedented proportions and requires, in order to be overcome, a tremendous effort — that of rethinking and reevaluating many of the presuppositions held hitherto to be self-evident—, the Orthodox vision of the world and of the state, as well as of the Church's relation to them, may be of some help.

2.

All historians would probably agree that the long and, more often than not, tragic history of the relations between the Church and the state has passed through three main stages: an open and acute conflict at the beginning, then a reconciliation that led to an organic alliance of the Church with a Christian state and finally, in our own "post-Christian era," a divorce between them resulting either in a more or less peaceful and "legal" separation or in a new conflict. But if these three stages are *grosso modo* common to both the East and the West, the meaning given them, the way they were and still are "experienced," is without any doubt deeply different. Our first purpose, then, is to outline briefly the Eastern experience insofar as it has differed from the Western one.

So much has been written about the conflict between the early church and the Roman Empire that we need not recall the bare facts. One point however, pertaining not to facts but to their interpretation, does require our attention, for on it ultimately depends the understanding of the whole history of the Church-world relationship, of its very basis. It has often been affirmed that the "rejection" of the Empire by the first Christians was rooted primarily in their eschatological worldview, in their expectation of an imminent *parousia*. It is our eschatology that allegedly made the entire outlook of the Church a world-denying one and prevented her from any participation and involvement in the "world." By the same token the subsequent reconciliation with the world, state, society and culture and a new and positive attitude towards them are ascribed to a radical change, a real *volte-face*, in Christian world-view, to its progressive liberation from the eschatological obsession of the earlier period.

This theory, in my opinion, is wrong on two counts: first, in its identification of early Christian eschatology with a mere "world-denying" attitude, and second, in its affirmation that this eschatology therefore had to be, and in fact was, dropped or at least radically altered before a positive Christian approach to the world and its components — state, culture, etc.— could take shape.

The crux of the matter here is the very notion of eschatology, a term so much used and also abused today. It seems to me that no other area of modern theology is more confused than that of eschatology. This confusion may be to some degree explained, if not excused, by the fact that for many centuries Christian theology simply lost its eschatological dimension. There existed, to be sure, in manuals of theology a chapter or rather an appendix entitled "de novissimis," in which all kinds of information about the end of the world and what comes after it were given. What disappeared, however, was eschatology as precisely a dimension, a coefficient of the entire theological enterprise, shaping and permeating the whole Christian faith as its dynamic inspiration and motivation. And thus when at first historians and then theologians rediscovered the tremendous importance that eschatology had in the early Christian faith, they either rejected it as precisely "past" — a passing phenomenon characteristic of the primitive church but of no value for our "scientific" theology — or then began to reinterpret and to "transpose" it according to their own understanding of modern "needs." Hence the paradox of the present situation: Everyone seems to attach a great importance to eschatology — past or present — but there is no consensus as to what it meant in the past and ought to mean for the Church today. To treat this crucially important subject, be it only superficially, is obviously beyond the scope of this paper. But since the whole problem of the Church and the world ultimately depends on it, one must state very briefly our own understanding of the meaning of eschatology in the development of the Eastern "experience."

I submit in the first place that the eschatology in whose light the early church indeed judged and evaluated everything in this world was not a negative, but a highly "positive," experience, not a denial of the world but a certain way of looking at it and experiencing it. For its ultimate content and term of reference was not the world, but the Kingdom of God, and thus rather than being "anti-world" it was a "pro-Kingdom" attitude, in which it differed from eschatologies that developed later. The Kingdom of God — announced, inaugurated and given by and in Christ — stands at the heart of the early Christian faith, and not only as something yet to come but as that which *has come*, is *present now* and *shall come at the end*. It has come in Jesus Christ, in His incarnation, death, resurrection, ascension and in the fruit of all this — the descent of the Holy Spirit on the "last and great" day of Pentecost. It comes now and is present in the Church, the "ecclesia" of those who having died through Christ in baptism can now "walk in the newness of life," partake now of the "joy and peace of the Holy Spirit," eat and drink at Christ's table in His Kingdom. And it shall come at the end, when, having fulfilled all His dispensation, Christ will "fill all things with Himself."

Thus it is the experience of the Kingdom of God and not a mere doctrine "de novissimis" — experience centered on the Church's self-fulfillment in the Eucharist, on the Lord's Day — that permeates the whole faith and the whole life of the early church and, supplying us with the key to the initial Christian attitude towards the world and its "components" — time, nature, society, state, etc.— explains the antinomical character of that attitude, the correlation within it of an emphatic *yes* to the world with an equally emphatic *no*. In the light of the Kingdom, the world is revealed and experienced on the one hand as *being at its end*. And not only because the Kingdom of God, which is the end of all things, has already been revealed and manifested, but also because by rejecting and condemning to death Christ, the Life and the Light of all life, it has condemned itself to die, to be the world whose form and image "fade away" so that the Kingdom of God "is not of this world." This is the Christian *no* to the world and, from the first day, Christianity proclaimed the end of "this world" and required from those who believe in Christ and want to partake of His Kingdom that they be "dead with Christ" and their true life be "hid with Christ in God." Yet, on the other hand, it proclaimed that the world is redeemed and saved in Christ. This means that for those who believe in Christ and are united to Him, this very world — its time and matter, its life, and even death—

have become "means" of communion with the Kingdom of God, the sacrament, i.e. the mode, of its coming and presence among men. "All is yours and you are Christ's." This is the Christian *yes* to the world, the joyful affirmation that "heaven and earth are full of God's glory."

I have tried elsewhere to show how this antinomical correlation of the *yes* and the *no* constitutes the very foundation, the initial *ordo* of the early Christian liturgy.[1] How, for example, the *sui generis* Christian institution of the Lord's Day, the "first" and the "eighth" as the Fathers call it, far from being a Christian substitute for the Jewish Sabbath (this it indeed became in later piety), places all of time in the perspective of the Kingdom, makes it "passage" towards the "day without evening" and thus fills each moment of it with meaning and responsibility; how Eucharist by being primarily the sacrament of the Kingdom, of Christ's *parousia*, i.e. coming and presence, refers the whole cosmos to eschatological fulfillment; how, in short, the fundamental liturgical experience of withdrawal from "this world" (Christ comes "the doors being shut") is understood not in terms of a spiritualistic or apocalyptic "escape," but as the starting point, as indeed the foundation, of Christian mission and action in the world, for it is this experience that makes it possible to see the world in Christ. It is impossible here to reproduce the entire argument. Let me simply state that in the light of the evidence as I see it, the early Christian eschatology, rather than rejecting the world, posits the foundation of a world-view which implies a "positive" attitude towards the world in general, and towards the state in particular.

3.

The state is, to be sure, wholly of "this world." It belongs to the level of reality which in the light of the Kingdom "fades away." This does not mean, however, that it is either evil or neutral, an enemy to be fought or an entity to be ignored for

[1] Cf. my *Introduction to Liturgical Theology* (Faith Press, London, 1966; repr. St. Vladimir's Seminary Press, Crestwood, N.Y., 1977).

the sake of "spiritual values." On the contrary, it is precisely the experience of the Kingdom that for Christians gives the state its real meaning and value. The fall consisted primarily in the disconnection of "this world" from God and in its acquiring therefore a pseudo-meaning and a pseudo-value which is the very essence of the *demonic*, the Devil being "the liar and the father of lies." To redeem the world, or anything in the world, is then to place it in the perspective of the Kingdom of God as its end and ultimate term of reference, to make it transparent to the Kingdom as its sign, means and "instrument." The eschatological world-view of the early church is never a "static" one. There is no trace in it of any distribution of the various essences of this world into good and evil ones. The essence of all that exists is good, for it is God's creation. It is only its divorce from God and its transformation into an idol, i.e. an "end in itself," that makes anything in this world evil and demonic. Thus, as everything else in "this world," the state may be under the power of "the prince of this world." It may become a vehicle of demonic lies and distortions, yet, as everything else, by "accepting" the Kingdom of God as its own ultimate value or "eschaton," it may fulfill a positive function. As an integral part of "this world," it exists under the sign of the end and will not "inherit the Kingdom of God." But its positive and indeed "Christian" function lies in this very recognition of its limit, in this very refusal to be an "end in itself," an absolute value, an idol, in its subordination, in short, to the only absolute value, that of God's Kingdom.

It is well known that from a purely legal point of view the crime for which Christians were condemned and denied the right to exist ("non licet vos esse") was their refusal to honor the emperor with the title of *Kyrios*, Lord. They did not denounce, reject or fight any other "defect" of the Roman Empire be it, to use our modern "fixations," *injustice* (slavery), *colonialism* (the regime of imperial *versus* the senatorial provinces), or *imperialism* (expansion at the expense of other states and nations). Yet what they denounced and fought by denying the emperor the divine title of Kyrios implied in fact much more than all this, for it challenged once and for all the self-proclaimed divinity of the state, its claim to be an absolute value, a divine "end in itself." And it implied therefore not only a negation, but also an affirmation.

In the first place it affirmed the coming into the world, into time and history, of the one and true Kyrios, Jesus Christ. "Thou alone art the Kyrios," says one of the earliest Christian hymns, and this means infinitely more than a general belief in divine providence or a remote divine government of the world. It means that the Kingdom of God has become the decisive factor of the "here and now," of the world's life and history, and that human history develops from now on under the sign of the *kairos*, the direct divine intervention into time and life. It thus lays the foundation for an ecclesiology, a doctrine of the Church, including into its scope and perspective the whole cosmos and the totality of history.

In the second place this denial affirms the state as also belonging to the dominion of the one Kyrios, Jesus Christ. In a deep sense it rejects the "separation" of Church and state, if that separation is understood not in "institutional" or "legal" terms (the only terms ultimately retained in the West) but in those of a common perspective, a common reference to the same "end." Limited as it is by its belonging to "this world," the state is nevertheless capable of reflecting the ideal of the Kingdom, of living by it, of truly serving the Kyrios of the universe. Early Christian writings are surprisingly free from either cosmical or historical "pessimism." They resound on the contrary with a joyful expectation of a cosmic victory of Christ. Nowhere in them does one find any longing for a peaceful isolation of the Church into a purely "spiritual" sphere, a separation from the world and its "worries." Christians know, of course, that they are a "tertium genus." All home is exile for them and all exile a home, but this leads them to no indifference or "neutrality" or pessimism. For their exile is in the Kingdom, and that Kingdom has been revealed in the midst of the world as its true meaning, redemption and salvation.

Finally, that Christian "denial" proclaimed and affirmed the Truth as the very power and "mode of presence" of the Kingdom in "this world," as the criterion for both its negation and its affirmation, as the source of true charity and justice, as

above all the criterion enabling men to "discern the spirits —
whether they are from God. . . ." The question "What is
truth?" of Pontius Pilate and behind him of the whole Roman
Empire implied indeed a distinction and a separation between
Truth on the one hand and Authority on the other; it also
implicitly denied the possibility for man to know the Truth
and to be guided by it. Hence the absolutization of Authority
and the divinization of Caesar. "What is Truth?" asked Pilate,
suggesting the relativity of that concept and *therefore* de-
manding an unconditional obedience to the emperor. "Authority is Truth," such was the significance of that demand.
To it Christians answered by affirming that Truth is Authority.
Such indeed was the meaning of the Christian *martyria*, of the
martyr's blood which ultimately destroyed the greatest, the
most demonic of all idols.

Thus, in my opinion at least, early Christian eschatology,
rather than "rejecting" the state, posited in fact the fundamental principles of the next historical chapter, that of a
"Christian" state. But it posited them only inasmuch as it kept
at the center of its "world-view" the experience of the Kingdom of God.

4.

The different interpretation given that "world-view" by
Western historians and theologians, who consistently view it
as incompatible with the subsequent reconciliation of the
Church with the world, as a particularity of the primitive community soon to disappear under the pressure of reality, is not
accidental. For it is here indeed that lies the fundamental
difference between the two *visions* of the Christian world as
they developed respectively in the West and in the East. I am
convinced that basically, i.e. in vision and intention, in *theoria*
if not always in reality, the Christian East preserved the eschatological perspective of the early church, making it the basis
of its attitude towards the world, whereas the Christian West
replaced it at an early date with a different "vision," whose
main ideological core and context can be termed *juridical.*

Is it not indeed characteristic of Western ecclesiastical development that the relations between Church and state were virtually from the beginning understood, discussed and formulated almost exclusively in juridical or legal terms — as a relation between two *institutions*, two *powers*, two *governments?* Is it not true that in spite of substantial differences, such historical phenomena as the medieval struggle between the Papacy and the Western emperors, Luther's doctrine of the two kingdoms, and the modern theories of separation of Church and state do ultimately belong to the same ideological level, for they all share as their basic presupposition a "juridical" understanding of the problem they try to solve. This legalism moreover is so deeply rooted in the Western ecclesiastical mind that even when trying to understand and to formulate other, non-Western patterns of Church-state relationship, Western historians almost without exception begin by reducing them in some way or another to "juridical" categories. Thus, for example, when speaking of Byzantium, few of them fail to define it as "Caesaropapism," i.e. to view it as a simple case of subordination of the ecclesiastical power to the imperial.

The truth, however, is that another type of Church-state relationship, not exclusively juridical in nature and in its ways of functioning, not only can, but in fact did exist, rooted in the world-view which we termed *eschatological.* Such precisely was the Eastern or Byzantine "type." Just as the initial conflict between the Church and the empire was not a legal, but an "eschatological" one, was focused not on rights and obligations, freedom of conscience or freedom of cult, but on the decisive meaning for the world of one Person, one Event, one Community, the subsequent reconciliation between Church and state could not in the Eastern conscience, or maybe better to say "subconscience," have had any other basis. It is this "eschatological continuity" which, in my opinion, constitutes the starting point and the ultimate term of reference of the entire Eastern "experience." The historical complexity, the tragedies and failures of that experience should by no means be silenced or minimized. But even their meaning cannot be fully grasped unless they are referred to and seen in the light of the experience from which they stem. To define that experience, be it only schematically, is thus our next task.

5.

Rather than with legal texts, this definition must begin with the event which formed the spiritual and psychological foundation of Byzantine "theocracy" and of its continuation in other Orthodox lands, the spectacular conversion to Christianity of the Emperor Constantine.

We are not concerned here with what "really" happened to Constantine on that mysterious afternoon, not even with how he himself understood and later explained it. The unique and indeed crucial significance of that event lies in its acceptance by the Byzantine Christian tradition as the self-evident and sufficient basis for the Church's reconciliation with the empire, or to use a Byzantine term, for their "symphony." Of the many and varied formulations of that acceptance one of the most explicit can be found in Byzantine liturgy, in that cycle of "imperial" feasts and prayers whose constant theme is Constantine's vision of the Cross and its implications for both the Church and the empire. It is here, in this emphasis on the election of Constantine "by God and not by men," that one grasps the continuity of the Byzantine experience with the early, "eschatological" attitude of the Church towards the empire.

"Like Paul, thou hast received the calling not from men. . . ." This in the eyes of the Eastern tradition is the decisive factor in Constantine's conversion. He is called directly by Christ, not even through the Church, and he is chosen not as an "individual," but precisely as emperor, for the event of that election occurs at a crucial moment of his imperial career, his acceptance of Christ being the condition of his victory over his enemies. In him, thus, the empire itself is called to accept Christ and to become His *politeuma*. But this means that in the person of the emperor, the empire acknowledges as its own Kyrios the Lord of heaven and earth, places itself in the perspective and under the dominion of His Kingdom. Thus *ab initio* the alliance between Church and state is based not on any "treaty," bargaining and agreement, not on any detailed definitions of mutual rights and obligations, but on *faith*. One does not "bargain" with God, and it is God who elected Constantine and in him revealed the empire to be part of His "dominion." And in the eyes of the Church this act of faith leading to the new attitude towards the empire not only by no means contradicted the earlier one, but was indeed in full continuity with it. For the Church, when she opposed the empire, did it not because of any political or social principles, not for the sake of any particular doctrine of the state, but uniquely in the name of Christ whom God made the Kyrios of all creation. In other terms, she opposed the demonic "misuse" of the state by the "prince of this world," and her very refusal to acknowledge the emperor as Kyrios implied, as we have said above, a positive attitude towards the state, faith in the possibility for the Messiah to be accepted by the entire "house of Israel." The Church in the Graeco-Roman world never gave up her hope to see it accept Christ and His Kingdom. The heresies she consistently fought were heresies not of exaggerated "optimism" but those of dualism, docetism, escapism and pessimism in all its forms. The conversion of Constantine and its joyful and confident acceptance by the Church meant therefore no change in faith, no alteration of its eschatological content. To use a term forgotten and dismissed today but absolutely essential in the language of the early church, the conversion of the emperor and the empire were of the order of "exorcism." The power of the Cross — the Church's essential weapon against the demons — liberated the empire from the power of the "prince of this world." By crushing the idols, it made the empire "open" to the Kingdom, available as its servant and instrument. But in no way, and this must be stressed, did it transform the empire *into* the Kingdom of God. For it is the property of the early Christian eschatology that, while experiencing the Kingdom of God as an *immanent* factor in the life of "this world," it maintains intact its totally *transcendent* character. It is always the presence in "this world" of the "world to come," never the transformation or the "evolution" of the former into the latter. That this distinc-

tion was fully preserved is proved best of all by the fact that
Constantine received baptism only on his death bed, some
twenty-five years after his "conversion." And when he died on
the day of Pentecost, dressed in his white baptismal garment,
it was as a Christian "neophyte," not as emperor. Later on,
the same symbol was preserved in the monastic tonsure received
by the dying emperors. The empire may be Christian, i.e. serve
the Kingdom, make it its own "highest value," but it is not
and cannot become the Kingdom, which, although always
present in "this world," remains forever "not of this world" —
at its transcendent end as judgement, goal and fulfillment.

6.

To remember all this is essential for the understanding of
Byzantine "symphony." Whatever the motivations of Constantine's policy towards the Church — and they certainly
changed and evolved, whatever the variations of the imperial
raison d'etat — and they were numerous, the Church, as we
said above, asked for no formal or juridical guarantees, no
agreements, but gladly surrendered herself to the care and
protection of him whom Christ Himself chose and appointed
to serve His Kingdom.

It is on purpose that I use here the strong term "surrender."
For it is absolutely true that the Byzantine Church gave up her
"independence" in the juridical connotations of that term.
Administratively, institutionally, she indeed merged with the
empire to form with it but one politico-ecclesiastical organism
and acknowledged the emperor's right to administer her. In
the words of a canonical text, "the administrative structure
of the Church followed that of the empire," and this meant
in fact a rather substantial transformation of the Church's
organization on all levels — the local, the regional and the
"universal." To analyze this transformation here is impossible,
but it is certainly not a mere terminological change that is
attested by the introduction into the ecclesiastical vocabulary
of civil terms such as "diocese," "eparchy," "exarchate," etc.
The spectacular rise of the hitherto unknown bishop of Con-

stantinople to the position of "ecumenical" (i.e. imperial) primacy is explicitly justified at the Second Ecumenical Council by the fact that he "dwells in the city of the emperor and senate." The emperor alone has the right to summon ecumenical councils, he legislates in matters of church discipline and welfare, he appoints bishops, and the formula of the imperial appointment is integrated into the ritual of episcopal consecration.

One could multiply *ad libitum* examples of this "surrender," and to Western historians they constitute unmistakable proofs of Byzantine "Caesaropapism," of the total subjugation of the Church by the state, of the Church's loss of "independence." In fact it is their own subjugation to an exclusively juridical concept of Church-state relationship that prevents them from discerning the true meaning of that relationship in Byzantium, to see it in its own light and according to its own presuppositions. They do not realize that for the Byzantine Church — and precisely because of the eschatological world-view which allowed her to accept Constantine's conversion — the problem of her relations with the empire was situated on an altogether different level where, it can be said in all objectivity, she not only preserved what she meant by her "independence" but, to use Western categories once more, truly "dominated" the empire.

To explain this, an ecclesiological footnote is in order. One of the reasons for the frequent misunderstanding and misinterpretation of Byzantine "symphony" in the West is a surprising ignorance of Orthodox theology and more particularly of Orthodox ecclesiology, the doctrine of the Church. Thus it is very important to understand the difference that exists between the Western and the Eastern approaches to the whole institutional or jurisdictional aspect of the Church. Whereas in the West for a long time and for reasons that we do not have to analyze here, this aspect virtually absorbed the whole of ecclesiology, in the East not only was it far less central, but the very approach to it was different. Here the Church was viewed primarily not as "power" or "jurisdiction," but as a sacramental organism whose function and purpose is to reveal, manifest and communicate the Kingdom of God, to communicate it as Truth, Grace and Communion with God and thus to fulfill the Church as the Body of Christ and the Temple of the Holy Spirit. The Church, to be sure, is *institution*, but of *sacramental*, and not *juridical*, nature. This means that it exists only in order to assure the Church's "passage" from "this world" into "the world to come," as the sign constantly to be fulfilled, as the "means" of the Church becoming all the time "that which she is." Essential as it is for the Church as *sign* and *sacrament*, the institution therefore cannot be simply identified with the Church. As institution the Church is of "this world," as fulfillment she is of "the world to come." This does not mean any separation within the Church between "institution" and "fulfillment," for the whole purpose of the institution is precisely to make fulfillment possible, to reveal as present that which is "to come." The fulfillment is impossible without the institution, just as the institution receives all its meaning from that which it fulfills. What this means, however, is that the Church's visible, institutional structure — episcopate, canonical order, etc.— is a structure not of power, but of *presence*. It exists in order to assure the fullness of that presence and its continuity in space and time, its identity and "sameness" always and everywhere. And this means finally — and we must stress this point — that the Church claims no "power" in this world and has no "earthly" interests to defend. On the one hand, the whole world, the entire creation belong to her because they belong to Christ, the Lord of creation, and are therefore in their totality the object of her mission. Yet, on the other hand, she does not *possess* them as her own "property," for her only mission is to reveal and to "represent," to make present in this world, the Kingdom which is not of this world and for the sake of which those "who possess should be as if they possessed not."

Thus, in the Eastern perspective the relation of the Church to the world is not "juridical" by its very nature and therefore cannot be expressed in juridical terms. There may be and there of necessity are "juridical persons" within the visible, institutional Church — diocese, communities, monasteries, etc. But as such they are "of this world" and, in their relation to the state or society, live according to earthly laws and principles, insofar as these do not prevent the Church from fulfilling her essential mission. If the Church "abides" in a non-Christian state, she claims, as we know already, nothing but the possibility to "be herself," i.e. to preach and to confess Christ, the unique Kyrios, and His Kingdom, to offer salvation to all men everywhere. Yet in the case of a Christian state — the one which by definition shares her "scale of values," her eschatological faith — the Church has no difficulty in leaving to it the "management" of her earthly life, the care and the administration of her earthly needs. And between the two attitudes there is no contradiction, for both are rooted precisely in the same "eschatological ecclesiology," in the same fundamental experience of the Church.

In the light of this "footnote," we may understand now why the basis for Church-state relationship in Byzantium was not a juridical principle but the notion of *Truth*. Juridically, let us repeat once more, the Church indeed "surrendered" herself to the empire and claimed no "independence" from it whatsoever. But — and here is the whole point — the one and absolute condition for that surrender was the acceptance by the empire of the faith of the Church, i.e. of the same ultimate vision of God, world and history; and this we call *Truth*. It was this Truth — expressed in doctrinal formulations, in the essential sacramental order, in worship, and last but not least (a point which we shall elaborate later) in the freedom of each man to "leave" the human society of "this world" for the sake of the Kingdom — that in the eyes of the Church "guaranteed" her real independence, the fulfillment by her of her mission. As long as the empire placed itself under Christ's judgement and in the perspective, essential for the Church, of the Kingdom of God, the Church saw no reason to claim any "juridical" independence from it and, in fact, gladly put the reins of ecclesiastical government and policy in the hands of the emperor. In his care for the Church, in the empire's function as the Church's earthly "habitation," the Church indeed saw the essential vocation of the Christian empire, the very "note" of it being Christian.

But what in their digressions about Byzantine Caesaropapism Western historians seem to overlook is the unique and indeed crucial role played precisely by the notion of Truth within that new relationship. Not only can one say without any exaggeration that the "surrender" always remained contingent on the empire's faithfulness to that Truth, but that, in another sense, it was itself transformed into the Church's "victory," or even into the empire's "surrender" to the Church. Every time the empire "tampered" with the Truth, tried to "adjust" it to its pragmatic needs, the Church, be it only in the person of her best representatives, protested and fought the empire, opposing it whenever necessary with the *martyria* of her blood and suffering. And ultimately each time it was the empire, and not the Church, that "surrendered" and gave up its claims and demands.

From this point of view the great doctrinal controversies which almost without interruption disturbed the life of Byzantium from the fourth century till the ninth, from Arianism to Iconoclasm, were a continuous crisis in Church-state relationship as well as a slow purification of Byzantine "symphony," the growth and deepening of that vision of Christian empire which the Church accepted in the conversion of Constantine. And on this level the real history of the Church was made, her genuine consciousness expressed, not by a perennially weak majority, not by bishops and clerics always ready to pay with a compromise for another state grant or privilege, but by men such as St. Athanasius of Alexandria, the three great Cappadocians, St. John Chrysostom, St. Maximus the Confessor and so many others. Yet — and this is the crucial point — it was their *martyria* that ultimately triumphed. It was they who were "canonized," not only by the Church but also by the empire, as bearers of Orthodoxy. It was their "truth" that sooner or later triumphed and was accepted by the entire Byzantine world.

That the effort of those martyrs and confessors was not lost, that there was a slow but steady purification of the Byzantine mind from the ambiguity of its pagan antecedents, that in other terms the Church progressively imposed her view, her concept of the Christian state, can be seen in Byzantine imperial legislation itself. Neither the code of Theodosius nor that of Justinian are free from the presuppositions and the

categories of the old, pagan "theocracy." Accepted and exalted
as it is, Christianity remains "ontologically" subordinated to
the empire, as the sign and means of its "victory," as a divine
sanction for its existence. From a purely legislative point of
view Christian religion is given the place vacated by the old
state paganism. In a way it is still Christ who is understood as
"serving" the empire. But in the ninth century, in a document
like the *Epanagoge*, or in later imperial iconography, the
situation is altogether changed. It is the emperor who, kneeling
before the Christ-Pantocrator, offers and dedicates to Him
the empire. It is the empire itself which, at least officially and
symbolically, knows no other purpose, no other function but
that of serving Christ and of being His "habitation." This
victory is, beyond any doubt, the fruit of the long fight for
Truth, of the Christian *martyria*, which cleared the initial
ambiguities of pagan theocracy, "exorcised" it from its impure
elements. The very concept of "Orthodoxy," which at the end
of early Byzantium becomes so central in Byzantine consciousness and forms henceforth the basis of all Byzantine "con-
stitutions," is in fact a direct result of that long fight, its most
significant and lasting consequence.

All this is said of course on the level of vision and theory.
In reality, in practice, the theory failed more than once and
was betrayed much too often. There is no need to recall here
the history of these failures. It fills virtually every book on
Byzantium. My purpose here is not to defend Byzantium or
to "idealize" it. Anyone who has consulted any of my other
writings on this subject would readily agree that I am not
guilty of any such idealization. My point here is simply that
to see the history of Byzantine Christianity merely as an example of Caesaropapism, to reduce it to a surrender of Church
to state, is not only to distort significantly the historical evidence, but also to miss, almost completely, the spirit and the
psychological "make-up" of a society, of a "world" which for
more than a thousand years of its existence was Christian, not
only in intention but also in content.

7.

We spoke of intentions. Let us now consider the "content." In what sense, to what degree, can it be termed "Christian"? It is clear, of course, that in the last analysis the answer to this question depends on the meaning given to the adjective "Christian," and it is precisely on this meaning that the mind and the conscience of Christians is deeply split today. The only objective approach therefore is to evaluate a society, an experience, in the light of its own criteria and presuppositions, and then to ask whether any aspect of that experience is of lasting value.

For the Byzantines the term "Christian" as applied to the empire meant, as we have seen, above everything else the acceptance by the empire of a certain "truth," a definite vision of the world and of history. We have satisfied ourselves that the empire indeed had *accepted* that vision. But now the question is: Did it "apply" that vision and live by it? Where is the proof that the Church's understanding and interpretation of Constantine's conversion was not a naive one and that ultimately she was not "fooled" by her partner?

Here again the proof is to be found, first of all, in an event which, in my opinion, is as crucial for the Eastern "experience" of the state as the conversion of the first Christian emperor. This event is *monasticism*, or rather the place and the function it acquired almost immediately in the Byzantine "world-view." Here again, as in the case of Constantine's conversion, we are concerned not with the content of monastic spirituality as such, but with the way in which the monastic ideal was incorporated into the Byzantine tradition.

One can consider as disqualified and abandoned the more or less "radical" theories which some liberal historians of the nineteenth century formulated concerning the origin of monasticism. Several first-rate studies have proved beyond any possible doubt the continuity which in spite of many differences existed between the early monastic ideal and the spirituality of the primitive Church. For us here the main point is that this continuity was precisely that of the eschatological world-view, of the faith centered primarily on the experience, expectation and anticipation of the Kingdom of God. The difference was one of "situation," not of "content." The early Christian community, because of the pagan context within which it lived, was itself in many ways "monastic," as K. Heussi has pointed out. To be separated from the world, one did not need to leave it physically. As to the monastic "exodus" and "anachorisis" of the fourth-fifth centuries, it was motivated by the reaction of the same Christian maximalism to the spiritual dangers created by the "reconciliation" of the Church with the world and, first of all, to the very real danger of a nominal and "easygoing" Christian life. What must be stressed, however, is the almost paradoxical mutual acceptance of monasticism by the empire and of the empire by monasticism, an acceptance which constitutes one of the basic dimensions of the entire Eastern "experience."

On the one hand, for all its maximalism and "world renouncing," monasticism did not either condemn or reject the very principle of the "Christianization" of the world which began with Constantine's conversion. On the contrary it is, in a way, for the sake of that Christian world, in order to keep alive the *martyria*, the testimony to the Kingdom of God by which the world is saved, that the monks "left the world," undertaking their spiritual fight. "How is the Church, how is the empire?" is the first question addressed to a priest who came to visit her in the desert by St. Mary of Egypt, the great hero of Byzantine monastic literature, after she had spent some forty years in total solitude. The question is by no means a merely rhetorical one. Apart from some radical and quasi-Manichean trends, quickly eliminated, the classical monastic tradition is totally alien to any utopianism, millenarianism or sectarianism and is in no way comparable to the later radical sects with their fanatical rejection of the state. Reading the texts in which this tradition was later formulated (cf. the Byzantine *Philokalia*), one is rather amazed by its balance, the absence from it of any exaggeration or "radicalism." The "world" which monks renounce is the one which all Christians, monks and non-monks alike, must renounce, for it is precisely the world which is an end in itself, an "idol" claiming the whole man for itself. The renunciation is based on the same and eternal Christian antinomy: *"in* the world but not *of* the world." In itself, however, this renunciation and constant fight are directed not against the "flesh and blood" of the world, but against the powers of darkness that deviated God's creation from God. They are means of liberation and restoration, not of "negation" and destruction. All students of Eastern mysticism stress the positive, joyful and in a sense "cosmical" spirit that permeates it and which, as late as a century ago, shone so brightly in a simple Russian monk, St. Seraphim of Sarov (d. 1832). It is this spirit, the "joy and peace in the Holy Spirit," that for centuries attracted millions and millions of Orthodox pilgrims to monasteries where, while "in this world," one could taste of the ineffable beauty and bliss of the "world to come." Monasticism thus was in continuation with that same eschatological world-view which made St. Paul and the early Christians, while fighting the imperial "idol," pray for the emperor and the "established powers."

Even more revealing was the attitude towards monasticism of the empire and the society it embodied. The Christian world born out of Constantine's conversion not only did not reject the monastic movement but, in an almost paradoxical way, placed the monastic ideal, the monastic "scale of values," at the very heart of its own life and consciousness. Very soon indeed the "desert" ceased to be limited to the wilderness at the outskirts of the "inhabited world" (*oikoumene*) and implanted itself, in the form of numberless monasteries and convents, in the "downtowns" of big cities, becoming thus the focus of spiritual guidance, leadership and inspiration. The Fathers of the desert became the "heroes" of the entire society and their *vitae*, the "bestsellers" of Byzantine popular literature. The monastic liturgy, the monastic piety invaded and reshaped the liturgy of the whole Church, which, it can be said without any exaggeration, "surrendered" herself to monasticism, just as, in another sense, she surrendered herself to the empire. Monasticism was thus "canonized" by the imperial-ecclesiastical organism as an integral part and expression of that Truth which, as we have seen already, formed the very basis of Byzantine "symphony." And nothing reveals better the depth of that acceptance than the symbolic monastic tonsure of the emperor at his hour of death. This ritual symbolized indeed the "hierarchy of values" acknowledged by the empire, its total subordination to the transcendent Kingdom of God, which the empire as such does not inherit, of which it can be an instrument or servant in "this world," but whose ultimate inheritance requires a total renunciation of everything "earthly."

My emphasis on monasticism as the main expression of the Byzantine world as Christian may seem strange and unconvincing to the "modern" man. What I am trying to say, however, is very simple. This "acceptance" of monasticism meant, in fact, the recognition of the ultimate *freedom* of man, not of course in our modern and formal definition of that term, but as recognition of man's transcendent destiny and vocation, of his belonging to God and to His Kingdom, and not to anything "in this world." It is not an accident that the iconoclastic emperors, the first proponents of a secular idea of both state and culture, led a violent attack not only against icons but also, and maybe primarily, against monasticism. They realized perfectly well that the latter's function within Christian society was precisely to affirm the transcendent freedom of man from the state, to preserve the eschatological world-view which alone makes this world Christian. The iconoclasts failed, as failed all those in the East who tried to reverse the "hierarchy of values." Therefore, it can be said of the empire that whatever its numberless failures, it lived by the "moto" inscribed by Justinian on the altar of Constantinople's St. Sophia: "Thine own Justinian and Theodora offer to Thee."

8.

A "built-in" tension and polarization between the empire and the desert: such could be the adequate definition of the Byzantine spiritual world, the context which makes it Christian. And the fruit of that tension, the tangible result of the Christian *politeuma*, is a civilization, a culture whose depth and meaning are being rediscovered today. This culture, in spite of all its limitations, can indeed be called Christian, not only nominally but essentially. It is a *sui generis* fruit of the Church in "this world." One must remark that Western interest in Byzantine civilization is of a relatively recent date. For too long the cultural and psychological self-centeredness of the West prevented it from seeing in Byzantium anything but an exotic and, to some, fascinating world. It is only today, through the efforts of a small group of Byzantinists, that the various aspects of the Byzantine experience — its art, thought, social and political organization, etc.—slowly begin to recover their place in the Western "curriculum." And although it is evident that there is no room here for even a most superficial description or analysis of that culture, three points which are relevant to the theme of this paper must be made.

I mentioned above the concept of Truth as the basis of the Byzantine theory and practice of Church-state relationship. But it would be wrong to see in this concept a mere set of rigid doctrinal formulations or "symbolic" texts. In reality the concept of Truth permeates the whole life of Byzantine society, constitutes its essential Christian "coefficient." Not by accident the Byzantine period of church history coincides with the patristic age, with the unique and truly unsurpassed effort of the human "logos" to "enter into the Logos of Truth," and, in a *synergeia* with grace, to find words "adequate to God." What from a purely formal point of view was a synthesis between Athens and Jerusalem, Hellenism and Christianity, meant on a deeper level the slow and creative transformation of the mind itself, the moulding of new fundamental thought forms, and not only for theology in the narrow, technical sense of this word, but for the entire intellectual enterprise of man. To the Byzantine mind Christianity is, above all, the revelation of divine Truth but, by the same token, of man's "adequacy" to it, of his ontological ability to receive it, to know it, to appropriate it and to transform it into life. The great theological controversies of the patristic age are never "abstract," never merely "intellectual." They are always *soteriological* and *existential* in their ultimate significance, for they deal with the nature of man, with the meaning of his life, with the goals of his *praxis*. This existential character of patristic theology, the certitude permeating it that Truth is always

Life, the absence from it of any separation of the "theoretical" from the "practical" — all this it may be good to remember today when in the mind of so many Christians the "practical" alone is exalted as if it had no need to be rooted in the *theoria*, the all-embracing vision of God, man and the world. When contemporary Orthodox theologians insist on a "return to the Fathers" (and it seems so often that theirs is a *vox clamans in deserto*), they call precisely to that vision and not to the contingent expressions of a past age. Together with the Fathers they affirm that "it all" ultimately depends on Truth, on knowledge as life and transfiguration. To a modern man, even to a modern Christian, the endless Byzantine debates on the "enhypostaton" or the two wills and two energies in Christ may appear as the very example of the "irrelevant." In the Eastern mind it is in these debates, in efforts to "appropriate" the great theandric mystery, that are to be found the roots and the presuppositions of all truly Christian "humanism," of a Christian vision of the world. To dismiss them as useless for our problems and needs may be the greatest danger for today's Christianity.

The second aspect related to the first one, yet also distinct from it, is the expression, the embodiment of that same Truth as Beauty: the *liturgical* expression of Byzantine civilization. But liturgy here means more than just worship or cult. It is indeed a way of life in which the "sacred" and the "secular" are not disconnected from one another, but the entire life is thought of as a continuation, a "follow-up" of that which is revealed and communicated in worship. For it is the very purpose of worship to manifest the Kingdom of God, to make people taste of its celestial beauty, truth and goodness, and then live, inasmuch as possible, in the light of that unique experience. It is enough to enter St. Sophia of Constantinople, even in its present "kenotic" state, to realize the vision and the experience from which it was born and which it aimed to communicate. It is indeed that of *heaven on earth*, of a Presence which transcends all human experience and categories, yet relates all of them to Itself and reveals the world as Cosmos, in which heaven and earth are truly full of divine glory. The paschal, doxological, "transfigurational" and, at the same time, deeply penitential character of Byzantine liturgy — which includes architecture, iconography, hymnography, time, space, movement, and whose purpose is truly to take the whole man and in a way the whole world into its rhythm and scope — makes it much more than "cult." It is the experience in "this world" of the "world to come." It assumes the whole of creation — matter, sound, color — and transfigures all of it in its sacramental *passage* and *ascension* into the glory of God's presence. As they leave the church, the Orthodox sing: "We have seen the true light, we have received the heavenly Spirit," and it is this light and this participation that are meant to act upon life itself, to transform it, according to one Russian religious thinker, into the "liturgy outside the temple." It is because in the liturgical mystery we are first given to see the *new* creation and to partake of it that we can then be its servants in "this world." When one considers in the light of this Eastern experience the modern liturgical chaos, the confusion about the very nature and purpose of Christian liturgy, one is tempted to say that maybe it is not the liturgy that we ought to make "relevant" to the world, but, on the contrary, it is again in the unique liturgical experience of the Kingdom — its light, truth, beauty and power — that the world could be rediscovered as a "relevant" place for Christian action.

Finally, a third aspect of the Byzantine Christian culture can be adequately termed *ascetical*. Man's sin and alienation from God, the radical illness of "this world," the narrow way of salvation — these are the essential components of Byzantine religious experience, shaping in more than one way the whole life of Byzantine society. It is, as I said already, a "monastic" society in the sense that it accepts the monastic ideal as the self-evident norm and criterion of all Christian life. The doxological spirit of worship, mentioned above, not only does not exclude, but on the contrary implies as its very condition a deep penitential emphasis: "I see Thy bridal chamber adorned, and I have no wedding garment to enter therein. . . ." It would be a mistake however — and I have mentioned it already — to view this ascetical and penitential aspect as made up of fear and pessimism. To be understood properly it must be referred to and judged by its goal: by the theme, central in Eastern spirituality, of *theosis*, the deification of man by the grace of the Holy Spirit. For there is indeed no higher idea of man than the one by which Byzantine society ultimately lives and measures itself. Asceticism here is the "art of arts," for it is the means by which man ascends to his true nature and calling, fulfills his eternal destiny. And if many a "modern" Christian rejects it today as "anti-human" and "anti-social" escapism, it is because this modern Christian for all his obsession with being "man-for-the-other," with serving man and mankind, paradoxically enough does not seem to feel the need to ask the preliminary question: to serve *what* man and for the sake of *what* ultimate destiny of that man? Yet long before the vague terms "freedom" and "liberation" became the *passe-partout* slogans of modernity, they stood — but filled with very concrete, very high and indeed "difficult" meaning — at the very heart of an entire civilization, as its ultimate aspiration and goal.

It is true, of course, that there was much injustice and cruelty in Byzantine society, that by our present standards it was "autocratic" rather than "democratic," that our concepts of freedom and rights were unknown to it. Byzantium most certainly did not solve all its political, economic, social and even "racial" problems. And yet, to use the key word of our modern approach to these problems, there was no *alienation* in that society and this precisely because of the one and unifying *vision* of man, of his nature and destiny, a vision which in spite of all injustice kept the society together, as one body. For in that vision all men were not so much equal as equally destined for the "honor of high calling." This vision they all received, day after day, week after week, in the *leitourgia*, in the common and corporate celebration of and participation in the Kingdom of God. A full — and long overdue — study of the social texture of Byzantine society, a deeper analysis of Byzantine legislation, a fresh approach to Byzantine institutions — in short, a new evaluation, based on the entire evidence, would show, I am sure, that in spite of the apparent rigidity of its social and political system, there existed in Byzantium, and later in other Orthodox lands, a sense of community and interpersonal relationship, a spirit of *philanthropia*, a constant opening towards a full human experience seldom achieved elsewhere. The rich, to be sure, were rich, and the poor much too often remained poor. Yet the poor, and not the rich, stood at the heart of the Byzantine experience as its inspiring ideal. One has only to read the funeral hymns of St. John of Damascus or the Byzantine mariological hymnology to grasp the tremendous wave of compassion and solidarity, mercy and brotherhood that never completely died in the daily existence of the Byzantines. No doubt it was a pre-industrial, "agricultural" and "primitive" society. But whether these definitions invalidate altogether *all* principles on which it was founded and render them totally "irrelevant" for us today, whether furthermore the principles and ideals which have replaced those of Byzantium have not, in fact, mutilated something essential in man and are the main reason for his present "alienation" — all this remains to be seen. Meanwhile it is my certitude that there is no reason to discard disdainfully an "experience" which, when all is said about it, can still teach and inspire us.

9.

The fall of the Byzantine Empire in 1453 by no means meant the end of the Eastern "experience." The latter had its continuation and also a creative development in states and nations which, having received Christianity from Byzantium, received together with it the Byzantine "theocratic" ideal.

Nowhere is this continuity seen better than in the self-identification of each of these nations with a "Constantine" of its own, seeing the fundamental experience of his "conversion" as an act of divine initiative and election. Boris, the first Christian "Kaghan" of Bulgaria, Vladimir, the Baptizer of Kievan Russia, St. Sava, the "Patron" of Orthodox Serbia — each of them remained in the history and memory of his nation as its "father in Christ," as the living symbol of its dedication to Christ's mission in the world. We find here again the same philosophy of history as in Byzantium, rooted in the same "eschatological" perspective in which nations and kingdoms are related to the Church not by "juridical" agreements but by a common "reference" to the ultimate Kingdom. Whatever the political motivations the historian finds behind many of those events, more important is their progressive transformation into a national myth, their interpretation by the nation's consciousness, interpretation which was the decisive factor in shaping the very "psyche" of Orthodox nations.

The Turkish conquest put an early end to the theocratic dreams of the Southern Slavs, and thus it is the Russian "experience" that remains the most significant and creative chapter in the history of the post-Byzantine Orthodox world. Here only a few remarks concerning this chapter can be made.

The Turkish "yoke," by isolating the Orthodox world for many centuries and by depriving it of its freedom, forced it into a kind of "non-historical" survival, into an implicit rejection of history which, as we know, was so central in the Byzantine theocratic consciousness. The sense of the universal mission, of the cosmic and historical scope of the Church, of her dynamic relationship with "this world," of her responsibility for it — all this vanished if not "dogmatically" then at least psychologically, and was replaced with a kind of non-historical "quietism" which came to be viewed, by the Orthodox and non-Orthodox alike, as the "essence" of Orthodoxy. Not noticing the tremendous political and cultural changes, the quick transformation of nearly everything in "this world," the Orthodox continued, and some still continue, to live in an unreal, imaginary, symbolic and purely "static" world, a static "empire," all the more static since, in reality, non-existent. The early "eschatology" which gave birth to that world and whose main content was precisely its "openness" to history and to God's action in it was now "reversed," aimed no longer at present and future, but at one particular "situation" of the past and thus deprived of its meaning. The old imperial cities and ecclesiastical centers — Constantinople, Alexandria, Antioch, now capitals of non-Christian states or sleepy Oriental villages—kept proclaiming their glorious ancient titles or claiming their "rights" as if nothing had happened, as if it were not the very nature of "this world" that its "fashion" always "fades away," as if God's purpose and will were revealed and decisively incarnated once and for all in one particular society, state and culture. The Orthodox historians and theologians, I repeat, do not seem fully to realize the depth of that metamorphosis of the Orthodox consicousness, of the tragic vanishing from it precisely of that which constituted its very foundation. And it is only against the background of that metamorphosis that one can grasp the unique significance and importance of the Russian "chapter."

Russia alone in the whole Orthodox world escaped the isolation and the historical "kenosis" imposed by the Turkish conquest and domination. Its political independence and growth on the one hand, the collapse of Byzantium and of Orthodox "empires" on the other hand, forced upon Russia a new historical awareness, challenged it with problems which in turn shaped its culture. Ultimately that challenge led Russia into a creative rethinking of the initial Byzantine "experience." This, however, would have never been achieved without another challenge, that of the West. For only through a restoration of the universal consciousness and perspective, through a return into "history" itself, could history become again the object of the Church's interest and mission, be related again to the central "experience" of the Kingdom of God. By his radical "Westernization" of Russia at the beginning of the eighteenth century, Emperor Peter the Great imposed on the Russian mind a search for identity, a radical reevaluation of both the "Western" and the "Eastern" historical and religious experiences, united and merged now within the same culture. And it is out of that search, out of its agony and often tragic depth that emerged little by little a vision, a trend, a spiritual and intellectual perspective which permeates and unifies, in spite of all its internal diversity and even polarity, the Russian culture of the nineteenth century and which Berdiaev termed "the Russian Idea."

There is no consensus yet about either the exact content of that "Russian Idea" or its meaning for Orthodox theology. Students of Russian history and culture, theologians and philosophers disagree on it and interpret it each in his own way. To some it means a creative progress of the Orthodox mind itself, to others a dangerous deviation from Byzantine patterns. No one denies, however, the fact itself of a tremendously meaningful spiritual and theological revival in Russia during the last century preceding the collapse of imperial Russia. No one questions its general orientation. And this orientation is precisely towards a new synthesis between *eschatology* and *history*, towards a reintegration of "this world" — of action, creativity and culture — into the perspective of the Kingdom of God. Whatever the value of answers given so far, the questions, the inspiration and the aspirations of that revival bring us back to the starting point of the Christian experience of the world, to the antinomical correlation of the *yes* and the *no* in the attitude towards it. The radiant and paschal spirituality of St. Seraphim of Sarov, the antinomical and prophetic world of Dostoievsky's writings, the daring intuitions of Russian religious thinkers, the dreams of Russian poets — each of these components of the "Russian Idea" can and must be studied, evaluated and interpreted separately. All together, however, they unmistakably reflect and point towards a common vision, challenge us with the same "ultimate questions." And these are about God and the world, the Kingdom and "history." In this sense the Russian spiritual phenomenon is more truly in continuity with the real Eastern and Byzantine tradition, with its eschatological roots and inspiration, than the pseudo-conservatism of those who make Byzantium and the Fathers a closed, rigid and absolute "world in itself," requiring nothing but repetition and archeological cataloguing. This continuity is proved by the facts. It was in Russia indeed that after many centuries of acute "Westernization" Orthodox theology recovered its genuine sources: the patristic thought, the liturgical tradition, the mystical realism of the spiritual *theoria*. It is not an accident that more and more of those who, in the "East" as well as in the "West," are thirsty and hungry for an authentic Christian vision, a vision in which the eternal and transcendent truth would at the same time be truly "relevant" for our age, begin to find it in this Russian "source."

But then what about the question we raised at the beginning of this paper? What about the historical collapse of that "Eastern" world, its catastrophic metamorphosis into the center of atheism and materialism, state totalitarianism and denial of all freedom? Does this not imply a failure also of the "world-view" by which it lived and which, as we tried to show, was its spiritual foundation? In trying to answer these questions, we encounter the last and at present probably the most serious Western misunderstanding of the East, rooted again in the same inability of the Western mind to see the Eastern reality except through Western categories. It is indeed the West, and not the East, not Russia at least, that identifies communism and the Soviet political system with Russia and makes that identification the basic presupposition of all its dealings with the communist world. In Russia itself long before the revolutionary collapse, that collapse was prophesied and then interpreted and understood as precisely a "Western" phenomenon, the result of the rejection by Russia, in the person of both its imperial bureaucracy and its "intelligentsia," of its true historical and spiritual foundation, the result thus of a surrender to alien ideas and "visions." Here the blindness of the West, of its "experts" and "analysts," is simply incredible. They do not seem to realize that if there is anything deeply "anti-Russian" and "anti-Eastern" it is precisely the entire psychological, intellectual and even emotional make-up of men like Lenin and Trotsky, that if there is an example of a total alienation of a group of men from their roots and tradition it is that of "bolsheviks" and that finally, the deep motivation of "Bolshevism" was and still is a real, almost irrational, hatred for "Russia." Maybe if they knew Russian a little better, these "experts" would have discovered that even the Russian language used by the Soviet officialdom is a language deeply, if not radically, alien from that of Russian culture and always sounds like a clumsy translation from a synthetic and unidentified Western prototype.

All this does not mean at all that an attempt is made here to make the West directly responsible for the Russian "collapse" and to present Russia as an innocent victim of a Western "conspiracy." This collapse is a Russian sin and Russia bears the responsibility for it. What I am affirming is that it is a sin *against*, and not a natural outcome and fruit of, the "Russian Idea" mentioned above. The sin itself, however, and this must be said, consisted primarily in a non-critical acceptance of a "Western" and not an "Eastern" idea. It was the acceptance of the specifically Western eschatology without the "eschaton," of the Kingdom without the King, which reduced man to matter alone, society alone, history alone, which closed his spiritual and intellectual horizon with "this world" alone. This reduction of man, his progressive alienation from his divine and transcendent destiny began in the West at the time of the Renaissance, continued through the Enlightenment, and found its fulfillment in the "this-worldly" enthusiastic utopianism of the nineteenth century. And the fact is that throughout the entire nineteenth century, from Chaadaiev to Dostoievsky, it constituted the very focus of the critique of the West by the most creative and original Russian thinkers. Yet at the same time it was more and more enthusiastically endorsed by the "Westernized" Russian intelligentsia. The latter, as Berdiaev well put it, "busied itself not with politics but with saving mankind without God," and this is exactly the scope and content of the Western "secularism" which today begins to engulf Western Christianity itself. It is time to realize that the Russian Revolution and the pseudo-messianic totalitarianism which grew out of it was the triumph on Russian soil of a "Western" idea, the *reductio ad absurdum* of a Western dream, the literal application of a Western program.

That this idea "succeeded" in the "East" and not in the "West," in Russia and not in Western Europe, was due to many complex factors, one of which, it must be conceded, was indeed the initial acceptance by many Russians of the Revolution as fulfilling the "eschatological" aspirations of the Russian people, the interpretation of the "Western" idea in "Eastern" terms, and this in spite of the total and outspoken frankness of the Bolsheviks themselves who systematically and violently rejected such intepretation. In his famous poem *The Twelve*, Alexander Blok, the most celebrated poet of the Russian poetical "renaissance" of the twentieth century, depicted Christ as leading the twelve Red soldiers through storm and snow, blood and murder. But—and this is of crucial importance — while in Russia this confusion came to a quick and tragic end, it lasted and in many ways still lasts in the West, preventing it from seeing the present Russian reality. When he realized the depth of the spiritual lie which in his *The*

Twelve he presented as truth, Blok literally died of despair and while dying kept asking his wife to destroy all copies of his poem. Esenin and Maiakovsky, the two other poets responsible for that confusion, committed suicide. Already in 1924 Berdiaev in his "Reflections on the Russian Revolution" denounced it as totally alien to the true Russian tradition and affirmed that "Russia becomes that which it never was before. . . ." But in the West the myth of the specifically "Russian" (if not "Eastern Orthodox"!) sources and nature of the Soviet reality remains the basic presupposition of all approaches to and dealings with "Russian communism."

The basic fact which the West and even the Christian West, because of its intellectual *a priori*, does not seem to acknowledge is the obvious fact of the *non-acceptance* by the Russian people in their overwhelming majority, and thus by "Russia" itself, of Soviet communism. The evidence supplied by thousands of books and testimonies is so conclusive that, considering the amazing blindness of the West towards it, one is almost tempted to apply the words of the Gospel: "Even if a man rises from the dead, they will not believe. . . ." Ironically enough, it may be a real disappointment for the Western Christians who, with their usual solemnity and seriousness, prepare themselves for a "dialogue" with Marxists to discover some day that there are no Marxists behind the Iron Curtain!

Thus we must reject as nonsense the interpretation of the Russian "collapse" in terms of that Eastern "experience" which we are trying to describe here. What happened in Russia is one event within the great crisis of Western civilization, a crisis which not only has not ended, but today enters its crucial stage. In Russia itself however, beneath the ruins of that spiritual collapse, one begins to detect a new and creative trend towards the recovery of the "Russian Idea" and the Eastern Orthodox sources that fed and shaped it. The return of the "Westernized" Russian intelligentsia to its spiritual fatherland, a return which began before the Revolution but was limited to a few "prophets," becomes today an important, even if silenced, factor in the life of Russia. Solzhenitzyn and other Russian writers, mimeographed publications of the *samizdat*, the renewed interest in Russian religious thought,

and so many other "signs" are an unmistakable proof of all
this as is also, on another level, the truly miraculous survival,
after half a century of persecution, of the Russian Orthodox
Church. It is obviously much too early to write off the Eastern
"experience" or to consider it as disqualified.

10.

If anything is obvious today, it is the impossibility of thinking of the future in terms of a "Christian state" or a "Christian
society." The *secularization* of the world, i.e. its divorce not
only from the Church but from all religious world-views as
well, is a fact and is therefore a self-evident presupposition of
all Christian thinking and planning. It is, however, in approaching and evaluating this phenomenon of secularism, in
reaction to it in thought and action, that the Christian West
and the Christian East, rooted as they are in their respective
"experiences," seem to come once more to different conclusions. To understand this difference, to "compare notes," to
restore if possible a common Christian vision of the world and
of Christian action in it, may constitute today one of the most
important "ecumenical" tasks. As an Orthodox sees him, the
Western Christian is increasingly preoccupied, not to say obsessed, with the world, society, history, etc. This preoccupation
may be "radical" or "moderate," "revolutionary" or "evolu-
tionary"; but a general consensus seems to exist as to the need
for the Church's reorientation towards the world, its needs
and its problems. Hence the acceptance if not of "secularism,"
then at least of the "secular" as the self-evident term of reference for both Christian thought and Christian action, as the
inner motivation and criterion of all Christian "renewal." This
consensus, since it becomes more and more the exclusive context of the ecumenical movement, is forced, so to speak, upon
the Orthodox, and it is here, no doubt, that a new ecumenical
"malaise" is bound to develop even if at present neither the
"Westerners" nor the "Easterners" seem fully to realize this:
the Westerners because they have **always** assumed that their
categories, theological fashions and approaches are *ipso facto*

universal; the Easterners because with a very few exceptions they are theologically silent and ecumenically passive. There is growing evidence, indeed, that behind this silence and this passivity a great majority of the Orthodox cannot help feeling that something is deeply wrong with what, to them at least, appears much more like obsession rather than preoccupation of their Western brothers with the "world" and its problems. So far this feeling has not been expressed in theological terms, given a responsible theological interpretation and justification. As so often happened in the past, the Orthodox reaction is split between, on the one hand, so radical a rejection of the Western approach that it distorts and vitiates Orthodoxy itself by reducing it to a fearfully "apocalyptic" rejection of the world, and, on the other hand, the search for a compromise which, as all compromises, only increases confusion. There is thus an urgent need to transpose this "feeling" into a more articulate and constructive critique, and this can be done only by referring the present Western trend to the Eastern "experience" in its totality.

Our initial distinction in describing the two "experiences" was between the *juridical* and the *eschatological*. We termed "juridical" the Western approach to Church-state relationship as it developed after the conversion of Constantine and the reconciliation of the Church with the empire. Now it must be stressed that this juridical approach was not limited to the state alone, but implied a much wider, in fact an all-embracing, "world-view" which from the Eastern standpoint can be defined as *non-eschatological*. The medieval Christian synthesis in the Latin West was based indeed on a progressive elimination of the Early Christian notion of the Kingdom of God, elimination, of course, not of the term itself but of its initial Christian understanding, as the antinomical presence in "this world" of the "world to come," and of the tension implied in that antinomy. For it is precisely the antinomy and the tension inherent in the patristic notion of *mysterion* that the West eliminated from its approach to faith, from its ultimate "intuition" of God and creation, from sacramental theology and the doctrine of sanctification, from ecclesiology and soteriology. If all the old controversies between the Orthodox East and the Latin

West — those about *Filioque*, original sin, created grace, essence and energies, purgatory, and even the papacy — controversies which to so many today appear totally irrelevant, were
transposed into an "existential" key, explained in terms of their
"practical" significance, it would become clear that their
"common denominator" in the Eastern mind is, first of all,
the rejection by the West of the *mysterion* — the holding-to-
gether, in a mystical and existential, rather than rational, synthesis of both the total *transcendence* of God and His genuine
presence. But this mystery is precisely that of the Kingdom of
God, the faith and the piety of the Church being rooted in the
experience *now* of that which is *to come*, in the communion
by means of "this world" with Him who is always "beyond,"
in truly partaking of "the joy and the peace of the Holy Spirit."

For reasons which we cannot analyze here, the West ra-
tionalized the *mysterion*, i.e. deprived it precisely of its antinomical or eschatological character. It replaced the tension,
essential in the early Church, between the "now" and the "to
come," between the "old" and the "new," with an orderly,
stable, and essentially extra-temporal distinction between the
"natural" and the "supernatural," between "nature" and
"grace"; and then, in order to assure God's total transcendence,
it viewed grace itself not as God's very *presence* but as a created
"medium." Eschatology thus became exclusively "futuristic,"
the Kingdom of God a reality only "to come" but not to be
experienced now as the new life in the Holy Spirit, as real
anticipation of the new creation. Within this new theological
framework, "this world" ceased to be experienced as *passage,*
as "end" to be transfigured into "beginning," as the reality
where the Kingdom of God is "at hand." It acquired a stability,
almost a self-sufficiency, a *meaning* of its own, guaranteed to
be sure by God (*causa prima, analogia entis*), yet at the same
time an autonomous object of knowledge and understanding.
For all its "other-worldliness," the Latin medieval synthesis
was based in fact on the alienation of Christian thought from
its eschatological source, or to put it more bluntly, on its own
"secularization."

Thus even before the formal "liberation" of the world
from the Church's control and dominion, before its "seculari-

zation" in the narrow meaning of that term, the "world" in the West was secularized by Christian thought itself. In the early Christian world-view the notion of "this world" is by no means identical with that of a "secular" world. In its separation from and rebellion against God, "this world" may be a sick, condemned and dying world, it may fall under the dominion of "the prince of the world" into a state of blindness, depravity and corruption, but it is never "autonomous." The term "this world" depicts a state, but not the nature, of creation, and for this reason "this world" is the scene of the eschatological tension between the "old" and the "new" and is capable of being experienced, in Christ, as the transfigured "new creation." Eschatology is thus the very "mode" of the Church's relationship with the world, of her presence and action in it. By abandoning this eschatological perspective, the West rejected in fact the possibility of any real "interpenetration" of the Church and the world, or, in theological terms, of the world's real sanctification. But then the only other possible relationship between the Church and the world is precisely the *juridical* one, in the deepest sense of this term, as a connection in which those who are connected remain ontologically extrinsic to one another. Within this type of relationship, the Church may dominate and govern the world, as she did in medieval society, or she may be legally separated from it, as she is in our modern era. In both cases and situations, the world as such remains essentially "secular."

From this point of view, the "secularization" which began at the Renaissance and continued without interruption throughout the entire "modern" era was in reality a second secularization, or rather a natural and inevitable result of the first one. For it was a "secular" world that the medieval Church dominated politically as well as intellectually. If politically she claimed a power superior to that of the state, and intellectually a source of knowledge superior to human reason, both claims were essentially "juridical," i.e. extrinsic to the nature of that which they claimed to dominate. Secularization changed a relationship of "power," not of "essence." What the "world," i.e. state, society, culture, etc., progressively rejected was an extrinsic submission to the *authority* of the Church, the

Church's ultimate "jurisdiction" over them, but not an essentially "Christian" idea of state, culture, etc. Revolutionary and criminal as this rejection may have appeared to the Church, accustomed as she was to her divine *power*, it meant no radical change in the Western world-view itself. And in this perspective, the Reformation with its radically "secular" concept of the world was in fact more in continuity with the medieval synthesis than post-Tridentine Catholicism with its belated struggle for power, dominion and control.

It follows from all this that the true novelty of the present Western situation lies not in "secularization" as the world's autonomy from the Church's power and not even in "secularization" as culture's autonomy from "religious values." It lies paradoxically enough in the recent acceptance by the Christian West, or at least by Western theology, of what could be termed the *secular eschatology* of the modern secular world. This indeed is the new fact, the true focus of the theological and ecumenical situation in the West. We call this situation paradoxical, for it was, in fact, for the sake of the world's "stability" and "order" that the Western Church gave up her eschatological world-view, replacing it with immovable and absolute norms, making "this world" a well-defined universe with a fixed and closed horizon. As a reward for respecting, i.e. not transgressing, this "law and order," man was given the promise of salvation in the "other world." Provided he preserved that "stability," i.e. kept the required balance between his "secular" and "religious" obligations, man could be at peace with God, the Church and the world. And yet this "solution" did not work. The most ironic and probably the most tragic development of all "Christian" history is this strange mutation of the eschatological world-view from the Church into the secular culture. It was indeed the Church, it was Christian faith, that "poisoned" the human mind with a certain vision and experience of cosmos and time, of matter and history, that made the "world" a notion, an experience correlated to that of the Kingdom of God and challenged man with a kind of "impossible possibility." And it was the Church in the West that "gave up" that vision and replaced it with a universe in which no room was left for history and movement, for the historically unique and irreversible, for the dynamic and disturbing *ruah* of the Spirit. But banished from the Church, the "poison" not only survived, but little by little became the very spirit, the very motivation of the world's "secularization," i.e. liberation from the Church. From the medieval sects and "revivals" through the Renaissance, Enlightenment, Rationalism, Romanticism, and the social and political utopias of the nineteenth century, the idea of the Kingdom stood as the center of the secular mind, but a Kingdom, and here lies the tragedy, progressively deprived of its King, more and more identified with "this world" as such. A secularized eschatology, a faith in the immanent fulfillment by man of his dreams and aspirations, a belief in "history," "justice," "freedom" and other pseudo-absolutes — such was, such still is, the secular faith of the secular man, a faith which miraculously survives and overcomes whatever wave of pessimism and disillusion shakes it at more or less regular intervals.

It is this "secularized eschatology" that the Western Christian, Catholic as well as Protestant, seems not only to accept but to accept on its own terms, i.e. as the criterion of Christian faith and action themselves, as the term of reference of all Christian "renewal," as a valid framework and content of Christian eschatology. As I already pointed out, after centuries of almost total neglect, "eschatology" is becoming again fashionable among Western theologians. The fashion, however, is based not on an interest in the early eschatology in which the transcendent Kingdom of God and not the world is the *eschaton*, but on the desire to find a common language with the secular world. Even where an attempt is made to preserve the transcendent Kingdom, it is preserved as a vague "horizon of hope" and not as the radical *reality* of all Christian experience. The obsession with "relevance" and "involvement," the incredibile discovery of Christ's social and political "radicalism," the enthusiastic "rethinking" of Christianity within the categories of secular utopian ideologies — it all looks as if having at first "secularized" the world for the sake of a totally transcendent God, the Christian West is about to give up the "transcendent" as the very content of Christianity.

11.

In the light of all that has been stated above, it hardly needs to be said that this whole perspective is alien to Eastern Orthodoxy. It is true that until now there has been no consistent and explicit response on the part of the Orthodox, only a general feeling of alarm and anxiety about the seemingly growing surrender of the Christian West to "secularized eschatology." The purpose of this paper, however, was to show, be it only in general terms, that the deep reason for that anxiety is not the often-alleged Orthodox indifference towards the world and its problems, indifference rooted as some Westerners affirm in the "liturgical," "sacramental" and "contemplative" character of Eastern Orthodoxy, but in an entirely different world-view, a different experience and vision of the world itself. We call this world-view *eschatological*, but not in the sense given this term in the deeply Westernized systems of postpatristic theology. This eschatological dimension is to be found in the total experience of the Church and primarily in her liturgical experience as well as in her unbroken spiritual tradition. These indeed were the real sources and the living content of patristic thought, which, when it is isolated from them, simply cannot be understood in its real significance. The ultimate meaning of that world-view can be expressed in a simple formula: to be fully *in* the world, to be of any "use" to it, to fulfill their historical, cosmic and any other "function," the Church and the Christian must be at the same time totally *not* of this world. This "not" implies no negativism, however, no connotations of escape, contempt, quietism, or, in short, no "spiritualistic" indifference. It is a highly positive notion for it means immersion in and partaking of the Kingdom of God, of the spiritual reality already "inaugurated" by the Holy Spirit, already given *now* although yet *to come.* Of this reality the Church, in "this aeon," is the sign and the sacrament, the gift and the promise. Without this reality nothing in this world has any ultimate meaning or value. Thus that which to a Western "activist" appears to be the cause of Eastern "otherworldliness" — the "liturgical," the "sacramental," the "contemplative" — is, in fact, the very condition of any true discovery of the world and the source of any genuine theology of Christian action and involvement in it.

It is in a way irrelevant to ask what a return to that eschatological world-view and experience may mean in "practical" terms, how it can "contribute" to the solution of the world's agonizing problems. The whole point of our argument is that without the recovery of that experience, no clear pattern of Christian thought and action can be detected. As long as the Church is imprisoned by the world and its ideologies, as long as she accepts and views all "problems" facing humanity in their secular and worldly formulations, we remain within a vicious circle without any hope of breaking through it. Before it can be put to any "use," the notion of the Kingdom of God is to be purified of all "utilitarianism." It is when, in the words of an Orthodox eucharistic hymn, we "lay aside all earthly cares" that the world and all its problems may be discovered again as the object of all Christian love, as the stage for Christian mission and action.

One thing, however, can and must be said. Only a recovery by Christians of their eschatology can, in the last analysis, be a response to the "secularized eschatology" of the modern world. One wonders indeed whether the Christian West in its enthusiastic endorsement of that "secularized eschatology" is not in reality misreading and misinterpreting its true significance. While Christians, in their eagerness to be "relevant," shift the emphasis from the "transcendent" to the "immanent," one detects in the world a growing thirst and hunger for that which can *transcend*, i.e. fill life with the ultimate meaning and content. Behind the sometimes cheap and romantically naive rebellion against "systems" and "establishment," behind the rhetoric of "revolution" and "liberation," there is a genuine longing not only for the Absolute but for *communion* with it, for its true possession. Behind the "juridical," it is for the "eschatological" that the modern man is longing, and this means for the Kingdom of God. But have we not "seen the true light," have we not "partaken of the Spirit"? Who else but the Church ought to be able to satisfy that hunger, to name the King and manifest the Kingdom?

III

THE WORLD IN ORTHODOX
THOUGHT AND EXPERIENCE

1.

The very fact that, after almost two thousand years of the Church's presence in the world, we feel compelled to ask ourselves about the meaning of that presence and about the role of theology in expressing it is a clear proof that something has "happened" (to the Church? to the world?) which requires from theology a new effort of reflection, a renewed "reading" of Tradition. What has happened? My purpose in this paper is to attempt to answer this question by trying to locate the problem whose pressure we all feel, and to outline, be it only in very general terms, my understanding of the ways leading to its solution.

Needless to say, my task is not an easy one. In the first place, strange and even paradoxical as this may appear, the very notions whose relation to one another, whose presence in one another, we are to elucidate: i.e. the *Church* and the *world,* have only recently made their appearance in Orthodox theology as objects of specific theological study and analysis, as distinct "chapters" within theological systems. We are just beginning to emerge from a long theological era whose main characteristic, it may be said without exaggeration, was precisely the absence of *ecclesiology,* i.e. of such reflection on the Church which implies — as its very basis — a radical distinction between

* A paper originally presented under the title "The Problem of the Church's Presence in the World in the Orthodox Consciousness," at the Second Congress of Orthodox Theological Schools, Athens, August, 1976; originally published in *St. Vladimir's Theological Quarterly* 21.1 (1977), pp. 3-17.

the Church and the world and therefore of necessity posits the problem of their relationship.

The first difficulty then is that we cannot even begin to discuss our problem ("the Church's presence in the world") without having first deciphered the meaning of that "ecclesiological silence." Is it, as some seem to think today, a mere deficiency of our theology, a deficiency which, however serious it may be, ought to be corrected by another massive injection into Orthodoxy of Western theological categories, by our acceptance of the current Western fixation on, if not a real obsession with, the Church-*versus*-the-world dichotomy and problematics? Or is that "silence" to be viewed as being itself part of our tradition, in which case it is no longer simply silence or absence, but an indication, maybe even an "eloquent" one, of an experience and vision substantially different from those adopted today in the West? Obviously the very understanding of the problem we are to discuss, and its formulation, primarily depend on which of these two approaches we adopt, and on how we justify our choice.

However tempting the first approach may appear to be (it has for a long time been the fate of Orthodox theology to be "tempted" by the West and to "find itself" mainly by reacting to those temptations), there is no doubt, in my mind at least, that it should be rejected. For whatever the numerous and sometimes very serious deficiencies, the truly tragical one-sidedness of our post-patristic and precisely heavily "Westernized" theology, the "ecclesiological silence" mentioned above clearly antedates its appearance and development within the Orthodox Church and has its roots in a much deeper level of Orthodox consciousness. The question is: Where?

My answer is: In that "Christian world" which shaped the historical consciousness of Orthodoxy and which still constitutes the essential context for the Orthodox experience of the Church, of the world and of their relationship with one another. If for several centuries our theology felt no need to reflect upon that relationship —and this means to distinguish between the Church and the world — the reason for this is to be found in the Christian *oikoumene* which grew out of the reconciliation between the Church and the Graeco-Roman Empire, and which throughout the entire "Constantinian period" remained the only self-evident expression and experience of the Church's "presence" in the world. Therefore it is that experience, or rather its ecclesiological significance, its place and meaning within our tradition, that constitute the equally self-evident starting point of any Orthodox reflection about the Church in her relationship to the world.

2.

To state this, however, is not to solve the problem. For if the historical knowledge of that "Christian world" in its various aspects and dimensions — political, cultural, social, etc.— has been steadily advancing, the same cannot be said of its theological understanding. The very question of its ecclesiological meaning — the question on which depends our own reflection upon the Church and the world — has hardly been raised. We know that the reconciliation between the Church and the empire resulted not in a juridical agreement, a contract which, while defining the respective rights and obligations of both parties, the Church and the empire, would have preserved their structural distinction from one another. We know that the result of that reconciliation was such an interpenetration of the Church and the empire, of their structures and functions, that this was consistently expressed in terms of an organic unity, comparable to that of the soul and the body. We know that this favorite Byzantine image was not a rhetorical exaggeration, that the Christian *oikoumene* truly was, in theory and consciousness as well as in reality, an organism within which neither the Church nor the world — state, society, culture — had a separate existence or could be "constitutionally" distinguished from one another. We know all this, and scores of historical books and dissertations are here to confirm this knowledge. The only thing we seem not to know is the meaning of all this for our own theological reflection about the Church's presence today in this present world.

The reason for this is simple, although to state it is to point out our second and truly major difficulty: the continuing power

which the "Christian world" of the *past* still has in shaping
and determining the *present* Orthodox consciousness, in remaining in fact a virtually unique, albeit subliminal source
of today's Orthodox mentality and world-view. To put it
bluntly, as Orthodox we still live in that "Christian world"
of the past, ignoring the historical fact of its collapse and
disappearance. And we ignore it because for us — and this is
essential — not only does the "Christian world" survive in and
through the Church, but also to make it survive, to assure its
continuing "presence," has in fact become the main, if not the
exclusive, function of the Church.

Do I have to prove this? Is it not evident that for an overwhelming majority of the Orthodox, whether individuals or
churches, the very word "Orthodox" is virtually meaningless
and abstract unless given substance by adjectives which, although formally they belong to the categories of the "world,"
are inseparable from an Orthodox Christian's experience of
the "Church," and in fact truly expressive of it. Greek, Russian, Serbian... These adjectives transcend, in their ecclesiastical usage, mere nationalism, understood as natural attachment to and interest in the destinies of a nation, a country,
a culture. If the Orthodox diaspora has eloquently proven
anything, it is precisely this: the Orthodox, even when they
willingly leave their "Orthodox" country, even when they
forget their original language and fully identify themselves
with the life and the culture of another nation, find it both
natural and desirable that their "Orthodoxy" remain Greek,
Russian, Serbian, etc. This is so not because they cannot imagine
any other expression or form of Orthodoxy, but because it is
precisely the quintessential "Hellenism" (and not Greek Orthodoxy) or "Russianism" (and not Russian Orthodoxy), of
which the Church is the only "presence," the only symbol in
the "modern world," that they love in Orthodoxy, that constitutes the treasure of their heart's desire. And this is true not
only of the "diaspora," which merely reflects and intensifies —
sometimes to the point of a *reductio ad absurdum* — the Orthodox mentality, but of Orthodoxy as a whole. Everywhere
Orthodoxy is experienced primarily as representing — as
"making present" — *another world*, the one of the past which,

although it can also be projected into the future as a dream
or as a hope, remains fundamentally alienated from the present one. Everywhere even the basic canonical structures of
the Orthodox Church remain determined by the geographical
and administrative organization of that "world" whose language and thought forms, culture, and indeed whose whole
ethos, still shape and color from within the present Orthodox
consciousness. And it is primarily because of that identification, because the "Church" itself is experienced as the ideal
and symbolic existence of a nonexistent "world," that it is so
difficult for us to understand the real meaning and values of
that past world, the meaning of our *past* for the *present*.

In the first place, this identification makes it almost impossible for the Orthodox consciousness to evaluate that "Christian world" in ecclesiological terms, to distinguish in it between that which, revealing its "success," remains normative
for us, truly a part of the Church's Tradition, and that which,
by deviating from and mutilating that Tradition, must be
termed "failure." It is here, in this inability to evaluate, that
we can grasp the unique and indeed crucial significance of an
event which is ignored by the Orthodox consciousness and
which, precisely because it is ignored, still dominates that
consciousness. This event is the historical end and disintegra-
tion of the Christian *oikoumene.*

Indeed the collapse, one after another, of the organic
"Orthodox worlds," beginning with that of their common
source and archetype, the Byzantine Empire, brought about a
profound transformation of their *experience* in the Orthodox
mind. That experience contained in itself, as its very focus —
and we shall speak of this later — the belief that the "Christian
world," born under the sign of victory (*en touto nika*), cannot
collapse, is indestructible, and has as its proper vocation to
last until the end of the world. This explains why the trau-
matic shock of its collapse, paradoxical as this sounds, resulted
in a *denial* of that collapse, not in its historical reality of
course, but as a "meaningful" event challenging the accepted
Orthodox world-view. Since the "Christian world" *cannot*
disappear, it has *not* disappeared. Its external collapse is but
a temporary "suspense," a God-permitted "temptation." Such

was — such still is — the content and the meaning of that denial which made, and still makes, Orthodoxy to live as if nothing happened, as if nothing changed.

In reality, however, what changed is the Orthodox consciousness itself. It is *after* the collapse of the Christian world, and *because* of the denial of that collapse, that the "Christian world" was transposed and transformed into an almost mythical and archetypal golden age, to be "restored" and "returned to," the ideal past projected therefore as the ideal future, as the only horizon of the Church's vision of history. And in this transformation the initial experience was reversed: If before its collapse, the value of that world for the Church lay in the fact that it accepted her as its "soul," as the ultimate content and criterion of its own existence, now it is the Church that began to be experienced as the "body" expressive of, and living by, the "Christian world" as its "soul."

From this springs the ecclesiological silence mentioned at the beginning of this paper, the inability of our theology to distinguish between the Church and the world, to evaluate the central Orthodox experience of the "Christian world," its "success" as well as its "failure." This silence is not broken and overcome by the noisy and confused controversies about the rights and privileges of this or that Church, the canonicity of this or that particular development — controversies which today, alas, seem to exhaust the life of the Orthodox Church. Rather they themselves are the result of that silence, of the absence from the present Orthodox consciousness of a clear ecclesiological perspective which would clarify the very terms and notions so indiscriminately used in those controversies, which would relate them to the whole of the Orthodox faith and experience.

Neither is that silence broken by the equally noisy Orthodox quarrels about the "world." Here the Orthodox consciousness seems to be polarized between the "optimists" and the "pessimists." Yet the whole point of that polarization is that it remains conditioned by, or — better to say — is itself a result of, that psychological enslavement to the past, to the golden age of the Christian world, which, paradoxically enough, is the common source of both the Orthodox "optimism" and the Orthodox "pessimism." For *grosso modo* the difference between them is this: that while the "optimists" believe in the forthcoming resurrection of the Orthodox world of the past, the "pessimists" have given up that hope, and for them the apparently irreversible triumph of the evil "modern world" acquires an apocalyptic significance, becomes the sign of the approaching End.

The "optimists" may condemn the "pessimists" as fanatics. The "pessimists" may excommunicate the "optimists" as apostates. Both may even be right to some extent, for if the Orthodox "optimism" results more often than not in a non-critical, passive and unconscious surrender to the modern world, the Orthodox "pessimism" leads to a Manichean and dualistic condemnation of that world. All this, however, remains in the deepest sense of the word irrelevant, for what is absent from that quarrel is precisely the "world" itself, the world as object of theological reflection, as the necessary and essential term of reference of ecclesiology: the reflection by the Church on herself, and therefore on her presence in and relation to the world.

3.

Only now can we raise the essential question: If such is our present theological situation, where and how are we to find for the problem which we discuss in this paper ("the Church's presence in the world") a ground, a context, a perspective that would be both objective and Orthodox? — "Orthodox" meaning here: rooted in the Orthodox faith and experience, and not in some artificially adopted Western categories, and "objective": free from that enslavement to that "Christian world" which, as we have tried to show, precludes proper ecclesiological evaluation of our own past, of its meaning for our present. Our difficulty at this point seems to stem from the apparent incompatibility of these two terms: "objective" and "Orthodox." For if, on the one hand, without having understood the situation we cannot properly formulate the essential question, to have understood it, on the other hand,

seems to make an answer to it impossible. Yet the whole point
of this paper is to try to prove that it is precisely this difficulty,
this apparent vicious circle that, once it is properly understood,
opens to us the only perspective which satisfies the two requirements mentioned above ("objective" and "Orthodox") and
leads us to the adequate, i.e. theological, formulation and
solution of our problem. Indeed, the real usefulness of that
vicious circle, and thus of the entire analysis that makes us
aware of it, lies in the fact that they literally force upon us
the discovery, or rather the rediscovery, of the third "reality":
the one which, although it infinitely transcends the "realities"
of the Church and the world, constitutes for the Christian
faith the ultimate term of reference for each of them, and
therefore the only permanent principle and criterion of their
distinction from one another as well as of their relation to one
another. This reality is the *Kingdom of God*, whose announcement precisely as reality, and not merely idea or doctrine, stands
at the very center of the Gospel or, better to say, *is* the Gospel
and also the eternal horizon: the source and the content of
Christian experience. As long as we do not relate all other
realities to that ultimate reality, as long as we try to understand and define the Church's presence in the world in terms
of a hopelessly "worldly" perspective and experience, i.e.
without seeing both the Church and the world in the light of
the Kingdom of God, we are bound to reach a dead end, to
find ourselves, consciously or unconsciously, in a vicious circle.
For there is — there can be — no true ecclesiology, i.e. no true
understanding of the Church, of the world and of their inter-
relationship, without eschatology, i.e. the Orthodox faith in
and experience of the Kingdom of God.

It may be useful and even necessary at this point to emphasize that by eschatology we do not mean merely the chapter
which we usually find at the very end of our theological
manuals, which deals almost exclusively with the fate of man's
soul after its separation in death from the body. In fact this
futuristic and individualistic reduction of eschatology is one
of the greatest deficiencies of our post-patristic theology, the
worst fruit of its long Western captivity. Properly understood,
eschatology is not so much a separate "chapter" or "doctrine"

(which, being distinct from all other Christian "doctrines," can and ought to be treated "in itself") as it is the essential dimension of the Christian faith and experience themselves, and therefore of Christian theology in its totality.

The Christian faith is essentially eschatological because the events from which it stems and which are its "object" as well as its "content": the life, death, resurrection and glorification of Jesus Christ, the descent of the Holy Spirit, and the "institution" of the Church, are seen and experienced not only as the end and the fulfillment of the history of salvation, but also as the inauguration and the gift of a new life whose content is the Kingdom of God: knowledge of God, communion with Him, the possibility while still living in "this world" to foretaste and really to partake of the "joy, peace and righteousness" of the "world to come." Thus eschatology, being the essential term of reference of the Christian faith itself, permeates the whole of Christian theology and indeed makes possible theology itself, i.e. the transformation of our human and hopelessly limited words into *theoprepeis logoi*, "words adequate to God," truly expressive of the eternally transcendent divine truth.

So also it is eschatology that "posits" the proper understanding of the Church and of the world and, in doing this, reveals the nature of their relation to one another. In the first place it reveals the Church as the epiphany, as the manifestation, the presence and the gift of the Kingdom of God, as its "sacrament" in this world. And again the whole Church, as both "institution" and "life," is eschatological because she has no other foundation, content and purpose but to reveal and to communicate the transcendent reality of the Kingdom of God. There is no separation in her between "institution" and "life": as institution she is the sign of the Kingdom, as life she is the sacrament of the Kingdom, the fulfillment of the sign into reality, experience, communion. Being in "this world" (*in statu viae*), she lives by her experience of the "world to come," to which she already belongs and in which she is already "at home" (*in statu patriae*).

The eschatological "being" of the Church explains the Orthodox "ecclesiological silence" during the classical, patristic period in the history of our theology. If, as it has often been noticed, the Fathers do not define the Church, do not make her into an object of theological reflection, it is because none of such definitions can truly or adequately comprehend and express the essential mystery of the Church as *experience* of the Kingdom of God, as its epiphany in "this world." Even the scriptural images of the Church: the Body of Christ, the Bride of Christ, the Temple of the Holy Spirit, cannot be construed as "definitions." To say that the Church is the "Body of Christ" is indeed perfectly meaningless to someone who has no experience of the Church and of her life. Thus the Church, for the Fathers, is not an "object" of theology but the very "subject" in them of their theologizing, the essential reality which by revealing the Kingdom of God, i.e. the ultimate and saving truth, makes it possible to have a new life and to bear witness to it. They do not define the Church because when abstracted from the experience of that reality, she becomes a pure form about which there is essentially nothing to say. And from the subsequent history of Christian theology, especially Western, we know what happens when ecclesiology, abandoning its eschatological dimension, foundation and content, selects as its proper "object" precisely the *form* of the Church, gives it, so to speak, an existence in itself, and by doing this, by changing ecclesiology into ecclesiolatry, mutilates the entire "experience" of the Church. All this, as we shall see, is of great importance for the proper evaluation of the "Christian world" and the place in it of the Church.

4.

Revealing the Church, her nature and her vocation, eschatology of necessity reveals the world or, better to say, the vision and understanding of it in the Christian faith. If the essential experience of the Church is that of the new creation, of a new life in a renewed world, that experience implies and posits a certain fundamental experience of the world. First of all, it implies the experience of the world as God's creation and therefore positive in its origin as well as in its essence, reflecting in its structure and being the wisdom, the glory and the beauty of the One who created it: "Heaven and earth are full of Thy glory!" There is no ontological dualism of any kind, no cosmic pessimism whatsoever in the Christian faith, which fulfills the essential biblical glorification of God in His creation. The world is *good.*

In the second place, the eschatological experience of the Church reveals the world as the *fallen* world, dominated by sin, corruption and death, enslaved to the "Prince of this world." This fall, although it cannot destroy and annihilate the essential goodness of God's creation, has nevertheless alienated it from God, made it into "this world" which, because it is "flesh and blood," pride and selfishness, is not only distinct from the Kingdom of God but actively opposed to it. Hence the essentially tragic Christian view of history, the rejection by the Christian faith of any historical optimism that would equate the world with "progress."

And finally, the ultimate experience: that of *redemption,* which God accomplished in the midst of His creation, within time and history, and which by redeeming man, by making him *capax Dei,* capable of the new life, is the salvation of the world. For as the world rejects, in and through man, its self-sufficiency, as it ceases to be an end in itself and thus truly *dies* as "this world," it becomes that which it was created to be and has truly become in Christ: the object and means of sanctification, of man's communion with and passage to God's eternal Kingdom.

5.

We can now return to the "Christian world" which, as I have tried to show, blocks the "Orthodox consciousness" by continuing to dominate it. The eschatological perspective as the common ground for the Christian experience and under-standing of the Church and of the world makes it possible for us truly to evaluate our *past* and, on the basis of that evalu-ation, to discern our *present*: the basic norms for an Orthodox approach to the world as it exists and challenges us today.

If to evaluate primarily means to distinguish "success" from "failure," to evaluate the complex reality of the "Orthodox world" of the past is to distinguish its truly Christian and therefore lasting achievements from its betrayal of its own Christian ideal. Yet it is that ideal itself which, I am convinced, constitutes the first and the essential "success" of the Christian world, and its lasting value for us and our own situation. If the Church so readily, so enthusiastically and without any reservations, without any legal or "constitutional" conditions, *accepted* the "world" which for more than two centuries denied her the very right to exist, if she accepted it as the form of her own existence and for all practical purposes merged with it, it is because in the first place that world, i.e. the Graeco-Roman Empire, *accepted* the Church's faith, and this means that it subordinated itself, its own values, its entire self-understanding, to the ultimate object and content of that faith: the Kingdom of God. In other terms, it accepted as its own foundation, as its *sui generis* basis, the Christian eschatological perspective. And this happened not only in theory, not only nominally. We are so accustomed to the "Western" evaluation of the "Christian world," i.e. its evaluation almost exclusively in terms of Church-state relations and more specifically in terms of the relationship within it between two *powers*, the *imperium* and the *sacerdotium*, that we are virtually incapable of discerning the real *locus* of that unique alliance between the Church and the world: their essential agreement as to what constitutes the ultimate value, the ultimate "term of reference," the ultimate horizon of human existence in all its dimensions.

Obviously to prove that this non-written and yet real "agreement" existed, and that, in spite of all human failures and betrayals, it *worked*, would require a detailed analysis of the entire culture and ethos of that "Christian world," analysis impossible within the scope and the limitations of this paper. I am convinced, however, that such analysis would establish beyond any doubt the fundamental *openness* of that culture and of the society which produced it to the Christian eschatological vision, as the unique inspiration, as indeed the "soul" of their very existence. Whatever aspects of that world we consider — its art, which in each given "society" is a main expression of its vision of life, its lifestyle, and, to use another of the favorite modern terms, the entire "discourse" of its culture — we find that their inner consistency, their style in the deepest sense of the word, comes to them, in the last analysis, from the Church's eschatological experience, from her vision and knowledge of the Kingdom of God. If monasticism, for example, is for that society its ideal pole, the "exceedingly good" way to perfection which shapes its worship, its piety and indeed its whole mentality, it is because the monk personifies the eschatological nature of the Christian life, the impossibility of reducing Christianity to anything in "this world" whose "fashion fades away." In this sense repentance, in the radical sense of the evangelical *metanoia*, constitutes the fundamental tonality of the "Christian world," permeating its prayer, its thought and the essential symbols of its whole life. This the modern Christians forget much too easily, although in the light of the reductionism characteristic of our modern civilization this should be remembered more than anything else.

6.

If such is the essential "success" of the "Christian world," the same eschatological perspective which reveals it to us also reveals that world's fundamental "failure." I call it "fundamental" in order to distinguish it from all other defects: crimes, cruelty, conflicts, of which the "Christian world," as any other human society, had its full share. What, however, transcends all those "human, all too human" deficiencies and tragedies is the inner betrayal by the "Christian world" of its own ultimate vision, its progressive subordination to a different vision, subordination which because it remained virtually subconscious was all the more tragical.

Using categories familiar to us today, I would define that betrayal as *denial of history*, and this means denial of that experience of time, of its meaning and function, which are implied in Christian eschatology. It is indeed the mark of Christian eschatology that, by revealing the *eschaton*, the ultimate *end* and thus the ultimate "term of reference" of the world, it posits the world as *history*, as a meaningful process within a linear time. The Christian world-view is dynamic. It liberates the world from its enslavement to a static "sacrality." By revealing the Kingdom of God as the Beyond which nevertheless is present within time as its leaven, as that which gives it its value, meaning and orientation, the Church generates in man the thirst and hunger for the Absolute, the unsatiable desire and search for perfection.

The initial "agreement" between the Church and the world not only contained this dynamic world-view but indeed was based on it. By accepting the Church's eschatological faith, the "world" accepted to be "journey" to the Kingdom, a world *open* to the prophetic vision, the prophetic voice of the Church. Even if, according to the biblical scheme applied to it by the Church, the Graeco-Roman *oikoumene* was to be the last in the sequence of the great empires that measured the history of salvation, even if, by accepting Christ as its supreme *Basileus* or *Pantokrator*, it thought of itself as the Christian *politeuma*, the ultimate response of the world to God, all this did not alter — for the Church — the empire's essential "historicity," its belonging to the world whose "fashion is fading away."

With time, however, that vision began to change. From a dynamic one it became, little by little and almost unconsciously, a static one. And although it would obviously be impossible even to mention here the various reasons which led to that metamorphosis, all of them are rooted, in one way or another, in the inertia that characterizes social organisms, in their "natural" tendency to divorce their form from the content which alone justifies that form and thus to absolutize the latter as an end in itself, as a sacred form-for-ever. Nothing illustrates better that metamorphosis than the change, and again an unconscious one, in the eschatological emphasis. It is precisely then that that individualistic and almost exclusively futuristic reduction of eschatology began to develop and to deprive even the sacraments, the Eucharist itself, of their eschatological dimension and to put it bluntly, to remove the Kingdom of God, at least in theological reflection, into the future alone, to make it into a mere doctrine of rewards and punishments after death.

The real context of that reduction, however, is not merely theological. It reflected the growing change in the very mentality, the very consciousness of the "Christian world," the progressive abandonment by it of its own eschatological vision. On the one hand, its self-understanding as the last earthly kingdom, as the providential *locus* of Christ's victory, began to be experienced — rather than interpreted — as the end of history: the end, not of time but precisely of "history," i.e. of that time which is open to new events, to meaningful developments. All such developments, all historical happenings, were now to be squeezed somehow into a static and unchanging pattern, denied their historical specificity and uniqueness. On the other hand, and simultaneously with that growing a-historicity, there developed within the Christian world a sense of its own perfection, not of course in its "members," who remain sinful, but in its forms and structures, which were experienced more and more as final, God-given and therefore unchangeable.

All this, I repeat, took place little by little and on a subconscious rather than conscious level. The theory did not change, only the "experience" of it. But the results of that change constitute without any exaggeration the greatest tragedy of Christian history. What it provoked was a progressive emancipation of the human mind — and of the "thirst" and "hunger" injected into it by Christianity — from the "Christian world," and therefore their growing secularization, their rebellion against Christianity itself. Prevented from developing within the framework — religious, cultural, psychological — of the "Christian world," blocked by the latter's static self-absolutization, the human mind, shaped and inspired by Christian eschatological maximalism, began to see in the "Christian world" the main obstacle to that maximalism, a structure of oppression and not of freedom. The sad history of the divorce between man and his "search" on the one hand and the "Christian world" on the other hand, has been told many times. What is important for us is, of course, the indelibly "Christian" mark on the "modern world," the one which grew out of this divorce, and this in spite of the world's rebellion and, sometimes, apostasy. This is truly a *post-Christian* world because, in the last analysis, even the most secular, the most anti-religious and anti-Christian ideas and ideologies by which it is moved, are in one way or another — "des verités chrétiennes devenues folles" — the fruit of a secularized eschatology. It is the Christian faith which, by injecting into man's mind and heart the dream — the vision — of the Kingdom of God, made possible the fundamental utopianism of the "modern mind," its worship of history, its almost paranoic belief in a forthcoming kingdom of freedom and justice.

7.

Now the last question: What does all this mean for us, for our own theological reflection on the Church's presence in our own "modern world"? Our task was to find the ecclesiological perspective implied, rather than formally expressed, in the central Orthodox experience: that of the "Christian World," of its "success" and "failure"; to discern its significance, its normative character for our present tasks.

It seems to me that the essential meaning of that which I termed "success" lies in the very fact of the "Christian world," which, above all, reveals the Orthodox belief in the possibility for the world to be sanctified — the belief, in other words, in the world not as a hopelessly "extrinsic" reality, alien and irrelevant to the uniquely "religious" preoccupations of the Church, but as the object of her love, concern and action. And this is very important especially in view of the dangerous and potentially even heretical tendency pervasive today among the Orthodox to accept an almost Manichean, dualistic view of the world and thus to make the Church into a self-contained and self-centered religious ghetto. Our own past, our own Tradition bears witness not only to the possibility of a "theology of the world" but indeed makes such theology an organic dimension of ecclesiology.

If, then, that "success" liberates us from Manichean dualism, it ought to liberate us also from the opposite, yet equally pervasive and equally dangerous temptation: that of a mere surrender to the world, acceptance of the world as the only content of the Church's life and action, setting — to use an expression popular today — "the agenda for the Church." That "success," to the extent to which it was "success," reveals that the function of the Church in the world is to make present within it the *eschaton*, to manifest the Kingdom of God as the ultimate term of reference, and thus to relate to it the whole life of man and of his world. The Church is not an agency for solving the innumerable "problems" inherent in the world, or rather, she may help solving them only inasmuch as she herself remains faithful to her nature and to her essential vocation: to reveal in "this world" that which by being "not of this world" is therefore the only absolute context for seeing, understanding and solving all human "problems."

As to the "fundamental failure" of the Christian world, it should make us fully aware that there is but one essential sin, one essential danger: that of idolatry, the ever-present and ever-acting temptation to absolutize and thus to idolize "this world" itself, its passing values, ideas and ideologies, to forget that as the people of God "we have here no lasting city, but we seek the city which is to come" (Heb. 13:14). It is the "failure" of the "Christian world" that should make it possible for us to see through the "modern world" and the spiritual reality shaping it, to discern in it what is positive: the cry that comes from its Christian subconscious, and also what is negative: its truly demonic rebellion against God.

There is, however, one precondition for all this, which is both "necessary and sufficient": it is that the Church herself return to the "one thing needed," to the essentially eschatological nature of her faith and of her life. No theological reflection on the world will be of any help, no theological reflection on the world will be possible unless we rediscover, make truly ours again, that reality which alone constitutes the Church and is the source of her faith, of her life and therefore of her theology: the reality of the Kingdom of God. The Church is *in statu viae*, in pilgrimage through "this world," sent to it as its salvation. But the meaning of that pilgrimage, as indeed the meaning of the world itself, is given and revealed to us only when the Church fulfills herself as being *in statu patriae*, truly at home at Christ's table, in His Kingdom.

This precondition requires, of course, a radical rethinking of our theological enterprise, of its very structure and methodology, of its ultimate roots, of that which makes it possible. It is not enough simply to quote the Fathers, to make them into "authorities" certifying our every theological proposition, for it is not quotations, be they scriptural or patristic, that constitute the ground of theology, but the *experience of the Church*. And since, in the ultimate analysis, she has no other experience but that of the Kingdom, since her whole life is rooted in that unique experience, there can be no other source, no other ground and no other criterion for theology, if it is truly to be the expression of the Church's faith and the reflection on that faith.

All this means a return to a very old, indeed eternal truth: The Church is never more present to the world and more "useful" to it than when she is totally free from it, free from it not only "externally," i.e. independent from its structures and powers, but also and primarily internally, i.e. free from her own spiritual surrender to its values and treasures. To accomplish such liberation, however, is not easy, for it presupposes that our hearts find the only true treasure, the experience of the Kingdom of God, which alone can restore to us the fulness of the Church and the fulness of the world, which alone makes us capable of truly fulfilling our calling.

IV

A MEANINGFUL STORM

> "Wherefore putting away lying,
> speak every man truth with his
> neighbor: for we are members one
> of another." Eph. 4:25

1.

The storm provoked by the "autocephaly" of the Orthodox Church in America is probably one of the most meaningful crises in several centuries of Orthodox ecclesiastical history. Or rather it could become meaningful if those who are involved in it were to accept it as an unique opportunity for facing and solving an ecclesiastical confusion which for too long was simply ignored by the Orthodox. For if America has suddenly become the focus of Orthodox attention and passions, it is because the situation of Orthodoxy here, being the most obvious result of that confusion, was bound to reveal sooner or later the true nature and scope of what is indeed a "pan-Orthodox" crisis.

Not many words are needed to describe the American "situation." By 1970, Orthodoxy in America existed in the form of: one Greek jurisdiction, three Russian, two Serbian, two Antiochian, two Romanian, two Bulgarian, two Albanian, three Ukrainian, one Carpatho-Russian and some smaller groups which we omit here for the sake of simplicity. Within every national subdivision each group claimed to be the only "canonical" one and denied recognition to others. As to

---

* Originally published in *St. Vladimir's Theological Quarterly* 15. 1/2 (1971), pp. 3-27.

criteria of this "canonicity," they were also quite diverse. Some groups saw it in their jurisdictional dependence on their "Mother Churches," some, which—like the Carpatho-Russian diocese—could not claim any identifiable Mother Church, on their "recognition" by the Ecumenical Patriarch, some on other kinds of "continuity" and "validity." Several of these "jurisdictions" did—while others did not—belong to the "Standing Conference of Orthodox Bishops," an unofficial, voluntary association established to promote the unification of Orthodoxy in the New World but which in ten years of its existence could not agree even on general principles of such a unification. This unique and quite unprecedented situation existed for many decades. But what makes it even more appalling is the fact that at no time did it provoke any noticeable alarm in the Church at large, at least in her "officialdom." Indeed, no one seemed either to see or to admit that American Orthodoxy had in fact become a blatant denial of all that learned Orthodox delegates to ecumenical gatherings were at the same time proclaiming to be the "essence" of Orthodoxy as the True Church and the Una Sancta. I am convinced that to future historians this "American situation," made up of progressive fragmentation, court trials, passionate polemics and mutual suspicion, will be a source of endless amazement.

The storm began early in 1970 when one of the largest and oldest "jurisdictions" brought to an end its long quarrel with its Mother Church by asking for and receiving a status of total administrative independence ("autocephaly"), dropped from her name a qualification ("Russian") which after 175 years of unbroken continuity on this continent was obviously obsolete, and adopted a geographical definition ("in America") corresponding both to its location and vocation. Yet if some fifty years of chaos and divisions, confusion and progressive deterioration, left the Church at large perfectly indifferent, this simple fact—the emergence of an Orthodox Church in America based on equally simple and empirical presuppositions, that the Church here, after almost two centuries of existence, might be *independent* and could be *American*—raised a storm which keeps gaining momentum and has by now involved the entire Orthodox Church.

Our purpose here is not to defend the "autocephaly."
It is rather to investigate the nature and the causes of the
storm it ignited, the deep and probably almost unconscious
motivations behind these passionate reactions. That "autocephaly" was met at first with insults, innuendos and interpretations *ad malem partem* was probably to be expected.
But insults never prove or solve anything. And I am convinced
that beneath them there is an immense and truly tragic
misunderstanding. My only goal now is to try to locate and to
assess it. Above all we need today a clarification. Only then
may a more constructive and meaningful discussion, a search
for common solutions, become possible.

2.

The natural and essential "term of reference" in Orthodoxy
is always *Tradition*. That the present controversy takes the
form of "appeals" to Tradition, of argumentation *ex tra-
ditione*, is therefore perfectly normal. What is less normal
but deeply revealing of the present state of Orthodoxy is the
fact that these "appeals" and arguments seem to result in
openly contradictory and mutually exclusive claims and
affirmations. It is as if we were either "reading" different Traditions or the same one differently. It certainly would be unfair
to explain these contradictions merely by ill-will, ignorance or
emotions. If to some the coming into existence of an "Orthodox Church in America" is a first step towards genuine Tradition, while to some others it is the beginning of a canonical
collapse, the reason for this must be a deeper one; not only,
indeed, do we differently read the same Tradition, but we also
appeal to different traditions. And it is this fact that we have
to understand and to explain.

Let us remember first of all that the Orthodox concept of
Tradition cannot be reduced to that of texts and regulations
which any one who wants to prove something has merely to
quote. Thus the "Holy Canons," i.e. that collection of canonical texts which is common to all Orthodox churches, does not
exhaust the canonical tradition. This observation is especially

important in view of the fact that the key words of our present debates — "autocephaly," "jurisdiction," etc.— are virtually absent from the Holy Canons, and current "appeals" and references are made almost exclusively to various "precedents" of the past. Now, such appeals to the past and to "precedents" have always been considered as perfectly legitimate from the Orthodox point of view, for Tradition most certainly includes *facts* as well as *texts*. It is also clear, however, that not all "past," simply by virtue of being "past," is to be identified with Tradition. In the eighteenth century the Ecumenical Throne "abolished" the Serbian "autocephaly." More recently it "recognized" the heretical "Living Church" in Russia. Muscovite bishops used to reconsecrate the bishop elected to the patriarchal office. At some time or another virtually all Orthodox churches established their "jurisdiction" in America. Are all these facts "canonical precedents" simply because they occurred in the past and were "institutionalized"? Is it not obvious, therefore, that "past" itself always needs evaluation, and that the criterion of such an evaluation is not "factual" ("it happened") but *ecclesiological*, that, in other words, it consists in a reference to the permanent and unchanging doctrine of the Church, to her "essence"? If the forms of the Church's life and organization change, it is in order precisely to preserve unchanged the "essence" of the Church; for otherwise the Church would cease to be a divine institution and become a mere product of historical forces and developments. And the function of Tradition is always to assure and to reveal this essential and unchanging "identity" of the Church, her "sameness" in space and time. To "read" Tradition is therefore not to "quote" but to *refer* all facts, texts, institutions and forms to the ultimate essence of the Church, to understand their meaning and value in the light of the Church's unchanging *esse*. But then the question is: What is the basic principle and the inner criterion of such a "reading," of our appeals to Tradition?

3.

Orthodox canonists and theologians have always agreed that for the canonical tradition such an inner criterion is to be found in the Holy Canons, i.e., that corpus which includes the Apostolic Canons, the decisions of ecumenical and some local councils, and rules extracted from various patristic writings. This corpus has been always and everywhere considered as *normative*, not only because it constitutes the earliest "layer" of our canonical tradition, but because its primary content and term of reference is precisely the "essence" of the Church, her basic structure and constitution rather than the historically contingent forms of her existence. This layer is thus the norm of any subsequent canonical development, the inner measure of its "canonicity," the very context within which everything else in the history of the Church, be it past, present or future, is to be evaluated.

If this is true, and until now it has always been held as true by the consensus of Orthodox canonists and theologians, we have a first methodological "clue" to our present controversy, one principle by which to evaluate the various "appeals" to Tradition. It is indeed quite significant then that references to this "essential" canonical tradition are very scarce, not to say non-existent, in the storm originated by "autocephaly." The reason for this is simple, and I have already mentioned it. The Holy Canons virtually ignore the terms which are at the heart of the debate: "autocephaly," "jurisdiction," etc. One is naturally tempted then to refer directly to those "layers" of the past and to those "traditions" which seem to be of greater help in providing "proofs" and "precedents." But it is here precisely that we must "locate" the initial weakness and the fundamental deficiency of this entire method of arguing. For on the one hand, it is probably possible with some know-how to find a "precedent" and a canonical "justification" for almost anything. Yet on the other hand, the whole point is that no "precedent" as such constitutes a sufficient canonical justification. If the notion of "autocephaly" came into existence after the fixation of the *normative* tradition, this does not mean that the former does not need to be "referred" to the latter, understood and evaluated in its ecclesiological context. One cannot meaningfully debate the question of who has the "right to grant autocephaly" unless one first agrees on the basic ecclesiological meaning of that "right" and of "autocephaly." One cannot speak of "autocephaly" as "canonical" or "uncanonical" unless one first sees and understands it in the light of the canons, i.e. the essential and universal canonical tradition. If "autocephaly"— and here everyone will agree — is one particular mode or expression of the churches' relationships to one another, where, if not in the *essential* tradition, is the fundamental nature of that relationship to be found?

                                    4.

My first conclusion is a simple one. If notions such as "autocephaly" or "jurisdiction" are absent from the canonical tradition which everyone accepts as normative, this very absence is a tremendously important factor for the proper understanding and evaluation of these notions. In the first place this absence cannot be termed "accidental"; if it were accidental, we would of necessity have been able to find an equivalent notion. It cannot furthermore be ascribed to, let us say, the "underdeveloped" character of earlier ecclesiology, for it would mean that for several centuries the Church existed without something essential for her very life. But then this absence can be explained by only one fact: a significant difference in the very approach to the Church between the *essential* tradition and the one which appeared at a later date. It is this difference that we must understand if we are to grasp the true ecclesiological meaning of "autocephaly."

Even a superficial reading of the canons shows that the Church they depict is not, as it is today for us, a network of "sovereign" and "independent" entities called patriarchates or autocephalous or autonomous churches, each having "under" itself (in its "jurisdiction") smaller and subordinated units such as "dioceses," "exarchates," "parishes," etc. This "jurisdictional" or "subordinationist" dimension is absent here because, when dealing with the Church, the early ecclesiological tradition has its starting point and its basic term of reference in the *local church*. This early tradition has been analysed and studied so many times in recent years that no detailed elaboration is needed here. What is important for us is that this local church, i.e. a community gathered around its bishop and *clerus*, is a *full* church. It is the manifestation and the presence in a given place of the Church of Christ. And thus the main aim and purpose of the canonical tradition is precisely to "protect" this fulness, to "guarantee," so to speak, that this local church fully manifests the oneness, holiness, apostolicity and catholicity of the Church of Christ. It is in function of this fulness, therefore, that the canonical tradition regulates the relation of each church with other churches, their unity and interdependence. The fulness of the local church, its very nature as the Church of Christ in a particular place, depends primarily on her unity in faith, tradition and life with the Church everywhere; on her being ultimately the *same* Church. This unity is assured essentially by the bishop whose office or *leitourgia* is to maintain and to preserve, in constant union with other bishops, the continuity and the identity in space and time of the universal and catholic faith and life of the one Church of Christ. For us the main point, however, is that although *dependent* on all other churches, the local church is not "subordinate" to any of them. No church is "under" any other church and no bishop is "under" any other bishop. The very nature of this dependence and, therefore, of unity among churches, is not "jurisdictional." It is the unity of faith and life, the unbroken continuity of Tradition, of the gifts of the Holy Spirit that is expressed, fulfilled and preserved in the consecration of one bishop by other bishops, in their regular synods, and, in brief, in the organic unity of the episcopate which all bishops hold *in solidum* (St. Cyprian).

The absence of "jurisdictional" subordination of one church to another, of one bishop to another, does not mean absence of hierarchy and order. This order in the early canonical tradition is maintained by the various levels of *primacies*, i.e. episcopal and ecclesiastical centers or focuses of unity. But primacy is not a "jurisdictional" principle. If, according to the famous Apostolic Canon 34, the bishops everywhere must know the *first* among them, the same canon "refers" this primacy to the Holy Trinity which has "order" but certainly no "subordination." The function of primacy is to express the unity of all, to be its organ and mouthpiece. The first level of primacy is usually that of a "province," i.e. a region in which all bishops, together with the metropolitan, take part in the consecration of the bishops of that region, and meet twice a year as synod. If we had to apply the notion of "autocephaly" to the early Church it should be properly applied to this provincial level, for the main mark of "autocephaly" is precisely the right to elect and to consecrate bishops within a given region. The second level of primacy is that of a wider geographical area: "Orient" with Antioch, Asia with Ephesus, Gaul with Lyons, etc. The "content" of this primacy is primarily doctrinal and moral. The churches of any given area usually "look up" to the church from which they received their tradition and in times of crisis and uncertainty gather around her in order to find under her leadership a common solution to their problems. Finally, there is also from the very beginning a universal "center of unity," a universal primacy: that of the Church of Jerusalem at first, then that of the Church of Rome, a primacy which even modern Roman theologians define, at least in that early period, in terms of "sollicitude" rather than in those of any formal "power" or "jurisdiction."

Such is the *essential* canonical tradition of the Church. And it is only in its light that we can understand the real significance of those subsequent "layers" which were added to it and complicated it during the long earthly pilgrimage of the Church.

5.

The early structure of the Church was substantially changed and "complicated," as everyone knows, by the event which still remains the most important single event in the history of the Church: the Church's reconciliation with the empire, and an alliance between them within the framework of a Christian *oikoumene*, a Christian "universe." Ecclesiologically this event meant, above all, a progressive organizational integration of the Church's structures into the administrative system of the empire.

Let me stress immediately that this integration, and the entire second "layer" of our canonical tradition which is derived from it and which can be termed "imperial," cannot be considered from an Orthodox point of view as a passing "accident," or, as some Western historians think, a result of a "surrender" of the Church to the empire. No, it is an integral part of our tradition and the Orthodox Church cannot reject Byzantium without rejecting something belonging to her very substance. But it must be understood that this layer is a *different* one, based on different presuppositions and having therefore different implications for Orthodox ecclesiology. For if the first layer is both the expression and the norm of the unchanging *essence* of the Church, the fundamental meaning of this second, "imperial" level is that it expresses and regulates the *historicity* of the Church, i.e. her equally essential relation to the world in which she is called to fulfill her vocation and mission. It belongs indeed to the very nature of the Church that she is always and everywhere *not of this world* and receives her being and life from above, not from beneath, and that, at the same time, she always *accepts* the world to which she is sent and adjusts herself to its forms, needs and structures. If the first layer of our canonical tradition refers to the Church in herself, to those structures which, expressing her essence, do not depend on the "world," the second one has as its very object her "acceptance" of the world, the norms by which she is related to it. The first deals with the "unchanging," the second with the "changing." Thus, for example, the Church is a permanent reality of the Christian faith and experience whereas the Christian Empire is not. But inasmuch and as long as this empire, this "Christian world," is a reality, the Church not only accepts it *de facto* but enters into a positive and in a sense even an organic relationship with it. The essential aspect, the "canonical" meaning of that relationship, however, is that it does not bestow on anything in this world the same essential value as the one the Church possesses. For the Church the "image of the world always fades away" (I Cor. 7:31), and this applies to all forms and institutions of the world. Within the framework of the Christian *oikoumene* the Church may easily accept the right of the Christian *basileus* to convoke ecumenical councils or to nominate bishops or even to change the territorial boundaries and privileges of the churches. All this does not make the emperor an essential category of the Church's life. In this sense the second canonical layer is essentially *relative*, for its very object is precisely the Church's life within relative realities of "this world." Its function is to *relate* the unchanging essence of the Church to an ever-changing world.

Now it is obvious that the *jurisdictional* dimension of the Church and of her life has its roots precisely in this second, "imperial" layer of our tradition. But it must be stressed immediately that this jurisdictional level did neither *replace* the earlier, "essential" one, nor merely *develop* it. Even today, after centuries of an almost complete triumph of "jurisdictional" ecclesiology, we say, for example, that all bishops are "equal in grace," denying thus that distinctions in rank (e.g. patriarch, archbishop, bishop) have any "ontological" content. It is absolutely important to understand that this "jurisdictional" layer, although perfectly justified and even necessary in its own sphere of application, is a *different* layer, not to be confused with the "essential" one. The source of that difference lies in the fact that the jurisdictional "power" comes to the Church not from her *essence,* which is not "of this world," and is, therefore, beyond any *jus*, but from her being "in the world" and thus in a mutual relationship with it. Essentially the Church is the Body of Christ, the Temple of the Holy Spirit, the Bride of Christ; but empirically she is also a *society* and as such a part of "this world" and in "relation" with it. And if any attempt to separate and to oppose to one another those two realities leads to a heretical disincarnation of the Church, her reduction to a human, all too human "institution," a confusion between the two is equally heretical, for it ultimately subordinates grace to *jus*, making Christ, in the words of St. Paul, "die in vain." The heart of the matter is that the "essence" of the Church—which is not "jurisdictional"—can and even must have "in this world" an inevitable "jurisdictional" projection and expression. Thus, for example, when the canon says that a bishop is to be consecrated by "two or three" bishops, this in itself is not a "juridical" norm but the expression of the very essence of the Church as an organic unity of faith and life. The full "reading" and understanding of this canon implies, therefore, of necessity its reference to the "essential" ecclesiology. Yet at the same time this canon is obviously a rule, a practical and objective norm, a first and essential criterion for discerning a "canonical" from a "non-canonical" consecration. As "rule," as *jus*, it is neither self-sufficient nor self-explanatory, and the essence of the episcopate cannot evidently be reduced to it. Yet it is that rule which—properly understood within the context of ecclesiology—maintains precisely the identity of the Church's "essence" in space and in time.

During the first centuries of her existence the Church was denied any "legal" status and "jurisdiction" by "this world" which persecuted her. But within the new situation—that of a "Christian *oikeumene*"—it was normal and inevitable for the Church to receive and to acquire such a status. Remaining "essentially" what she was, what she always is and always will be in any "situation," "society" and "culture," the Church received within a given situation a "jurisdiction" which she did not possess before and which is not "essential," although beneficial, for her to possess. The state, even a Christian state, is entirely "of this world," i.e. of the order of *jus*, and it cannot express its relationship with the Church in any but a "jurisdictional" manner. In the world's categories the Church is also primarily a "jurisdiction"—a society, a structure, an institution with rights and obligations, privileges and rules, etc. All that the Church can require from the state is that this "jurisdictional" understanding not mutilate and reform her "essential" being, that it be not contrary to her essential ecclesiology. It is therefore within this new "situation" and, in fact, *from* the Christian empire that the Church received in addition, so to speak, to her "essential" structure a *jurisdictional* one, meant to express primarily her place and function within the Byzantine "symphony": the organic alliance in one *oikoumene* of the state and Church. The most important feature of that jurisdictional aspect is that organizationally and institutionally the Church "followed" the state, i.e. integrated itself into its own organizational structure.

The best example, indeed the "focus" of that integration and of the new "jurisdictional" order is, without any doubt, the place and function of the Patriarch of Constantinople within the Byzantine *oikoumene*. No historian would deny today that the quick rise of the see of Constantinople was due exclusively to the new "imperial" situation of the Church. The ideal of "symphony" between the *imperium* and the *sacerdotium*—the very basis of Byzantine "ideology"—required an ecclesiastical "counterpart" to the emperor, a personal "focus" of the Church corresponding to the personal "focus" of the empire. In this sense the "jurisdiction" of the bishop of Constantinople as the Ecumenical (i.e. "imperial") Patriarch is an *imperial* jurisdiction, whose true context and term of reference is, above all, the Byzantine theocratic ideology. And it is very interesting to note that there is an obvious difference between the imperial legislation concerning the role and the function of the patriarch and the canonical tradition of the same period. Canonically, i.e. in reference to "essential" ecclesiology, the patriarch of Constantinople, in spite of his unique "imperial" position, remained the primate of the Eastern Church, although even this primacy was given him because his city was that of the "emperor and the senate" (Chalcedon canon 28), and also the primate of his own "diocese." "Imperially," however, he became the head of the Church, her "spokesman" to the empire and her link to it, the "focus" not only of the Church's unity and agreement, but also of her "jurisdictional" government.

We know also that this "imperial" logic was not accepted easily and without resistance by the Church: the fight against Constantinople of the old "centers of unity" or "primacies"—

those of Alexandria and Antioch—is here to witness it. The
historical tragedy which transformed these once flourishing
churches into mere remnants put an end to that resistance;
and for several centuries the New Rome became the center,
the heart and the head of one "Imperial" Church—the religious projection of the one universal Christian empire. The
"jurisdictional" principle, although in theory still distinct
from the essential ecclesiology, occupied the center of the
stage. Local bishops like civil governors became more and
more the representatives and even the "delegates" of a
"central power": the patriarch and his by now permanent
synod. Psychologically, in virtue of the same imperial and
"jurisdictional" logic, they became even his "subordinates,"
as well as the subordinates of the emperor. What was primarily
a *mode* of the Church's relationship to a particular "world"
began to permeate the Church's mentality itself and to be
confused with the Church's "essence." And this, as we shall
see later, is the main source of our present confusion and
disagreements.

6.

We are coming now to the third historical "layer" of
our tradition, a layer whose formative principle and content
is neither the local church, as in the early tradition, nor the
empire, as in the "imperial" tradition, but a new reality which
emerged from the progressive dislocation of Byzantium: the
Christian nation. Accordingly we shall define this third layer
as *national.* Its appearance added a new dimension, but also
a new complexity, to Orthodox ecclesiology.

Byzantium thought of itself, at least in theory, in universal
and not national terms. Even on the eve of its final collapse a
Byzantine patriarch wrote to a Russian prince a long letter
explaining to him that there can be but one emperor and one
empire under heaven, just as there is but one God in heaven.
Ideologically and ideally the empire was *universal* (inci-
dentaly "Roman" and not "Greek" according to official imperial language), and it was this universality that was the

main "basis" for its acceptance by and alliance with the Church.

But we know today that this Byzantine universalism began, and this at a relatively early date, to dissolve itself into a rather narrow "nationalism" and exclusivism which were naturally fed by the tragic events of Byzantine history: the Arab conquest of its provinces, the unceasing advance of the Turks, the Latin invasion of 1204, the appearance of the Slavic challenge in the North, etc. In theory nothing changed; in practice Byzantium was becoming a relatively small and weak *Greek* state whose universal claims were less and less comprehensible to the nations brought into her political, religious and cultural orbit: Bulgars, Serbs and later, Russians. Or rather these very claims, this very Byzantine ideology was to become, in a truly paradoxical fashion, the main source of a new Orthodox nationalism (the second source being the later transformation of this nationalism under the influence of the "secular nationalism" of 1789). Less and less impressed by the ailing empire, more and more impatient with its religio-political claims, these "nations" which were born of Byzantine ideology began to apply this very ideology to themselves. From that complex process there emerged the idea of a *Christian nation*—with a national vocation, a kind of corporate "identity" before God. What is important for us here is that only at this stage in the history of the Eastern Church there appeared the notion of "autocephaly"—which, if not in its origin (it was used in various senses before but always "occasionally"), at least in its application, is a product not of ecclesiology, but of a *national* phenomenon. Its fundamental historical connotation is thus neither purely ecclesiological, nor "jurisdictional," but *national*. To a universal empire corresponds an "imperial" church with its center in Constantinople: such is the axiom of the Byzantine "imperial" ideology. There can therefore be no political independence from the empire without its ecclesiastical counterpart or "autocephaly": such becomes the axiom of the new Orthodox "theocracies." "Autocephaly," i.e. ecclesiastical independence, becomes thus the very basis of national and political independence, the status-symbol of a new "Christian nation." And it is very significant that all negotiations concerning the various "autocephalies" were conducted not by churches, but by states: the most typical example here being the process of negotiating the autocephaly of the Russian Church in the sixteenth century, a process in which the Russian Church herself took virtually no part.

We must stress once more that this new "autocephalous" church, as it appears in Bulgaria and later in Russia and in Serbia, is not a mere "jurisdictional" entity. Its main implication is not so much "independence" (for in fact it is usually totally dependent on the state) but precisely the *national* church, or, in other words, the church as the religious expression and projection of a nation, as indeed the bearer of a *national identity*. And again there is no need to think of this as a "deviation"—in merely negative and disparaging terms. In the history of the Orthodox East, the "Orthodox nation" is not only a reality, but in many ways a "success"; for in spite of all their deficiencies, tragedies and betrayals, there indeed were such "realities" as "Holy Serbia" or "Holy Russia," there truly took place a national birth in Christ, there appeared a national Christian vocation—and, historically, the emergence of the national church, at a time when the ideal and the reality of the universal Christian empire and its counterpart, the "imperial" church, were wearing thin, was perfectly justified. What is not justified, however, is to confuse this historical development with the essential ecclesiology and, in fact, to subordinate the latter to the former. It is when the very essence of the Church began to be viewed in terms of this nationalism and reduced to it, that something which in itself was quite compatible with that "essence" became the beginning of an alarming ecclesiological deterioration.

7.

It may be clearer now what I meant when, at the beginning of this essay, I stated that in our present canonical and ecclesiastical controversies we appeal in fact to different "traditions." It is an obvious fact indeed that these appeals are made to one of the three "layers" briefly analysed above as if each one of them were a self-sufficient embodiment of the entire canonical tradition. And it is another obvious fact that at no time was an effort made within the Orthodox theological and canonical consciousness to give these three layers, and especially their interrelation inside Tradition, a serious ecclesiological evaluation. It is this strange fact that constitutes the main source of our present tragic misunderstandings. Now, the historical reason for that total lack of ecclesiological "reflection" and clarification is again a rather simple one. Virtually until our very time and in spite of the progressive disappearance of the various "Orthodox worlds," the Orthodox churches lived within the spiritual, structural and psychological context of these organic "worlds"—and this means by the logic of either the "imperial" or the "national" traditions, or else a combination of both. And the plain fact is that for several centuries there was in Orthodoxy an almost total atrophy of ecclesiological thinking, of any real interest in ecclesiology.

The collapse of Byzantium in 1453 provoked no such ecclesiological reaction and we know why: the Islamic concept of a "religion-nation" (*milet*) assured for the entire Byzantine world, now under Turkish domination, the continuity of the "imperial" tradition. In virtue of this principle the Ecumenical Patriarch assumed not only *de facto*, but even *de jure*, the function of the *head* of all Christians; he became, so to speak, their "emperor." This even led at one time to the liquidation of former "autocephalies" (Serbian, Bulgarian), which had never really become an integral part of the Byzantine system (the Greeks even today rarely use the term "autocephaly" as a clearly defined ecclesiastical concept) and were always granted "reluctantly" and under political pressure. One can say that this Byzantine "imperial" system was indeed reinforced by the Turkish religious system, for it made the Greek "imperio-ethnic" self-consciousness even greater. As to the "church-nations" born before the downfall of the empire, they were either absorbed by the monarchy of the Ecumenical Throne or, as in the case of Russia, made this very downfall the basis of a new national and religious ideology with messianic overtones ("the Third Rome"). Both developments clearly excluded any serious ecclesiological reflection, a common reevaluation of the universal structures in the light of the radically new situation. Finally the impact on post-patristic Orthodox theology of Western thought forms and categories shifted ecclesiological attention from the Church as the Body of Christ to the Church as "means of sanctification," from the canonical tradition to the various systems of "canon law," or, more sharply, from the *Church* to ecclesiastical *government.*

All this explains why for many centuries the Orthodox churches lived in a variety of *status quos* without even trying to relate these to one another or to evaluate them within a consistent ecclesiological tradition. One must add that these centuries were also the time of an almost total lack of communications between the churches, of their mutual alienation from one another and of growth, consequently, of mutual mistrust, suspicion—and let us admit it—sometimes even hatred! The Greeks, weakened and humiliated by the Turkish dominion, became accustomed—and not always without reason—to see in every Russian move a threat to their ecclesiastical independence, a "Slavic" threat to "Hellenism"; the various Slavic groups, while antagonistic to one another, developed a common hatred for the Greek ecclesiastical "dominion." The fate of Orthodoxy became an integral part of the famous "oriental question" in which, as everyone knows, the Western "powers" and their Christian "establishments" took a great and by no means disinterested part. Where, in all this, was any place left for ecclesiological reflection, for a serious and common search for canonical clarification? There are not many darker pages in "pan-Orthodox" history than the ones dealing with the "modern age," the age which for Orthodoxy was—with a few remarkable exceptions—that of divisions, provincialism, theological sclerosis, and last but not least: a *nationalism* which by then was almost completely secularized and therefore paganized. It is not surprising then that any challenge to *status quo*, to the tragically unnoticed and normalized fragmentation, was inescapably to take the form of an explosion.

8.

That America became both the cause and the focal point of such an explosion is only too natural. Chances for an open crisis were indeed very small as long as Orthodox churches lived in their respective "worlds" in almost total isolation from one another. What happened to one church hardly mattered to the others. Thus the peculiar Greek "autocephaly" of 1850 was viewed as an internal Greek affair, not as an event with ecclesiological implications for all the churches. The same attitude prevailed towards the complex ecclesiastical developments within the Austro-Hungarian Empire, the "Bulgarian schism," the purely administrative "liquidation" by the Russian government—not by the Church—of the venerable Georgian "autocephaly," etc. All this was politics, not ecclesiology. And indeed the Russian foreign office, the Western embassies in Istanbul and Athens, the imperial court of Vienna, the obscure interests and intrigues of the Phanariot families, were at that time a greater factor in the life of the Orthodox Church than the lonely meditations on her nature and essence by a Khomiakov.

In America, however, this situation was bound to reach a "moment of truth." Here in the main center of Orthodox diaspora, of Orthodox mission and witness to the West, *the* ecclesiological question—that of the *nature* and *unity* of the Church, that of the relationship within her between her canonical order and her life, that ultimately of the true meaning and true implications of the very term *Orthodox*—was finally revealed as an existential, not academic, question. Here the tragic discrepancy between the various "layers" of the Orthodox past, the multisecular lack of any serious ecclesiological reflection, the absence of a "common mind," were revealed in their truly tragic dimension.

In the first place the American situation revealed the hypertrophy of the *national* principle, its virtually total disconnection from the "essential" ecclesiology. The national principle which, in a different ecclesiological context and in continuity with the genuine canonical tradition, had been indeed a principle of unity and thus a valid form of the Church's self fulfillment ("one Church in one place"), became in America exactly the opposite: a principle of division, the very expression of the Church's subordination to the divisions of "this world." If in the past the Church *united* and even *made* a nation, here nationalism *divided* the Church and became thus a real denial, a caricature of its own initial function. This *reductio ad absurdum* of a formerly positive and acceptable principle can best be shown by the example of churches which in the "old world" were virtually free from "nationalism." Take, for instance, the Patriarchate of Antioch, which never had any nationalistic "identity" comparable to that of the Russian or Serbian churches. Paradoxically enough it is this patriarchate's almost sporadic extension into "new worlds" that created little by little a "nationalism" *sui generis,* that at least of a "jurisdictional identity."

In America the national principle resulted in something totally new and unprecedented: each "national" church now claimed a *de facto* universal jurisdiction on the basis of national "belonging." In the "old world," even at the height of ecclesiastical nationalism, the rich and powerful Russian monasteries on Mount Athos never questioned the jurisdiction of the Ecumenical Patriarch, or the very numerous Greek parishes in southern Russia that of the Russian Church; and as to the Russian parish in Athens, it is still in the jurisdiction of the Church of Greece. Whatever their inner nationalism, all the churches knew their *boundaries.* The idea that these boundaries are exclusively national, that each Russian, Greek, Serb or Romanian *belongs* to his church wherever he may live, and that *ipso facto* each national church has canonical rights everywhere is therefore a new idea, truly the result of a *reductio ad absurdum.* There appeared even "churches-in-exile" with "territorial" titles of their bishop and diocese; there appeared national extensions of non-existent churches; there appeared finally a hierarchy, a theology, even a spirituality defending all this as something perfectly normal, positive and desirable.

If in the early and essential tradition the territorial principle of the Church's organization (one church, one bishop in one place) was so central and so important, it is because it

was indeed the essential condition for the Church's freedom
from "this world," from everything temporary, accidental
and non-essential. The Church knew herself to be simultaneously at home and in exile everywhere, she knew that she
was primarily and essentially a new people and that her very
structure was the expression of all this. The rejection of this
principle in the diaspora inescapably led to a progressive
enslavement of the Church to, and her identification with,
that which is precisely accidental—be it politics or nationalism.

The incompatibility between this mentality and the very
idea of an American "autocephaly" is so evident that it does
not need to be explained or elaborated. It is thus in the "national" layer of our tradition, a layer, however, almost completely detached from the essential tradition of the Church
and even "self-sufficient," that we find the first *locus*, cause
and expression of our present ecclesiastical crisis.

9.

The first but not the only one. If nearly all the Orthodox
churches are in various degrees victims of hypertrophied nationalism and appeal almost exclusively to the national "precedent" in the Orthodox past, the moment of truth which
descended upon us concerns also the "layer" which we termed
imperial. It is here indeed that we find the deep root of the
syndrome which is at the very heart of the specifically *Greek*
reaction to the present storm.

It is not a mere "accident," of course, that the most violently negative reaction to "autocephaly" has been that of the
Ecumenical Patriarchate. This reaction, however, is at such
variance with the entire personal "image" of Patriarch
Athenagoras, an image made up of ecumenical generosity,
universal understanding and compassion, opposition to
narrow-mindedness in all its forms, openness to dialogues and
reevaluations, that it certainly cannot be explained by anything
petty and personal. Neither can this reaction be ascribed to a
lust for power, a desire to rule the Orthodox Church in the
"papist" fashion, to subjugate *under* Constantinople all

Orthodox Christians in the diaspora. Indeed, during several decades of jurisdictional and national pluralism in America and elsewhere, the Ecumenical Patriarch neither condemned it as "uncanonical" nor made any direct and consistent claims on all these lands as belonging to his jurisdiction. Even in the most recent documents issued by the patriarchate the main theme is the defense of the *status quo* and not a direct jurisdictional claim. The idea of charging the Ecumenical Throne with the solution of the canonical problems of the diaspora was in fact developed some twenty years ago by a group of Russian theologians (including this writer) but met, on the part of the Greek and Phanariot circles, with total indifference. All this means that the real motivations behind the Greek "reaction" must be sought elsewhere. But where?

The answer to this question lies, I am convinced, in the developments analysed in the preceding pages. It is indeed in the *imperial* layer of that development that we must seek the explanation of something essential in the Greek religious mentality: its almost total inability to understand and therefore to *accept* the post-Byzantine development of the Orthodox world. If for virtually all other Orthodox the basic "term of reference" of their ecclesiastical mentality is simply national, the nationalism of the Greek mentality is precisely *not simple*. The roots of this nationalism are not, as in the case of other Orthodox, in the reality and experience of "Church-nation," but primarily in those of the Byzantine *oikoumene*, and this means in that layer of the past which we termed *imperial*. Thus, for example, the churches of Greece or of Cyprus or even the patriarchates of Alexandria and Jerusalem are, technically speaking, *autocephalous* churches; but to them this "autocephaly" has a meaning deeply different from the one attached to it by Russians, Bulgarians or Romanians and, in fact, the very seldom, if at all, use that term. For whatever their jurisdictional status or arrangement, in their consciousness—or shall we rather say subconsciousness?—they are still organic parts of a greater whole; and this "whole" is not the Church Universal but precisely the Byzantine "world" with Constantinople as its sacred center and focus.

Indeed the central and the decisive fact in the post-

Byzantine religious history of the Greeks is this almost unconscious yet obvious *transformation* of the "imperial" layer
of the Orthodox tradition into an *essential* one, the transformation of Byzantium into a permanent, essential and
normative dimension or *nota* of Orthodoxy itself. The reasons
for that paradoxical process are too numerous and too
complex to be enumerated here. Some have their roots in
Byzantium itself, some in the long Turkish captivity, some in
more recent layers of Greek history. But the fact is here:
the tradition which we described earlier as conditioned by
the fundamental *historicity* of the Church, i.e. the "acceptance"
of the contingent and relative "worlds" to which she is
"related" during her long earthly pilgrimage, resulted in its
very opposite: the equally fundamental *anti-historical* or
a-historical character of the Greek religious world-view.
Byzantium for the Greek is not a chapter, however central,
important and in many ways decisive, in the history of the
Church, in her unending "pilgrimage," but the fulfillment
of this history, its permanent *terminus ad quem* beyond which
nothing significant can "happen" and which therefore can
only be preserved. The *reality* of this unique and ultimate
"world" does not depend on history. The historical collapse
of the empire in 1453 not only did not destroy it but, on the
contrary, by depriving it of all that is merely "historical,"
i.e. temporary and contingent, transformed it into a truly supra-
historical reality, an "essence" no longer subject to historical
contingencies. "Historically" the imperial city may have been
called Istanbul for half a millenium. For the Greek it *is*
Constantinople, the New Rome, the heart, the center and the
symbol of a "reality" which is beyond all "history."

But the truly paradoxical character of that "reality" is
that it cannot be easily identified with either a "form" or a
"content." It is certainly not the Byzantine Empire as such,
not the "political" dream of its eventual restoration. Greeks
are too practical not to understand the illusory nature of such
a dream. In fact they expatriate themselves more easily than
many other Orthodox, their "adjustment" to any new situation
is usually more successful, and they certainly have not transferred any Byzantine and "theocratic" mystique to the modern

Greek state. But it is not "content" either—in the sense, for example, of a particular faithfulness to or interest in the doctrinal, theological, spiritual and cultural traditions of Byzantium, in that "Orthodox Byzantinism" which constitutes indeed an essential part of the Orthodox tradition. Greek academic theology has been not less, if not more, "Westernized" than the theology of other Orthodox churches; and the great patristic, liturgical and iconographic revival of our time, the new and passionate rediscovery of the Byzantine "sources" of Orthodoxy, did not originate in Greece or among Greeks. Thus the "Byzantine world" which consciously or mainly unconsciously constitutes the essential "term of reference" for the Greek religious mentality is neither the *historical* Byzantium nor the *spiritual* Byzantium. But then what is it? The answer—of decisive importance for the understanding of the Greek religious and ecclesiastical "world-view"—is: Byzantium as both the foundation and the justification of Greek *religious nationalism*. It is indeed this unique and truly paradoxical amalgamation of two distinct, if not contradictory, layers in the historical development of the Orthodox world that is at the very heart of that immense and tragic misunderstanding which, in turn, determines in many ways our present ecclesiastical crisis.

I call it paradoxical because, as I have said already, the very essence of the Byzantine "imperial" tradition was not national, but *universal*. And it is only this *universality*, however theoretical and imperfect, that made it possible for the Church to "accept" the empire itself and to make it her earthly "habitation." The Byzantines called themselves Romans, not Greeks, because Rome, not Greece, was the symbol of universality, and for this reason the new capital could only be a "New Rome." Until the seventh century the official language of the Byzantine chanceries was Latin, not Greek. Finally, the Church Fathers would have been horrified if someone were to call them "Greeks." It is here indeed that lies the first and deepest misunderstanding. For when a Fr. Florovsky speaks of "Christian Hellenism" as a permanent and essential dimension of Christianity, when a Philaret of Moscow puts in his *Catechism* the definition of the Orthodox

Church as "Greek-Catholic," they obviously do not refer to something "ethnic" or "national." For them this "Christian Hellenism" — that of theology, liturgy, iconography — is not only not identical with the "Greek" but, in fact, is in many ways its very "antidote," the fruit of a long and sometimes painful and critical transformation of the Greek categories. The fight between the "Greek" and the "Christian" is indeed the very content of the great and eternally normative patristic age, its real "theme." And it is the "Greek" revival, the appearance of a Greek nationalism no longer "referred" to Christian Hellenism, which, in the last years of Byzantium, was one of the essential factors behind the tragedy of Florence.

What happened in the Greek mentality was the result thus not of an evolution or development but of a metamorphosis. The tragic events in the history of the empire, the bitter experience of the Turkish domination, the fight for survival and liberation transformed the Byzantine "imperial" tradition, gave it a meaning exactly opposite to the one it had at the beginning and which justified its acceptance by the Church. The universal was replaced with the national, Christian Hellenism with Hellenism, Byzantium with Greece. The unique and universal Christian value of Byzantium was transferred to the Greeks themselves, to the Greek nation which, because of its exclusive identification with "Hellenism," acquired now a new and unique value. It is very characteristic, however, that when even Greek hierarchs speak of "Hellenism" they refer not so much to the "Christian Hellenism" of Byzantium, but to "ancient Greek civilization," to Plato and Pythagoras, to Homer and the "Athenian democracy" as if being "Greek" makes one in an almost exclusive sense an "heir" and a "bearer" of that "Hellenism."

But in reality this "Hellenism" is the Greek expression of the secular nationalism common to all modern nations and whose roots are in the French Revolution of 1789 and in European Romanticism. As every nationalism of that type it is built upon a mythology partly "secular" and partly "religious." On the secular level the myth is that of a unique relationship between the Greeks and that "Hellenism" which constitutes the common source and foundation of the entire Western civilization. On the religious level the myth is that of a unique relationship to Byzantium, the Christian *oikoumene*, which is the common foundation of all Orthodox churches. And it is this double mythology, or rather its impact on Greek ecclesiastical thinking, that makes ecclesiological dialogue so difficult.

10.

The first difficulty lies in the different understanding of the place and function within the Orthodox Church of the Ecumenical Patriarch. All Orthodox churches without any exception assent to his primacy. There is, however, a substantial difference in the understanding of that primacy between the Greek churches and all others.

For the non-Greek churches the basic term of reference for this primacy is the "essential" ecclesiology which has always and from the very beginning known a universal center of unity and agreement and therefore a *taxis*, an order of seniority and honor among churches. This universal primacy is thus both *essential*, in the sense that it always exists in the Church, and *historical*, in the sense that its "location" may vary and indeed has varied; for it depends on the historical situation of the Church at a given time. The primacy of Constantinople was established by ecumenical councils, by the "consensus" of all the churches; this makes it "essential" for it is truly the expression of the churches' agreement, of their unity. It is equally true, however, that it was established within a particular historical context, as an ecclesiological response to a particular situation: the emergence of a universal Christian empire. And although no one today in the whole Orthodox Church feels and expresses the need for any change in the churches' *taxis*, such changes have taken place before and, at least theoretically, may happen tomorrow. Thus, for example, in the case of a "conversion" to Orthodoxy of the Roman Catholic Church, the "universal primacy" may—or may not—return to the first Rome. Such is in its simplest form the ecclesiological stand of the non-Greek Orthodox churches. The fully accepted primacy of the Patriarch of Constantinople does not imply here either any "national" implication, nor that of some divinely instituted and therefore eternal *taxis* of the churches. The "consensus" of the churches expressed through an ecumenical council may, if necessary, change this *taxis*, as it did before—in the case of Antioch and Jerusalem, of Ephesus and Cyprus, and of Constantinople itself.

This theory, however, is "anathema" to the Greeks, and it is here that the fundamental ambiguity of contemporary Orthodox ecclesiology becomes obvious. For the Greeks the "term of reference" for the primacy of the Ecumenical Throne lies not in any particular ecclesiological tradition, be it "essential" or "imperial," but in the unique position held by the Ecumenical Patriarch within that "Hellenism" which, as we have just seen, constitutes the "essence" of their religious "world-view." For if the "secular" center of that "Hellenism" is Athens, its religious focus and symbol is most certainly Constantinople. For long centuries of the Turkish dominion the patriarch was the *religious ethnarch* of the Greek nation, the focus and the symbol of its survival and identity. And thus the Ecumenical Throne remains for the Greeks today a reality not so much of an ecclesiological and canonical, but primarily of a spiritual and psychological order. "Canonically" the Greeks may or may not "belong" to the patriarchate. Thus the Church of Greece is independent from the patriarchate, whereas every Greek in Australia or Latin America is in the latter's "jurisdiction." But whatever their "jurisdictional" status they are all *under* Constantinople. Here it is not Constantinople as the universal center of unity and agreement that is essential. It is Constantinople as such, the Ecumenical Throne as the bearer and guardian of "Hellenism." The primacy of Constantinople is ascribed now to the very *esse* of the Church, becomes in itself a *nota Ecclesiae*. The ecclesiological formula: "there *is* Constantinople, to which the Church has entrusted the universal primacy" becomes: "there *must* be Constantinople." But the tragic ambiguity of this situation is precisely that the primate, whose function is to assure the *universality of the Church*, to be guardian of that "Christian Hellenism" which preserves every Church from a total identification with "nationalism," is at the same time for one particular nation the bearer and the symbol of its very *nationalism*. The ecumenical primacy becomes the primacy of the "Greek."

It is this ambiguity in the Greek religious and national mentality that made it—and still makes it—so difficult for Greeks to understand the true meaning of the post-Byzantine Orthodox world, of its real problems, of its unity as well as diversity. Essentially they failed to understand that the collapse of the Byzantine Empire was not necessarily the end of Orthodox unity based on the common acceptance of Orthodox Byzantium, i.e. "Christian Hellenism." For the whole point is that the Slavs, for example, who sought their independence from the empire were, in fact, not less "Byzantine" than the Greeks, and were seeking independence from the Greeks but not from "Christian Hellenism." The first Bulgarian Empire—that of Boris and Symeon—was truly "Byzantine" in its entire ethos, culture and, of course, religious tradition. Fr. Florovsky in his *Ways of Russian Theology* speaks of "early Russian Byzantinism." All these new nations had no cultural tradition comparable to the one which the Greeks had in Ancient Greece, and their initial and formative tradition, the one that gave them their national "birth" and made them into Orthodox nations, was the Christian Byzantine tradition. And in spite of all conflicts, misunderstandings and mutual isolation, this unity in the Byzantine tradition has never been really broken or forgotten, but has always constituted the common foundation, the very form of unity, of the entire Orthodox East.

But for the Greeks, imprisoned as they progressively became by the identification of the "Byzantine" with the "Greek," by the national and even ethnic reduction of Byzantinism, any attempt to establish political and ecclesiastical independence from the empire—on the part of Slavs, or Arabs, or Romanians—meant almost automatically a threat to "Hellenism," an attempt to destroy the "Greeks" and their birthright within Orthodoxy. They never understood that the essential unity of the Orthodox world is neither national, nor political, nor even jurisdictional, but the unity precisely of

"Christian Hellenism," the Orthodox embodiment of the
essential Christian Tradition. And they did not understand
it because they identified this "Christian Hellenism" with
"Hellenism," i.e. with the Greek national and ethnic "identity." The Slavs in this perspective were viewed as an alien
and essentially "barbarian" force aimed at the destruction of
"Hellenism." And since the Slavs were strong and the Greeks
weak, this view took sometimes almost paranoic forms. After
the liberation of Greece in the nineteenth century and the
emergence of a new "Western" Greek nationalism, "Pan-
Slavism" became—not without the help of the Western
powers—a real catchword, the synonym of *the* Threat and *the*
Enemy. One must add here that Russian imperial policy in the
"Oriental question" was not always of great help in alleviating
these fears, and was certainly guilty of many a tasteless tactic,
but it is equally true that at the very height of Russia's own
messianic and imperialistic nationalism, never did the Russian
Orthodox consciousness question the primacy of Constantinople and of the venerable Eastern patriarchates or press for
a change in the *taxis* of the Orthodox churches. On the contrary, the nineteenth century in Russia was marked by a revival
of precisely "Byzantine" interests, by a return to "Christian
Hellenism" as the source of Orthodoxy, by a return to a truly
universal Orthodox ecclesiology, by progressive liberation
from the narrow, pseudo-messianic nationalism of the "Third
Rome." Whatever the various "diplomatic" difficulties, ecclesiologically the real obstacle to a recovery by the Orthodox
Church of her essential unity lay, at that time, not in any
mythological "Pan-Slavism" but in the narrowly nationalistic
reduction, by the Greeks, of "Christian Hellenism" to "Hellenism."

All this explains why the Greek ecclesiastical "officialdom" (we do not speak here of popular feelings, which have
always somehow preserved the intuition of Orthodox unity)
never really *accepted* post-Byzantine ecclesiological development, never integrated it into its own "world-view." The
various "autocephalies" granted during and after the Byzantine period were "concessions" and "accommodations," not
the acknowledgement of something normal, of something as

"adequate" to the new situation as the acknowledgement of the "Imperial Church" was "adequate" to the previous situation: that of a Christian empire. For that new situation really had no room within the Greek religious mentality, and was viewed indeed as accidental and temporary. For this reason no "autocephaly" has ever been granted freely but has always been the result of fight and "negotiation." For this reason also, even today the principle of "autocephaly," which constitutes the basic principle of the Church's present organization, is never quite understood by the Greek "officialdom," whether in its "principium" (the "right to grant autocephaly") or in its "modality" (its implications for "inter-church relations").

One thing is clear, however, and constitutes the ultimate paradox of this entire development. Having reluctantly recognized this principle *de facto*, the Greek "officialdom" seems to justify it by that very reasoning which in the past made the Greeks reject and fight it: the idea of an *essential* difference between the Hellenic and the various non-Hellenic "Orthodoxies." If in the past they fought "autocephalies" because they rejected the idea that "Christian Hellenism" — as essence of Orthodoxy—may have any other ecclesiological expression than that of one "Imperial Church" which is Greek, today they accept them because, having in fact replaced "Christian Hellenism" with "Hellenism," they believe that the other "Orthodoxies" must necessarily be the expression of some other "essences": "Russian Orthodoxy," "Serbian Orthodoxy," etc. And just as the vocation of "Greek Orthodoxy" is to preserve Hellenism, the vocation of the other churches is to preserve their own—ultimately "national"— essences. Having thus completed its full circle, the "imperial" mentality joined the "national" one. And this was inevitable if one remembers that the real source of modern "nationalism" lies not in Christianity but in the ideas of the French Revolution of 1789, the true "mother" of the petty, fanatical and negativistic "nationalisms" of the nineteenth and twentieth centuries. What makes, however, this new (not Byzantine but *modern*) Greek nationalism distinct from other Orthodox nationalisms is the certitude, surviving in it from its "imperial" antecedents, that within all these Orthodox "essences" the

Greek "essence" has a primacy, occupies *jure divino* the first place. Having forgotten that it is not "Hellenism" as such but "Christian Hellenism" that constitutes the real unity of Orthodoxy and has a spiritual and eternal "primacy" over all other "expressions," having identified this "Hellenism" with themselves, the Greeks claim a "primacy" which indeed might have been theirs but on entirely different presuppositions. This is today the fundamental ambiguity of the "universal primacy" in the Orthodox Church. Does it belong to the first among bishops, the one whom the "consensus" of all the churches respects, loves and venerates in the person of the Ecumenical Patriarch, or does it belong to the spiritual head and bearer of "Hellenism" whose Christian value and affiliation is as questionable as that of any modern and half pagan nationalism?

11.

Here we can interrupt our reflections on the true nature and causes of our present ecclesiastical storm. I am convinced that as long as the questions raised in this article are not answered, all our polemics and controversies about the new "autocephaly" will remain superficial, non-essential, and ultimately meaningless. To answer them, however, necessarily means to achieve a deep and constructive clarification of Orthodox ecclesiology itself.

What happened, or rather what happens, in America can indeed be reduced to a simple formula: it is an almost *forced* return to the "essential" Orthodox ecclesiology, to its very roots, to those fundamental norms and presuppositions to which the Church always returns when she finds herself in a new situation in "this world" whose "fashion" is passing. I use the term "forced" because this return is the fruit not of abstract "academic" thinking but of life itself, of the circumstances in which the Church discovers—painfully and not without torments and sufferings—that the only way of survival for her is precisely to be the *Church*, to be that which eternally shines and illumines us in the primordial and essential ecclesiology in which the unique and eternal experience, form and consciousness — the very being — of the Church, have found their expression.

That only one "part" of the Orthodox Church in America has up to now been "forced" into that return because its own situation made it inevitable; that this has provoked passions, fears, suspicions; that some of the external "factors" make some of these fears understandable: all this is natural, all this was probably inevitable. Fear, however, is a bad counsellor. Only if we are able to raise our questions to that level which alone can make them answerable and which is that of "essential" ecclesiology, only if we are able to see and to evaluate facts in this essential perspective, will the storm be revealed as meaningful, will it lead to a common victory.

Sooner or later it will become clear to all that it is not by concentrating on the preservation of "Hellenism," "Russianism" or "Serbianism" that we will preserve Orthodoxy; but, on the contrary, by preserving and fulfilling the demands of the Church we will salvage all that is essential in all incarnations of the Christian faith and life. If Fr. Florovsky, a Russian theologian living and working "in exile," had the courage in his *Ways of Russian Theology* to denounce and to condemn the deviations of "Russianism" from "Christian Hellenism" and thus to liberate an entire generation of Russian theologians from the last hangups of any pseudo-messianism and religious nationalism, is it not time for a Greek to perform the same painful yet necessary and liberating operation with the ambiguities of "Hellenism"?

Sooner or later it will become clear to all that the Ecumenical Patriarch, if he is to fulfill his "universal primacy," will achieve it not by defensive and negative reactions, not by questionable "appeals" to equally questionable and inapplicable "precedents" and "traditions," but by constructive leadership towards the fulfillment by the Church of her essence in every place of God's dominion. Personally I have spent too much of my theological life "defending" the universal primacy of the Patriarch of Constantinople to be accused of any "anti-Constantinopolitanism." This primacy, its necessity for the Church, its tremendous potential for Orthodoxy, I once more solemnly confess and affirm here. This primacy, however, to become again "what it is," must be purified of all ambiguities, of all non-essential "contexts," of all nationalistic connotations, of the dependence on anything—in the past, present and future—which is not the Church and only the Church. This is perhaps the most urgent task of the universal primacy today: to liberate us from pagan and heretical nationalisms which choke the universal and saving vocation of the Orthodox Church. We should cease to speak of our "glories." For glory in the essential Tradition of the Church belongs to God alone, and it is for the glorification of God, not of herself, that the Church was established. Once we have realized this, things impossible with men become possible with God.

V

THE TASK OF ORTHODOX
THEOLOGY TODAY

> "Do not quench the Spirit, do
> not despise prophesying, but test
> everything; hold fast to what is
> good . . ."
>
> I Thess. 5:19-21.

1.

What do we mean when we speak of the task of Orthodox theology today? It is proper to begin with this question because this phrase may seem to suggest a theological orientation of which Orthodoxy is suspicious, but which seems to predominate in the West today. It is the reduction of theology to a given "situation" or "age," a stress on "relevance" understood almost exclusively as a dependence of theology, its task, method and language on "modern man" and his specifically modern "needs." From the beginning, therefore, we must emphasize that Orthodoxy rejects such a reduction of theology, whose first and eternal task is to search for Truth, not for relevance, for words "adequate to God" (*theoprepeis logoi*), not to man. Theology is truly relevant—because truly Christian—when it remains a scandal for the Jews, foolishness for the Greeks and is at odds with this world and its passing "cultures" and "modernities." This does not mean, however, that theology operates in a cultural vacuum. For it is one thing to depend

---

* A paper read at the First Conference of Orthodox Theologians in America, September, 1966, and originally published in *St. Vladimir's Theological Quarterly* 10.4 (1966), pp. 180-188.

on the world and quite another to be related to it. If the first attitude, the acceptance of the world as the only criterion of theology, is to be rejected, the second (which, in the last analysis, is but the basic Christian concern for the world and its salvation) is the very *raison d'être* of theology. In this sense, all genuine theology has always been pastoral, missionary and prophetic, and whenever it has lost these dimensions, it has become a mere intellectual game justly ignored by the "real" Church. The task of theology at any given moment is necessarily determined by the needs of the Church, and the first task of the theologian is always to discern and to accept these needs, to become aware of what the Church expects from him.

As a small group of Orthodox theologians living and working in the West, far from the ancient and "organically" Orthodox worlds and cultures, we are justified therefore in asking this preliminary question: What are the needs of the Church to which we must respond and around which we are to organize and plan our theological work? How are we to obey here in the West the eternal demands—pastoral, missionary and prophetic—of Orthodox theology? This essay is a brief attempt to inaugurate a common search for a common answer.

2.

Probably everyone will agree that our theological task is determined primarily by the fact that, as theologians, we work within and for an Orthodox community which, for the first time in the long history of our Church, has to live in a non-Orthodox world, Western in its religious traditions, secularistic in its culture, and pluralistic in its "world-view." This for Orthodoxy is an unprecedented situation, and it challenges the whole Church and consequently us, her theologians, with a set of problems unknown to the Orthodox communities of the "old world."

First of all, this new situation substantially affects the *pastoral* responsibilities of theology. I venture to affirm that for several centuries theology was not needed as vitally—and on virtually every level of the Church's life—as it is today. The reason for this is simple. In Greece or Russia or any other Orthodox country, culture itself, i.e. the complex of values, norms and ideas by which man evaluates his life, was related in some deep sense to the Orthodox faith, was in continuation with the Church's "world-view." One can and must criticize the obvious shortcomings and sins of those Orthodox "worlds," but one cannot deny that, in spite of many betrayals, they remained for a long time organically shaped by Orthodoxy. But this is not so in the West. Here the rupture between the Orthodox world-view and secularistic culture is so radical that the former finds virtually no "point of application," and the language by which it is transmitted, that of the liturgy, spirituality and ethics, remains "alien," even if it is English or any other western language. As the integration of Western "way of life" progresses, there develops a truly schizophrenic situation in which deep attachment to Orthodox symbols and "externals" (e.g. worship, music, architecture) easily coexists with an almost totally secularistic philosophy of life. Needless to say, such a situation cannot last long, and a mere faithfulness to Orthodox externals will not save Orthodoxy from being dissolved sooner or later into that peculiar blend of secularism and vague religiosity which seems to emerge as the new pattern of Western religion. To those who have ears to hear and eyes to see, it is already abundantly clear that in the West one cannot be Orthodox by "osmosis." A spiritually alien culture makes Orthodoxy here a challenge, and the faith, if it is to be true to itself, must be consciously accepted, clearly understood in its implications for life, and constantly defended against the pressures of secularism. It is here, therefore, that theology is called to recover the *pastoral* dimension, to supply, or rather to be, that understanding, that essential link between the Tradition of the Church and real life, to assure the acceptance of the faith by the faithful.

It would be a mistake to think, however, that what is meant here is a kind of theological "digest" for quick consumption by the laity, a mere descent of theology to a "popular level." It is exactly the opposite that I have in mind: the uplifting of the whole life of the Church into theological consciousness, a vital relation to theological reflection of every aspect and every level of the Church's life. But to achieve this, we must give some thought to that which, at least in my opinion, constitutes the basic defect of our theology: its almost total divorce from the real life of the Church and from her *practical* needs. By his very upbringing and training, the theologian is accustomed to looking at everything "practical" as virtually opposed to theology and its lofty pursuits, and this attitude has been adopted for so many centuries that it is almost taken for granted. Since the breakdown of the patristic age, our theology (and not without Western influence) has become exclusively "academic," "scholastic" in the literal sense of the word. It is confined to a narrow circle of professional intellectuals, writing and working, in fact, for each other (who else reads theology, or, even if he wished to, is capable of reading its highly professional and esoteric language?) and, as time goes by, more and more anxious to satisfy and please their peers in other academic disciplines rather than the less and less theologically-minded Church. They are reconciled to the supreme indifference of the Church at large to their work because, in their unshakable self-righteousness, they put the blame on the anti-intellectualism of the clergy and laity. What they do not seem to realize, however, is that this "anti-intellectualism" is in a way a direct result of their own exclusive "intellectualism," of their quasi-Manichean contempt for the "practical" needs of the Church, of their reduction of theology to a harmless intellectual game of "interesting points of view" and scientifically impeccable footnotes. And the sad irony of the situation is that, ignored by the Church, they are not truly accepted by the so-called "intellectual community" either, for which, in spite of all their efforts *ad captatiam benevolentiae*, they remain non-scientific "mystics." And as long as such is the state and the inner orientation of our theology, the hope that it will fulfill its pastoral function and respond to the crying needs of our situation is, of course, vain.

But it is at this point, perhaps, that we can turn our eyes to those whom we always claim to be our examples and teachers, the Holy Fathers of the Church, and look a little deeper into their understanding of the theological task. Most certainly they were not less intellectual. And yet, there is one decisive difference between them and modern theological scholars. To all of them, that which we call "practical" and virtually exclude from our academic concerns meant nothing else but the unique and indeed very practical concern of Christianity: the eternal salvation of man. Words and ideas were for them directly related not simply to Truth and Error, but to the Truth that *saves* and to the error that brings with it death and damnation. And it is their constant, truly "existential" preoccupation with, and their total commitment to, salvation of real, concrete men that makes every line they wrote so ultimately serious and their theology so vital and precisely pastoral. Intellectual as it is, their theology is always addressed not to "intellectuals" but to the whole Church, in the firm belief that everyone in the Church has received the Spirit of Truth and was made a "theologian"—i.e. a man concerned with God. And the lasting truth of their theology is that in it ideas are always referred to the "practical" needs of the Church, revealed in their soteriological significance, whereas the most "practical" aspects of the Church are rooted in their ultimate theological implications.

For us in the West, to recover the pastoral dimension of theology means then not a change of level ("write on a more popular level"), but above everything else a change in the inner orientation of the theological mind, of the basic theological concern itself. First of all, we must aim our theological effort at the real Church and at real man in the Church. We must care about the situation of that man and not only about his becoming "more educated" and "proud of Orthodoxy." For as long as we ourselves are not convinced that many ideas and philosophies by which he lives today lead him to spiritual death, and that the knowledge of Truth is to *save* him and not merely to adorn our Church with a respectable intellectual elite, we certainly will not find the words which can reach him. As luxury and status symbol, theology is not needed in a religion which challenges man with the choice between life and death, salvation and damnation.

This means also that the "pastoral" revitalization of

theology must begin with a deep evaluation and critique of the culture in which the Orthodox man is immersed today and which indeed makes Christianity irrelevant. It is not accidental, of course, that patristic theology is rooted in a healthy apologetical purpose, in the defense of the faith against its external and internal enemies. As for us, we fight with great wit the battles which the Fathers have already won, but politely smile at the truly demonic implications of some of the modern philosophies and theories. We are unaware of the obvious fact that under the influences of these philosophies even some of the basic Christian terms are used in a meaning almost opposite to the ones which they had in the past. Salvation means self-fulfillment, faith—security, sin—a personal problem of adjustment, etc. Our culture, which recently has been described as a "triumph of therapeutics," has deeply changed the quest of even a religious man, and this makes it almost impossible for him to hear and to understand the true teaching of the Church. And finally, we do not seem to notice that this metamorphosis of religion takes place not in some mythical Western man, but in our own parishes, in the preaching of our priests. We must begin, therefore, with what patristic theology performed in its own time: an exorcism of culture, a liberating reconstruction of the words, concepts and symbols, of the theological language itself. And we must do it in order not to make our theology more "acceptable" to the modern man and his culture, but, on the contrary, to make him aware of the ultimately serious, truly soteriological nature and demands of his faith.

Only theology can accomplish this, and that is why it is so badly needed today. But it will succeed only when it again becomes *pastoral*, i.e. identified with the Church and her life, attentive to the real needs of man, when, putting aside the academic "straining at a gnat" which has never prevented anyone from "swallowing a camel," it accepts, in humility and with courage, its proper function in the Church.

3.

I defined the second task of our theology as *missionary*. To keep with the spirit of the time, I should have probably called it "ecumenical." But the word "ecumenical" has of late become so general and so ambiguous that it itself needs to be investigated and redefined. I prefer the slightly outmoded term "missionary" for several reasons. It indicates that Orthodox theology has a *mission* in the West. It has always been the consensus of Orthodox theologians that their participation in the ecumenical movement has as its goal to bring an Orthodox witness to the non-Orthodox, and there is no reason to deny that this implies the idea of conversion to Orthodoxy. I know very well that in current ecumenical thinking the term "conversion" has a bad reputation. But the Orthodox would simply betray both their Orthodoxy and the ecumenical movement if now, under the impact of a superficial ecumenical euphoria, they concealed the fact that in their approach conversion is one of the basic components of a genuine ecumenical perspective. More than ever, and precisely for deep ecumenical reasons, we must uphold our conviction that only a deep and genuinely Christian idea of *conversion*, i.e. of a decisive crisis, choice, and commitment to Truth, can give meaning and ultimate seriousness to all "dialogues," "rapprochements," and "convergences." That this term and the reality behind it are regarded today by many as "un-ecumenical" reveals, in fact, an alarming trend, a shift of the ecumenical movement from its original goal: organic unity in Christ, to a different one: the smooth functioning of pluralistic society. Excellent and useful as it may be, this second goal has very little to do with the fundamental Christian values of unity, faith and truth. Our "mission" then remains the same: to make Orthodoxy known, understood and, with God's help, accepted in the West. This mission stems naturally and, so to speak, inescapably from our truly awesome claim that we are *Orthodox* and that ours is the *true Church*. This claim is incompatible with any provincialism of thought and vision, ethnic self-consciousness, and self-centeredness.

For several decades the "ecumenical mission" has been, in fact, a monopoly of a small group of theologians, and it remained virtually unknown to and ignored by the Orthodox Church at large. I think that the time has come to put an end to this rather abnormal situation which, in addition to many other dangers, simply misleads the non-Orthodox by giving them the impression of an "ecumenical" Orthodoxy that does not exist in reality. A missionary orientation must be added to the whole theological structure of the Church and become an organic part of our theological "curriculum." This brings me to the second meaning of the term "missionary," to the "modality" of our approach to the West.

"Mission" has always meant, at least in the Christian connotations of that term, not only the effort to convert someone to true faith, but also the spiritual disposition of the missionary: his active charity and his self-giving to the "object" of his missionary task. From St. Paul to St. Nicholas of Japan there has been no mission without self-identification of the missionary with those to whom God has sent him, without a sacrifice of his personal attachments and his natural values. *Mutatis mutandis* the same must be said, it seems to me, about the Orthodox mission in the West, and more particularly, about the mission of Orthodox theology. This mission is impossible without some degree of love for the West and for the many authentically Christian values of its culture. Yet we often confuse the Universal Truth of the Church with a naive "superiority complex," with arrogance and self-righteousness, with a childish certitude that everyone ought to share our own enthusiasm for the splendors of Byzantium," for our "ancient and colorful rites," and the forms of our church architecture. It is sad and shocking to hear the West globally condemned and to see a condescending attitude towards the "poor Westerners" on the part of young people who, more often than not, have not read Shakespeare and Cervantes, have never heard about St. Francis of Assisi or listened to Bach. It is sad to realize that there is no greater obstacle to the understanding and acceptance of Orthodoxy than the provincialism, the human pride and the self-righteousness of the Orthodox themselves, their almost complete lack of humility and self-criticism. Yet Truth always makes humble, and pride in all its forms and expressions is always alien to Truth and is always a sin. It is obviously inconceivable to say that we are "proud of Christ," but we constantly preach and teach "pride of Orthodoxy." It is time to understand that if the Orthodox mission is to progress, we must not only transcend and overcome this spirit of self-righteousness, but we must, without denying any genuine value of our Eastern cultural and spiritual heritage, open ourselves towards Western culture and make our own whatever in it "is true, whatever is honorable, whatever is just, whatever is pure, whatever is lovely, whatever is gracious" (Phil. 4:8).

The missionary task of Orthodox theology must thus be guided by two equally important and interdependent imperatives: the emphasis on Truth as the only genuine ground of all "ecumenical" concern, and a real openness to Western Christian values. At a time when a serious temptation appears to sacrifice Truth for a very sophisticated, very qualified and, because of this, only more dangerous relativism, to replace the search for unity with a search for a religious "peaceful coexistence," when the very possibility of error and heresy is virtually ruled out by a pseudo-ecumenical doctrine of "convergence," the Orthodox theologian must stand, alone if necessary, in defense of the very concept of Truth, without which Christianity, for all its "relevance," denies in fact its own absolute claim. To do this, however, he must himself be open and obedient to *all* Truth, wherever he finds it.

4.

The third task of Orthodox theology today must be defined as *prophetic*, even if the word sounds presumptuous. The prophets were sent to the people of God not only to announce future events, but also to remind the people of their true mission and to denounce their betrayals of the divine will. And if, with the coming of Christ, who is "the fulfillment of all law and the prophets," their first function has become obsolete, the second remains as needed as ever. And properly understood, theology must always share in this prophetic function. For the eternal task of theology is to *refer* the life of the Church to the absolute Truth of the Church's own Tradition, to keep alive and operative a criterion by which the Church judges herself. Immersed in human history, the Church is always full of temptations and sins and, what is even more serious, of compromises and accommodations with the spirit of "this world." The temptation is always to prefer peace to truth, efficiency to rectitude, human success to the will of God. And since, in the Orthodox Church, there exists no visible center of infallible authority like the papacy, since her ultimate criterion and recourse is always the Truth abiding in her, it certainly belongs to those whose specific ministry is the study of and search for that Truth to make it known and manifest in all its purity and clarity. There is no arrogance, no pride in that claim. The theologian has no rights, no power to govern and to administer, this being the function of the hierarchy. But it is his sacred duty to supply the hierarchy and, indeed, the whole Church with the pure teaching of the Church and to stand by that truth even when it is not considered "opportune." It must be admitted that much too often our official "academic" theology has failed to accept this "obedience" and preferred quiet complacency. It has thus become accomplice to many deviations and distortions from which the whole Orthodox Church suffers today. But again, it was not so with the Fathers. Almost to the one, they suffered at the hands of the various "power structures" of their day for their refusal to opt for compromise or to accept silent obedience to evil. And the fact is that ultimately the Church followed them and not those who, then as today, have a thousand excellent reasons for avoiding the "abstract principles" and preferring the "demands of reality."

Today this prophetic function of theology is needed more than ever. For, whether we want it or not, the entire Orthodox Church is going through a deep crisis. Its causes are many. On the one hand, the world which for centuries framed and shaped her historical existence is crumbling and has all but vanished. The ancient and traditional centers of authority are threatened in their very existence and most of them are deprived of even elementary freedom of action. An overwhelming majority of Orthodox people live under the pressures and persecution of openly and militantly atheistic regimes, in situations where mere survival and not progress is the only preoccupation. A minority living surrounded by an alien sea seems to have become the rule rather than the exception for Orthodoxy almost everywhere. Everywhere, and not only in the West, it is challenged by a secularistic, technological, and spiritually antagonistic culture. On the other hand, a large Orthodox diaspora has appeared, putting an end to the multi-secular isolation of Orthodoxy in the East, challenging Orthodoxy with problems of ecclesiastical organization and spiritual "adjustments" unprecedented in the whole history of the Church. Only the blind would deny the existence of the crisis, yet not too many seem to realize its depth and scope, least of all—let us face it—the bishops who continue in their routine work as "if nothing happened." At no time in the past has there existed such an abyss between the hierarchy and the "real" Church, never before has the power structure so little corresponded to the crying spiritual needs of the faithful. And here the American Orthodox "microcosm" seems an excellent example. How long are we to live in a multiplicity of jurisdictions either quarreling with each other or simply ignoring each other? How long shall we leave unnoticed the rapid decay of liturgy, spirituality and monasticism—the traditional sources of Orthodox piety and continuity? How long, in short, shall we accept and respectfully endorse as normal and almost traditional a situation which, if we are honest, must be described as a scandal and a tragedy?

In spite of what too many Orthodox people think today, this is the hour of theology. Only a deep, fearless and constructive evaluation of this situation in the light of the genuine Tradition of the Church, only a creative return to the very springs of our dogma, canons and worship, only a total commitment to the Truth of the Church can help us overcome the crisis and transform it into a revival of Orthodoxy. I know that this task is difficult and that a long tradition has taught theologians to avoid hot issues and not to "get involved." I know also that a certain traditionalism which has nothing to do with Tradition has made self-criticism and spiritual freedom a crime against the Church in the eyes of many. I know that too many power structures have a vested interest in not allowing any question, any search, any encounter with Truth. The forces of inertia, pseudo-conservatism and plain cynicism are formidable. But the same was true of the time of St. Athanasius the Great, St. John Chrysostom and St. Maximus the Confessor. As for the issues we face today, they are not less important than those which they had to deal with. And it depends on us to choose between the pleasant prestige attached to mere academic scholarship and the response to the will of God.

VI

THEOLOGY AND LITURGY

1.

The time has come for a deep re-evaluation of the relationship between theology and liturgy. My purpose here is to explain the reasons for that affirmation, and to indicate, be it only tentatively, its meaning for the Orthodox theological enterprise as a whole, and also for the liturgical problems whose existence and urgency are acknowledged today by nearly everyone.

Very few people, I am sure, would deny that the Orthodox Church is in a state of crisis; yet very few also are those, it seems to me, who realize that at the bottom of this crisis, as one of its main sources, lies the double crisis of theology and liturgy.

A crisis of theology! Is it not obvious indeed that the confusion and the divisions we witness today on virtually every level of the Church's life—the canonical, the administrative, the educational, the "ecumenical"—are rooted, first of all, in the absence of commonly accepted and acknowledged terms of reference or criteria which normally are to be supplied precisely by theology? Contemporary Orthodox theology is unable to supply such norms because it is itself "broken." It is characterized, on the one hand, by an unhealthy pluralism and, on the other hand, by a peculiar inability to communicate with the "real" Church. I call this pluralism unhealthy because there can exist and there has existed in the past a healthy

---

* A paper presented at the First International Conference of Orthodox Theologians, at Holy Cross Greek Orthodox School of Theology, Brookline, Mass., in 1970, and originally published in *The Greek Orthodox Theological Review* 17.1 (1972), pp 86-100.

theological pluralism perfectly compatible with a fundamental unity. For example, there certainly were substantial differences among the Fathers, but they did not break the basic unity of a common experience and vision. Today, however, it is precisely such common vision that seems to be lacking. To put it somewhat sharply, Orthodox theologians do not seem to understand one another, so different are the respective "keys" in which they approach the same problems, so opposed to one another their basic presuppositions and thought forms. This leads either to meaningless polemics—for to be meaningful polemics would require a minimum of agreement as to the basic terms of reference—polemics in which the awesome word "heresy" is used more and more often without any discrimination, or to a kind of "peaceful coexistence" of theological orientations mutually ignoring one another.

Whatever its "key" or orientation, Orthodox theology moreover seems deeply alienated from the Church, from her real life and needs. Although taught in official ecclesiastical schools, its impact on students usually evaporates on the day of graduation. It is viewed as an intellectual abstraction nowhere to be really applied; as an intellectual game which the people of God—clergy and laity—simply ignore. In our Church today, professional theologians constitute a kind of *Lumpenproletariat* and, what is even more tragic, seem to be reconciled to this status. Theology is no longer the conscience and the consciousness of the Church, her reflection on herself and on her problems. It has ceased to be *pastoral* in the sense of providing the Church with essential and saving norms; and it has also ceased to be *mystical* in the sense of communicating to the people of God the knowledge of God which is the very content of life eternal. A theology alienated from the Church, and a Church alienated from theology: such is the first dimension of today's crisis.

2.

The situation of the liturgy is not much better. It has, to be sure, remained the focus, the "holy of holies" of the

Church's life; it is still the main—one almost could say the exclusive—"occupation" of the Church. Yet a deeper analysis would reveal here also a very serious crisis which cannot be resolved by the hasty and superficial liturgical reforms advocated by many today. A first aspect of this crisis is the growing nominalism of liturgical life and practice. In spite of its apparent conservatism and even archaism, this practice is hardly expressive of the genuine *lex orandi* of the Church. Entire and essential strata of the liturgical tradition, while faithfully preserved in liturgical books, are little by little disappearing from practice or else preserved symbolically and transformed beyond recognition. Eucharist and the sacraments, liturgical seasons and the celebration of feasts, rites of blessing and sanctification of life—everywhere one finds the same pattern: a "selection" of certain elements, a rejection of others; a selection, however, based not on the principles of the *lex orandi* itself but on considerations totally alien to it. If the average church-goer may not notice this rapid erosion of Orthodox worship, the specialist cannot help being worried by the discrepancy between the demands of Tradition on the one hand, and the nominalism and minimalism of the liturgical piety and practice on the other hand.

What is more serious, however, is the fact that the liturgy—central as it may be among the activities of the Church—has ceased to be connected with virtually all the other aspects of the Church's life; to inform, shape and guide the ecclesiastical consciousness as well as the "world-view" of the Christian community. One may be deeply attached to the "ancient and colorful rites" of Byzantium or Russia, see in them precious relics of a cherished past, be a liturgical "conservative," and at the same time completely fail to see in them, in the totality of the Church's *leitourgia*, an all-embracing vision of life, a power meant to judge, inform and transform the whole of existence, a "philosophy of life" shaping and challenging all our ideas, attitudes and actions. As in the case of theology, one can speak of an alienation of liturgy from life, be it from the life of the Church or the life of the Christian individual. Liturgy is confined to the temple, but beyond its sacred enclave it has no impact, no power. All other ecclesiastical activities—

in a parish, a diocese, a local church—are based more and more on purely secular presuppositions and logics, as are also the various "philosophies of life" adopted by professed Christians. Liturgy is neither explained nor understood as having anything to do with "life"; as, above all, an *icon* of that new life which is to challenge and renew the "old life" in us and around us. A liturgical pietism fed by sentimental and pseudo-symbolical explanations of liturgical rites results, in fact, in a growing and all-pervading secularism. Having become in the mind of the faithful something "sacred" *per se*, liturgy makes even more "profane" the real life which begins beyond the sacred doors of the temple.

This double crisis—of theology and of liturgy—is, I submit, the real source of the general crisis which faces our Church today, and which must shape our agenda, if theology is for us more than a quiet "academic" activity, if we understand it as our specific charism and ministry within the Body of Christ. A crisis is always a divorce, a discrepancy, between the foundations and the life which is supposed to be based on these foundations; it is life drifting away from its own foundations. The Church's life has always been rooted in the *lex credendi*, the rule of faith, theology in the deepest sense of that word; and in the *lex orandi*, her rule of worship, the *leitourgia* which always "makes her what she is": the Body of Christ and the Temple of the Holy Spirit. Today, however, there rapidly develops a dangerous alienation of the "real" Church from these two sources of her life. Such is our situation. Such is the crisis whose challenge is upon us— whether we acknowledge it or not. To understand it in its deep causes is, therefore, the first and necessary step. Our question thus must be: why and how did it occur?

3.

I have no doubts as to the answer. If today both theology and liturgy have ceased, at least to a substantial degree, to perform within the Church the function which is theirs, thus provoking a deep crisis, it is because first of all they have been divorced from one another; because the *lex credendi* has been alienated from the *lex orandi*. When did this happen? During that post-patristic "Western captivity" of Orthodox theology, which in my opinion constitutes one of the main tragedies on the historical path of Eastern Orthodoxy. This "Western captivity" consisted primarily in what Fr. Florovsky so aptly termed the "pseudomorphosis" of the Eastern theological mind—the adoption by it of Western thought forms and categories, of the Western understanding of the very nature, structure and method of theology. And the first and indeed the most fateful result of that "pseudomorphosis" was precisely a mutual alienation from one another of the *lex credendi* and the *lex orandi*.

The purpose of theology is the orderly and consistent presentation, explication and defense of the Church's faith. This faith is thus both its source and its "object," and the entire structure and method of theology depend therefore on how one understands the nature of its relationship to that "source," i.e. to the faith of the Church. It is at this point that a radical difference exists or, better to say, existed between the East and the West — a difference later obscured, if not entirely removed, by the "Western captivity" of Eastern theology. It was in the West at first, and for reasons inherent to the Western religious and intellectual development, that the "source" of theology, i.e. the Church's faith, began to be identified with a specific number of "data," mainly texts—scriptural, patristic, conciliar—which as *loci theologici* were to supply theological speculation with its subject matter and criteria. With the entire theological enterprise in the West being aimed primarily at constructing an *objective* or *scientific* theology, it was both natural and essential for it to establish itself on an equally objective and clearly defined foundation. Hence, the identification of faith, in theological terms, with "propositions"; hence also the rejection from the theological process of any reference to or dependence upon *experience*.

Yet it is precisely faith as *experience*, the total and living experience of the Church, that constitutes the source and the context of theology in the East, of that theology at least which characterized the patristic age. It is "description" more than "definition" for it is, above all, a search for words and concepts adequate to and expressive of the living experience of the Church — for *reality* and not "propositions." It is itself a part and a fruit of that experience, and it is in this sense that Vladimir Lossky calls it "mystical theology." Its criteria lie not in formal and, therefore, autonomous "authorities," but in its adequacy to and consistency with the inner life and experience of the Church. This understanding of theology stems from the very nature of its "source," i.e. the faith of the Church. For the faith which founds the Church and by which she lives is not a mere assent to a "doctrine," but her living relationship to certain events: the life, death, resurrection and glorification of Jesus Christ, His ascension to heaven, the descent of the Holy Spirit on the "last and great day of Pentecost"—a relationship which makes her a constant "witness" and "participant" of these events, of their saving, redeeming, life-giving and life-transfiguring reality. She has indeed no other experience but the experience of these events, no other life but the "new life" which they always generate and communicate. Her faith thus is not only not detachable from her experience, but is indeed that experience itself—the experience of that "which we have heard, which we have seen with our eyes, which we have looked upon and touched with our hands" (I John 1:1). For none of these events can be known, in the rational meaning of that word, nor even believed in outside the experience which reveals their reality and makes us "witness to these things." But then theology cannot be anything else but the "description" of that experience, its revelation in human words and concepts. The Church is not an institution that keeps certain divinely revealed "doctrines" and "teachings" about this or that event of the past, but the very *epiphany* of these events themselves. And she can teach about them because, first of all, she knows them, because she is the experience of their reality. Her faith as teaching and theology is rooted in her faith as experience. Her *lex credendi* is revealed in her life.

4.

I can now come to the main thesis of this paper: this *experience* of the Church is primarily the experience given and received in the Church's *leitourgia*—in her *lex orandi*. That today we must defend and prove this thesis is indeed the most bitter result of the "pseudomorphosis" of our theology mentioned above. What centuries of "Western captivity" did was not only alter the theological "mind" but, by the same token, tragically narrow and obscure the very concept and experience of liturgy, of its place and function within the life of the Church. To put it abruptly: the liturgy ceased to be viewed and experienced as the *epiphany* of the Church's faith, as the reality of her experience as Church and, therefore, as the source of her theology.

If indeed liturgy has remained at the center of the Church's life and activity, if it has changed very little as to its form and content, it has acquired a "coefficient," has begun to be comprehended and experienced in a "key" substantially different from that of the earlier patristic age. It suffices to consult any post-patristic manual of dogmatics to find the sacraments, for example, treated in the chapters devoted to "means of grace" and nowhere else, as if they had nothing to do with the faith itself, the structure of the Church or knowledge of God. As to the liturgical tradition in its totality, it has in the same manuals no place whatsoever, the implication being obviously that it belongs to the area of *cult* or *piety*, essentially different from that of dogma and theology. It is precisely this reduction of the liturgy, or the *lex orandi*, to "cult," its understanding exclusively in cultic categories, that reveals the new coefficient, is the new key of both liturgical practice and liturgical piety, and a major obstacle to its theological understanding, to a living communication between liturgy and theology.

In the early Church, however, even the term *leitourgia* was not, as it is today, a mere synonym of *cult*. It was applied indeed to all those ministries and offices within the Church in which she manifested and fulfilled her nature and vocation;

it had primarily ecclesiological and not cultic connotations. And the very fact that subsequently it was identified especially with "Divine Liturgy," the central act of Christian cult, reveals above all the peculiar character, the uniqueness of that cult itself, of its place and function within the Church. From the very beginning, this unique function was precisely to "make the Church what she is": the witness and the participant of the saving *event* of Christ, of the new life in the Holy Spirit, of the presence in "this world" of the Kingdom to come.

To baptize by water and spirit in the likeness of Christ's death and resurrection; to "come together as Church" on the Lord's Day, to hear His Word and "to eat and drink at His table in His Kingdom"; to relate, through the "liturgy of time," all time, all cosmos—its time, matter and life—to Christ who is to "fill all things with Himself": all this was not understood as mere "cultic acts" but, above all, as the fulfillment by the Church of her very nature, of her cosmical and eschatological calling.

Here is the essential point: in the early patristic Church, ecclesiology is cosmical and eschatological. The Church is the mystery of the new creation and she is the mystery of the Kingdom. It has often been said that there is no ecclesiology, in the modern sense of this word, in the writings of the Fathers. The reason for this, however, is not a lack of interest in the Church, but the Fathers' understanding and experience of the Church as the new life of the new creation and the presence, the *parousia*, of the Kingdom. Their attention is not focused on the "institution" because the very nature and purpose of that institution is not to exist "in itself" but to be the "sacrament," the *epiphany*, of the new creation. In this sense, their whole theology is ecclesiological, for it has the Church, the experience of the new life, the communion of the Holy Spirit, as its source and context. From this point of view the post-Tridentine treatise *De ecclesia*, mother and pattern of all modern ecclesiology both Western and Eastern, is indeed the downfall of patristic ecclesiology, for by focusing attention almost exclusively on the "institution," it obscures the cosmical and eschatological nature of the Church. It makes "institution" an end in itself, and in doing this, in apparently exalting the

Church, it in fact tragically mutilates her, making her as we see it today more and more "irrelevant" for the world, less and less "expressive" of the Kingdom of God.

What is important for us at this point is the relationship between this cosmical and eschatological nature of the Church and her *leitourgia*. For it is precisely in and through her liturgy—this being the latter's specific and unique "function"—that the Church is *informed* of her cosmical and eschatological vocation, *receives* the power to fulfill it and thus truly *becomes* "what she is": the sacrament, in Christ, of the new creation; the sacrament, in Christ, of the Kingdom. In this sense the liturgy is indeed "means of grace," not in the narrow and individualistic meaning given this term in post-patristic theology, but in the all-embracing sense of always making the Church what she is, a realm of grace, of communion with God, of new knowledge and new life. The liturgy of the Church is cosmical and eschatological because the Church is cosmical and eschatological. But the Church would not have been cosmical and eschatological had she not been given, as the very source and constitution of her life and faith, the *experience* of the new creation, the experience and *vision* of the Kingdom which is to come. And this is precisely the *leitourgia* of the Church's cult, the function which makes it the source and indeed the very *possibility* of theology.

5.

The theological and liturgical tragedy of the post-patristic age is that the Church's cult was deprived of its *liturgical* function, reduced to cultic categories alone. More precisely this means that the theological mind as well as piety ceased to see in it, to experience it, as the very epiphany of the cosmical and eschatological "content" of the Church's faith and thus of the Church herself. Yet once detached from this, its essential cosmical and eschatological content, the liturgy of the Church, her *lex orandi*, simply cannot be properly "heard" and understood. Then inevitably a deterioration of theology and piety begins, their own "pseudomorphosis" takes place—

the more dangerous because it takes place not in the forms of the liturgy, but in their inner comprehension and usage by the faithful. Paradoxical as it may seem, it is very often the liturgical "conservative," the passionate lover of rubrics and externals, the amateur of "ancient and colorful" rites, that is most hopelessly blind to the true meaning of these very rites, to the "Truth and Spirit" which gave them birth and of which they are both manifestation and gift.

Signs and symptoms of that deterioration are too many to be enumerated here. A few, however, ought to be mentioned. Take Baptism, for example. If today so many priests, not to speak of laymen, see no need whatsoever for the baptismal blessing of water and are perfectly satisfied with pouring some holy water into the baptismal font, it is because they do not experience this blessing as the sacramental re-creation of the cosmos so that it may become that which it was intended to be, a gift of God to man, a means of man's knowledge of God and communion with Him. Yet when deprived of this cosmical connotation, the understanding of Baptism itself begins to be altered, and this is exactly what we see in post-patristic theology as well as in post-patristic piety. From regeneration and re-creation, new birth and new life, attention shifts to original sin and justification, and thus to an altogether different theological and spiritual content. If the initial and organic connection of Baptism with Pascha and Eucharist has been all but forgotten, if Baptism has ceased to be a paschal sacrament and Pascha a baptismal celebration, it is because Baptism is not experienced as a fundamental act of *passage* from "this world" into the Kingdom of God—an act which, making us die here "in the likeness of Christ's death," makes our life to be hidden with Christ in God. But again, deprived of this eschatological connotation, Baptism is less and less connected—in theology and piety—with Christ's death and resurrection, and indeed post-patristic manuals hardly even mention that connection, as well as the connection of Chrismation with the pentecostal inauguration of the "new aeon."

Take Eucharist as another example. If it has become one "means of grace" among many, if its aim has been reduced,

in theology and piety, to individual edification and sanctification to the virtually total exclusion of any other aspect, it
is because its ecclesiological—and this means cosmical and
eschatological—dimensions have been simply ignored within
the new and "Westernized" theological perspective. It is
amazing how the sacramental theology which developed within
that perspective neglected — to say the least — such essential
aspects of the eucharistic *ordo* as the Synaxis, the proclamation
of the Gospel, the Offering, the Eucharist itself, the interdependence of all these aspects and their organic connection
with consecration and communion, as well as the relationship
of Eucharist to time, as manifested in the uniquely Christian
institution of the Lord's Day. All this is simply absent from
theology; but then the Eucharist ceases to be experienced as
the sacrament of the Church, of her very nature as *passage*
and ascension into the Kingdom of God. Theology exhausts
itself in purely formal and truly irrelevant definitions of
sacrifice and transubstantiation, while piety little by little
subordinates Eucharist to its individualistic and pietistic demands.

To that kind of theology and that kind of piety, meaningless indeed would appear the affirmation that the Eucharist
and all sacraments and the entire *leitourgia* of the Church
always place us at the beginning and at the end of all things,
revealing thus their true meaning and destiny in Christ; that
it is the very function or *leitourgia* of the Church's cult—
in its structure and rhythm, in its ineffable and celestial beauty,
in its words as well as its rites—to be the true epiphany of
the new creation redeemed by Christ, the presence and power
in "this world" of joy and peace in the Holy Spirit, of the
new aeon of the Kingdom, and being all this, to be the source
and the focus *par excellence* of the Church's faith and theology.

All this is neither "heard" nor understood today, be it by
theology or by liturgical piety. The former is imprisoned in
its own "data" and "propositions," and having eyes does not
see and having ears does not hear. The latter is entangled in
all kinds of liturgical experiences save the one expressed in
the *lex orandi* itself. And if today the Christian community
is being alienated more and more from both, if in theology

it sees nothing but intellectual speculations interesting to professionals alone, if liturgy is for it, at best, "inspiration" and, at worst, a meaningless "obligation" to be reduced, if possible, to a valid minimum, the reason for all this is the mutual alienation from one another of theology and liturgy, their surrender to Western categories and dichotomies. My last question is: Can this alienation be overcome?

6.

Enough has been said above, I think, to enable us to give this question a positive answer: Yes, it can. But only if the theological mind recovers its "wholeness" broken by centuries of Western captivity, if it returns to the old yet always valid expression of that wholeness: *lex orandi lex est credendi*. And this implies, as its first condition, a double task: a liturgical critique of theology and a theological critique of the liturgy. In this paper I can only briefly outline my understanding of this double task.

To affirm that liturgy is the source *par excellence* of theology does not mean, as some seem to think, a reduction of theology to liturgy, its transformation into "liturgical theology." The latter appeared only as a result of the unhealthy mutual alienation between theology and liturgy, and is therefore an illegitimate child of an illegitimate situation. All theology, indeed, ought to be "liturgical," yet not in the sense of having liturgy as its unique "object" of study, but in that of having its ultimate term of reference in the faith of the Church, as manifested and communicated in the liturgy, in that catholic vision and experience which now, in its alienation from liturgy, it lacks.

The Western influence upon our theology expressed itself, first of all, in the organization of theological work. Theology, in fact, was broken into a multiplicity of virtually "autonomous" disciplines each depending on its own set of "data" and on its own method, without any clear principle of coordination and theological "integration" into a common vision—indeed, without any common goal. While in the Roman Church such a principle lies in the hierarchical *magisterium*, understood as an authority extrinsic to theology itself, while Protestants do not even claim to have, beyond sufficiently vague "confessions," any consistent theology as theology of the Church, Orthodox theology found itself in a peculiar and unhealthy situation. It adopted, on the one hand and quite uncritically, the Western "scientific" organization of theological work, which meant in fact its progressive atomization into a number of uncoordinated and independent "disciplines." Yet, on the other hand, it failed to seek and to determine the criteria and methods that would integrate these disciplines not only into a consistent whole but also into an adequate and living expression of the Church's faith itself. While adopting methods hitherto alien to it, Orthodox theology did not ask the preliminary question: How are they to express the *experience* of the Church? Thus we have dogmatic theology built more or less after the pattern of scholastic theology with its dependence upon "data" and "propositions"; scriptural theology split between a surrender to and a violent rejection of Western "criticism," leading either to a mere rejection of Western critical theories or to an equally Western fundamentalism; and, finally, a host of "historical" and "practical" disciplines whose relationship to theology as such remains chronically ambiguous and problematic. Not only is there virtually no communication between these disciplines, but their very structure and self-definition prevents each one of them and all of them together from being the *catholic*, i.e. whole and adequate, expression of the Church's faith and experience.

If, however, as I tried to indicate above, it is the very function of the *leitourgia* to be the "epiphany" of the Church's faith, to "make the Church what she is," then theology must find its way back to that source, and rediscover in it precisely that common ground, that initial wholeness and vision which it so obviously lacks now in its topical and methodological fragmentation. If a certain degree of specialization is obviously necessary because it is beneficial to theology's scientific progress, this specialization not only does not exclude, but indeed requires as the very condition of its success and as its inner justification the convergence and interdependence of all disciplines as to their common source and their common goal. This common source is the experience of the Church; this common goal is the adequate, consistent and "credible" presentation, explication and, if necessary, defense of that experience. If theology stems from the Church and her experience, it must also lead to the Church and into that experience. In this sense it is never autonomous, never self-contained and self-sufficient. Its credibility lies not in its rational consistency, but in the fact that it points beyond itself — to that experience and reality which alone gave birth to these words and alone can "authenticate" them.

What then does all this mean in practical terms? In reference to the *leitourgia* as a common source of all theological disciplines, it means that whatever the object of theological scrutiny and investigation, the first and most important "datum" is its liturgical experience, its place and connotations within the liturgy. To take but one example, the liturgy of the Paschal *triduum*—Holy Friday, Great and Holy Saturday and Sunday—reveals more about the "doctrines" of creation, fall, redemption, death and resurrection than all other *loci theologici* together; and, let me stress it, not merely in the texts, in the magnificent Byzantine hymnography, but precisely in the very "experience"—ineffable yet illuminating— given during these days, in their inner interdependence, in their nature indeed as epiphany and revelation. Truly if the word *mystery* can still have any meaning today, be experienced and not merely "explained," it is here, in this unique celebration which reveals and communicates before it "explains," which makes us witnesses and participants of the one all-embracing Event from which stems everything else: understanding and power, knowledge and joy, contemplation and communion. It is this experience which then illuminates the theological work proper, be it the exegesis of scriptural or patristic texts, or the elaboration of sacred doctrine and of its application to the life and the problems of man. It is in the Eucharist, in its *ordo* and movement, in its connection with all other sacraments and cycles of worship, that one discovers the only true and catholic source of ecclesiology in its cosmical as well as eschatological, institutional as well as sacramental, dimensions. It is finally in the "liturgy of time," in the cycles aimed at the sanctification of life, that one first *experiences* the true content of the Christian doctrine of the world and the true meaning of Christian eschatology, before one begins to explain and to elaborate them.

It is obviously impossible for us to give here anything but the most superficial analysis of this initial and organic connection between theology and the liturgical experience of the Church as the primary spring and "ignition" of theology. The liturgical critique of theology is precisely to supply us with such analysis, to rediscover the once living and efficient interdependence of these two essential *leitourgias* of the Church.

As to the liturgy as the common goal of the various theological disciplines, the affirmation *lex orandi lex est credendi* means that it is again in the mystery of the Church that theology finds its inner fulfillment both as theological synthesis and as experience, which—although it itself is beyond theology proper, beyond its words and formulations—not only makes them "credible" but indeed *essential* and *authentic*. Theology is always an invitation "to taste and see," an announcement and a promise to be fulfilled in communion, vision and life. Biblical exegesis, historical analysis, doctrinal elaboration ultimately converge in and prepare the celebration: the act of witnessing to and participating in the *mystery* itself, in that epiphany of life, light and knowledge without which all words remain inescapably "human," all too human.

All this, however, requires not only a "conversion" of theology itself, of its structure and methods, but, first of all, of the *theologian*. He has mastered to perfection the necessary *akribeia* of intellectual discipline and integrity, the humility proper to all genuine rational effort. He now has to learn how to immerse himself in the joy of the Church, that great joy with which the disciples returned to Jerusalem to be "continually in the temple blessing God" (Luke 23:52-53). He has to rediscover the oldest of all languages of the Church— that of her rites, the rhythm and the *ordo* of her *leitourgia* in which she concealed from the eyes of "this world" her most precious treasure: the knowledge of that which "no eye has seen, nor ear heard, nor the heart of man conceived, what

God has prepared for those who love Him" (I Cor. 2:9).
He has to become again not only the student of the Church's
faith but, above all, its *witness*.

More than that, if theology needs a liturgical critique,
liturgy—to be again the *leitourgia* of the Church in the full
meaning of that term—needs a theological critique. During the
long centuries of its divorce from theology, this meaning, as
was said already, has been obscured by several strata of
pseudo-theological and pseudo-pious explanations and interpretations, by a superficial pseudo-symbolism, by individualism
and legalism. And it is not easy today—when so much of all
this has been identified by so many with the very essence of
Orthodoxy, has almost become the touchstone of "true" piety
and "conservatism"—to rediscover and to communicate the
real "key" of the Orthodox liturgical tradition, to connect
it again to the *lex credendi*.

Here the task of theology is needed. Here its tradition of
intellectual integrity, historical criticism and *akribeia* can make
its greatest contribution. To do so, however, theology must
turn its attention to the *lex orandi*, consider it not only as a
source but also as an *object* of its research and study. It is a
paradox that the universally admired liturgical tradition of
the Eastern Church has been virtually ignored in both its
history and its theological "content." Not only has theology
been divorced from liturgy as "source," but it has paid very
little attention to it even as to one of its "objects." We still
have not so much as a complete and critical history of Byzantine worship in all its aspects. Even here the only interest
shown so far has come from the West, so that Orthodox
liturgiology remains determined by Western scholarship. Yet it
is precisely the task of Orthodox theologians to show in their
study of our liturgical tradition its overall significance within
the Tradition of the Church, to reveal its true place within
the Orthodox theological enterprise.

To achieve this, however, the study of the liturgy must,
on the one hand, break through the typically Western "fixation" on certain themes and problems to the exclusion of
many others, and, on the other hand, overcome the dead-ends
of self-sufficient "historicism." It so happened, for example,

that under the influence of Western theological options, the approach to the Eucharist was reduced to two or three aspects, those of sacrifice, validity, and communion—while all that which constitutes the only context for the proper formulation of these aspects, i.e. the liturgical *ordo* of the eucharistic celebration, the interdependence within it of the Synaxis, the liturgy of the Word, the Offertory, the Eucharist, etc., has been virtually ignored. But perhaps the most important omission was that of the essentially *eschatological* nature of the *leitourgia*—its relation to and dependence upon the central object of Christian faith, i.e. the Kingdom of God; its anti-nomical relation to time, relation constituting virtually the very content of the Typikon and all its "rubrics"; its expression in *beauty:* singing, hymnography, iconography, ritual, solemnity, which indicates that its organic link with matter is not "accidental," but indeed *essential*—so that the epiphany of "heaven on earth," the icon and fragrance, the beauty and the *ruah* of the Kingdom of God, was concealed, so to speak, from theology and reduced, as it were, to the legalistic and rational categories of the Western approach to liturgy.

The same can be said of the *historical* reduction of more recent liturgiology, its fixation on the historical interest and attention. Absolutely indispensable as it is, this historical aspect not only can never be an end in itself, but, in the last analysis, it is only from a theological perspective that it can receive its most important and proper questions. Very good and knowledgeable historians, because of their theological ignorance, have produced monuments of nonsense comparable to those produced by the theologians of liturgy ignorant of its history.

At this point, therefore, it is the liturgiologist that must again become a theologian and adopt a theological context and depth for his work. It is indeed the entire Church—clergy and faithful alike—who, in spite of all "pseudomorphoses," still continue to live by the liturgy, who must in the *lex orandi* rediscover the *lex credendi*, must make their liturgical piety a way of theological knowledge and understanding.

Ultimately, the liturgical problem of our time is thus a problem of restoring to liturgy its theological meaning, and to theology its liturgical dimension. Just as theology cannot recover its central place and function within the Church without being rooted again in the very experience of the Church, liturgy cannot be rescued from its present decay by hasty, superficial and purely external reforms aimed at meeting vague and doubtful "needs" of a mythological "modern man." For what this "modern man," his culture and his society ultimately seek is not a Church that would serve them by adopting their "image," but the Church that would fulfill the divine mission by being always and everywhere the *epiphany*, the gift and communication of the eternal mystery of salvation; and by being this, would reveal to man his true nature and destiny. Theology must rediscover as its own "rule of faith" the Church's *lex orandi*, and the liturgy reveal itself again as the *lex credendi*.

VII

RENEWAL

1.

Reading the enormous and ever-growing renewal literature
of our time, one cannot help coming to the conclusion that
its main, if not exclusive, term of reference is *the world*. To
make Christianity relevant to the world, aware of its coming
of age, responsive to its needs, problems and anxieties, adequate to its thought forms—such is the basic content and the
orientation of the idea of renewal, whether we follow it on
the level of theology (where its aim has been formulated as
"recasting traditional Christian doctrine in the light of modern
man's new self-understanding"), of apostolate or even of
spirituality. Whatever the difference between the various
concrete programs of renewal (and they range from a radical
rethinking of nearly everything in traditional Christianity,
including the concept of God, to a moderate adjustment to the
needs of our time), the consensus, the common denominator
and the working principle here is not only a new and acute
sensitivity to the world, but its acceptance as virtually the only
criterion of the Church's faith, life and action. If in the past
the world was evaluated by Christians in terms of the Church,
today the opposite is true: to many Christians, it is the world
that must validate the Church. And even if one does not accept
the idea of secularization as it is understood by some radical
theologians, it is this term that is probably coupled more often
than any other with the term "renewal."

---

* A paper read under the title "Prayer, Liturgy, and Renewal," at the
Congress on the Theology of Renewal, Toronto, 1967, and originally published in *Theology of Renewal*, Vol. II: "Renewal of Religious Structures,"
by the Pontifical Institute of Medieval Studies in Toronto (Palm Publishers,
Dorval, P.Q., Canada, 1968), pp. 77-88.

My purpose in this paper is to question not the new awareness of the world in Christian consciousness, but that which,
to me at least, appears as a dangerous one-sidedness in that
awareness. I have no doubts about the urgent need for the
Church to remember that she exists not for herself but for
the world and its salvation. I am not sure, however, that all
aspects of this necessary renewal in the Church-world relationship have been given equal attention. I even wonder whether
one really begins at the beginning. Speaking of liturgy and
prayer, I am not trying simply to add a touch of piety to an
otherwise healthy process but to raise what I am convinced is
the fundamental question of all renewal. This paper is written
by an Eastern Orthodox, and, therefore, in a perspective which
may differ from that of the Christian West. It is hoped, however, that here as elsewhere, the Orthodox point of view may
contribute to the clarification of the basic issues.

2.

The first question is: What is the *world* which is spoken
of so much today? It is strange, indeed, that in our present
preoccupation with the world we seem to ignore the fundamental antinomy traditionally implied in the Christian usage
of that term. We seem to forget that in the New Testament
and in the whole Christian tradition the world is the object
of two apparently contradictory attitudes: an emphatic acceptance, a *yes*, but also an equally emphatic rejection, a *no*.
"God so loved the world that he gave His only Son . . .God
sent the Son into the world, not to condemn the world, but
that the world might be saved through Him" (John 3:16-17)
and then—"Do not love the world or the things in the world.
If anyone loves the world, love for the Father is not in him"
(John 2:15). Texts like these could be multiplied *ad libitum,*
and rooted in them is the whole history of the Church with
its polarization between the affirmation of and the care for
a "Christian world," and its rejection and negation for the
sake of "one thing needed." The question is, therefore, whether
this polarization gives us a simple choice, that is, whether it

permits us to opt for one of the two positions, the *yes* or the *no*, to the exclusion of the other. Such a reduction is always tempting. If in the past a certain tradition considered every opening towards the world as sign of betrayal and apostasy, today we hear voices denouncing any withdrawal from the world (monasticism, contemplation, even liturgy) as irrelevant and harmful, and calling us to a kind of unconditional surrender to the world and its values. But the whole point precisely is that the New Testament and the Christian tradition allow no choice and no reduction. They accept and reject the world simultaneously, they present the *yes* and the *no* as one, and not two, positions, and it is this paradox that of necessity constitutes the starting point of all Christian approaches to the world and thus to all renewal.

But is there really a paradox? Have we not forgotten that the ultimate term of reference in Christianity is not the world but the Kingdom of God, and that the two apparently contradictory attitudes towards the world are reconciled theologically and existentially when we refer their object—the world—to the central Christian notion of the Kingdom of God? The *yes* and the *no* appear then as two aspects, both essential and necessary, of one and the same attitude. For, on the one hand, the world created by God and made *good* by Him is revealed to us as the "matter" of the Kingdom of God, called to be fulfilled and transfigured so that ultimately God may be "all in all things." As such, the world is *accepted* as a gift of God, as the object of man's love and care, for it belongs to man, the king of creation, the representative of God in the cosmos, to fulfill the world. Thus the world is the "sacrament of the Kingdom"; it is oriented towards the Kingdom, and for this reason dualism and Manicheism have consistently been condemned by the Church as heresy. Yet, on the other hand, the same world, once it becomes — again through man — self-sufficient and self-centered, an end in itself and not in God, once it rejects its ontological subordination to the Kingdom of God, or in other words, its transcendent vocation and destiny, is revealed as not only the enemy of God but as a demonic and meaningless realm of self-destruction and death—"the lust of the flesh and the lust of eyes and the pride

of life . . ." (I John 2:16). And thus the acceptance of the true
world as the "passage into the Kingdom" implies as its very
condition the negation and rejection of that which in the New
Testament is called "this world" and the love of which is the
sin par excellence and the source of all sin.

All this, of course, is commonplace. Unless, however, one
returns to that commonplace, one cannot overcome the incredible confusion in which we find ourselves today and which,
in spite of the best intentions, deprives the world—be it modern,
technological, "come-of-age" or anything else—of any clear
Christian meaning, so that although we are called to sacrifice
for the sake of the world all that we cherish, we still do not
know for the sake of *what* it itself exists and what is its ultimate destiny.

It is here, however, that we encounter our major difficulty.
To refer the world to the Kingdom of God and to look for the
meaning of our action in the world in the light of the Kingdom is tantamount to asking: What is the Kingdom of God?
Are we not trying to find the meaning of one unknown simply
by replacing it with another unknown? If the notion of the
world is to be clarified by that of the Kingdom, how is the
Kingdom to be comprehended and accepted as the *ultima
ratio* of all our thought and action, the moving power of our
renewal. "Thy Kingdom come . . .": Since the foundation of
the Church there has been no day, indeed no hour, when this
prayer has not been repeated thousands of times. But has its
meaning remained clear and identical to itself throughout all
that time? Are we still praying for the same reality? Or, more
simply, for what are we praying? These questions are not
rhetorical. To anyone who has eyes to see and ears to hear,
it must be obvious that in the course of history something
strange happened to the central concept of the "Kingdom of
God"; little by little it simply lost its central position and
ceased to be the ultimate term of reference. It was Dom
Gregory Dix, I think, who put his finger on this development
when—with some exaggeration—he spoke of the "collapse" of
the early Christian eschatology. It is not an accident indeed
that the treatises *De novissimis* are among the vaguest and
the least developed in Christian dogmatics and that eschato-

logy achieved a bad reputation by taking refuge in all kinds
of apocalyptic sects? Whatever the reasons for all this (and
we cannot analyze them here) the fact remains that the idea,
or let us say, the *experience* of the Kingdom of God, so
overwhelmingly central in the early Church, was progressively
replaced by a doctrine of the "last things," of "another
world"—centered almost entirely on the salvation of individual
souls. But this, in turn, led to a shift and also to a "split" in
Christian piety. There were, on the one hand, those who for
the sake of the soul and its salvation not only rejected but also
ignored the world, refused to see in it anything but the lust
of the flesh; and, on the other hand, there were those who for
the sake of the world began to ignore more and more, if
not to reject, the "other world." The crisis of Christianity,
I am convinced, is not that it has become irrelevant to the
world—for in a way it always remains "scandal to the Jews
and foolishness to the Greeks" — but that the Kingdom of
God, as value of all values, the object of its faith, hope and
love, the content of its prayer: "Thy Kingdom come!" has
become irrelevant to Christians themselves. And thus, before
one can speak of any renewal, one must return to *the* question:
What is the Kingdom of God, and where and how does one
experience it so that it may be the power of our preaching and
action?

3.

To this question the early Church, at least, had an answer:
to her the Kingdom of God was revealed and made known
every time she gathered on the eighth day—the day of the
Kyrios—"to eat and drink at Christ's table in His Kingdom"
(Luke 22:29-30), to proclaim His death and confess His resurrection, to immerse herself in the new aeon of the Spirit.
One can say that the uniqueness, the radical novelty of the
new Christian *leitourgia* was here, in this entrance into the
Kingdom which for this world is still to come, but of which
the Church is truly the sacrament: the beginning, the anticipation and the *parousia.* And the liturgy, especially the

Eucharist, was precisely the *passage* of the Church from this world into heaven, the act by which and in which she fulfilled herself, becoming that which she is: entrance, ascension, communion. But—and this is the most important point—it was precisely this eschatological, that is, this Kingdom-centered and Kingdom-oriented character of the liturgy that made it (in the experience and the understanding of the early Church) the source of the Church's evaluation of the world, the root and the motivation of her mission to the world. It is because Christians—in their passage and ascension to heaven—knew the Kingdom and partook of its "joy and peace in the Holy Spirit" that they could truly be its witness in and to the world.

In my opinion, one of the greatest tragedies of Church history, a tragedy not mentioned in manuals, is that this eschatological character of the Christian *leitourgia* was little by little obscured in both theology and piety, which squeezed it into categories alien to its primitive spirit. It is here indeed that one must look for the major cause of the process mentioned above: the progressive weakening of the idea of the Kingdom of God, its replacement with an individualistic and exclusively futuristic doctrine of the last things. In the history of post-patristic theology, nothing I am sure was more one-sided and simply deficient than its treatment of sacraments and liturgy in general, of the Eucharist in particular. And the deficiency lay precisely in a double dissociation: of the liturgy from ecclesiology, and of the liturgy from eschatology. First from ecclesiology, that is, from the doctrine and the experience of the Church. Within the purely rational and juridical categories of the theology, which at first developed in the West but later had a deep impact in the East also, liturgy ceased to be understood and presented as the means of the Church's fulfillment, as the *locus Ecclesiae par excellence.* The sacraments now came to be seen as means of grace, as acts performed in and by the Church, to be sure, but aimed at individual sanctification rather than the edification and the fulfillment of the Church. But this also and of necessity meant their disconnection from eschatology. The initial understanding and experience of the liturgy as passage from the old into the new, from *this world* into the *world to come,* as procession and ascension to the Kingdom, was obscured and replaced by its understanding in terms of a cult (public *and* private) whose main aim is to satisfy our religious needs. The *leitourgia*—a corporate procession and passage of the Church towards her fulfillment, the sacrament of the Kingdom of God—was thus reduced to cultic dimensions and categories among which those of obligation, efficacy and validity acquired a central, if not exclusive, position. Finally, to this orientation of sacramental and liturgical theology there corresponded an equally non-ecclesiological and non-eschatological orientation of liturgical piety. If the liturgy remained very much the heart and the center of the Church's life, if in some ways it became its almost unique expression, it was no longer comprehended as the act which existentially refers us to the three inseparable realities of the Christian faith: the world, the Church, the Kingdom.

4.

I can now make my chief point, which is very simple and which will, no doubt, appear naïve to many a sophisticated ideologue of renewal. If renewal is to have a consistent orientation, and this means precisely a theology, this theology must be rooted, first of all, in the recovered Christian eschatology. For eschatology is not what people have come to think of it: an escape from the world. On the contrary, it is the very source and foundation of the Christian doctrine of the world and of the Church's action in the world. By referring the world, every moment of its time, every ounce of its matter, and all human thought, energy and creativity to the eschaton, to the ultimate reality of the Kingdom of God, it gives them their only real meaning, their proper entelechy. Thus, it makes possible Christian action as well as the judgment and evaluation of that action. Yet the locus of that recovery is the liturgy of the Church. For eschatology is not a doctrine, not an intellectual construction, not a chapter (*De novissimis*) simply added and juxtaposed to other chapters of dogmatics, but a dimension of all faith and of all theology, a spirit which permeates and inspires from inside the whole thought and life of the

Church. And the proper function of the Christian *leitourgia,*
as I tried to show, is precisely to generate that spirit, to reveal
and to communicate that eschaton without which the Church
is but an institution among other human institutions, an institution, however, with strange and indeed irrelevant claims,
and the Christian faith a helpless, if not ridiculous, attempt
to force an elusive respect on the part of Pascal's *savants et
philosophes.*

At this point one may ask: But is this possible? Have you
not admitted yourself that the eschatological power of the
liturgy has been obscured and, for all practical reasons, lost
in the course of history? Can we simply return to an experience
which seems to have been the particular grace of the Church's
childhood? To these questions two answers can be given:

In the first place, no changes in theological interpretation
or in liturgical piety have been able radically to alter the
nature of Christian liturgy and its original inspiration. We
would not have been able to speak about the real spirit of the
liturgy, and no liturgical renewal would have been possible,
if there did not exist a self-evident discrepancy between certain
theological thought forms and a certain liturgical piety, on
the one hand, and the liturgy itself as it was preserved in spite
of all developments and metamorphoses, on the other hand.
The unique and truly exciting meaning of the liturgical movement as it began and developed during the last fifty years lies
precisely in its breaking through the theological and pietistic
superstructure to the genuine spirit of the liturgy. As one of
the pioneers of the movement wrote: "I was a priest for several years and yet I did not know the meaning of Pascha."
Pascha was there all the time, but it was impossible to experience its existential meaning within the framework of a
theology alienated from Pascha. The most important aspect
of the movement, however, is that this rediscovery of Pascha
was not a simple return to the past, not archeology and anti-
quity, but the spring of a truly new vision of the Church and
of her mission in the world. The whole record of the liturgical
movement bears witness to this fact. What is true of Pascha
is true, in fact, of the whole liturgical tradition of the Church.
I mention Pascha, however, because it is precisely this paschal

dimension and root of the liturgy, its fundamental nature as passage and passover, that constitutes the most valuable achievement of the liturgical movement. Whatever aspect of Christian worship we study today—the liturgy of initiation, the Eucharist, or the liturgy of time—we discover more and more that the basic shape or *ordo* of each of them, the principle which permits the understanding of both their origin and their development, lies in their nature as acts of passage, as mysteries of the Kingdom of God. Thus, liturgical renewal *is* possible and it makes possible a renewal of the theology of the world as source and condition of a new vision of the Church-world relationship. Let me stress once more that it is not a mere interest in liturgy, its forms and spirit, that I have in mind here, but in liturgy as the source of a new vision and experience of the Church and of the relation to the world. As I have written elsewhere: ". . . the *lex orandi* must be recovered as *lex credendi.* The rediscovery of the Eucharist (and I will add here—of the whole liturgy) as the sacrament of the Church is, in other words, the rediscovery of the Church *in actu*, the Church as the Sacrament of Christ, of His '*parousia*'—the *coming* and *presence* of the Kingdom which is *to come* . . . It means that in the life of the Church, the Eucharist is the *moment of truth* which makes it possible to see the real 'objects' of theology: God, man and the world." [1]

5.

My second answer brings me to another reality: prayer. It will not be disputed that prayer is to the individual Christian what the liturgy is to the Church *in corpore,* and that there is no Christian life without prayer. What needs to be stressed, however, is that Christian prayer, just like the Christian *leitourgia*, and for the same reasons, is in its essence eschatological; it is an effort towards and an experience of the Kingdom of God. If by "prayer" we mean here not only an external rule and practice, but, above all, a total inner orienta-

[1] "Eucharist and Theology," in *St. Vladimir's Theological Quarterly* 5.4 (1961), p. 22.

tion of man towards God—and such is, of course, the content
of the entire world of Christian spirituality—there can be no
doubt that its object and experience is precisely the "peace
and joy in the Holy Spirit" which according to St. Paul is the
very essence of the Kingdom of God. When St. Seraphim of
Sarov, one of the last and greatest Orthodox saints and teachers
of spirituality, defines Christian life as the "acquisition of the
Holy Spirit," he merely sums up a tremendously rich spiritual
tradition which transcends the category of historical development, the division between East and West, the accidents of
theological fashions, for it is one consistent, unchanging and
radiant testimony to the reality of the Kingdom of God, to
its transcendent immanence and immanent transcendence.

But is it not strange that in the present discussions of renewal so little place is given to this testimony or, more exactly,
that its inescapable relation to the very idea of renewal seems
so often to be ignored? Is it not the result again of a particular
theological deformation, of another dissociation, this time of
theology and spirituality? Is it not clear that the same theology
which, in its triumphant intellectualism ignored liturgy as the
locus theologicus par excellence, had to ignore *ipso facto* spirituality? The latter was thus isolated in a particular com-
partment, that of mysticism, and ruled out as a source of
theology. What we discover today, however, is that theology,
when reduced completely to a self-sufficient rational structure,
becomes, in fact, defenseless before secular philosophies and
finishes by accepting them as its own criterion and foundation.
It literally cuts itself off from its sources, from that reality
which alone makes words about God *theoprepeis*, i.e. adequate
to God. At this point, renewal risks becoming surrender.

My point here is thus again a simple one. There can be no
renewal in any area of Church life or, simply, of the Church
herself, without first a *spiritual renewal*. But this emphatically
is *not* a mere pietistic statement, a call for more prayer. It
means, above everything else, the overcoming of the tragic
divorce between the *thought* of the Church and the *experience*
of the Kingdom of God which is the only source, guide and
fulfillment of that thought, and the only ultimate motivation
of all Christian action. At the risk of shocking many a Chris-

tian, one can say that the Church as *institution*, as *doctrine* and as *action* has no ultimate meaning in itself. For all these point beyond themselves to a reality which they represent and describe and seek, which is fulfilled, however, only in the new life, in the *koinônia* of the Holy Spirit.

And this experience is not to be "rediscovered" in books and at the conferences. It has always been, it is still *here* in the midst of us, independent of the fluctuations of theology and of collective piety. It is indeed the only *real* continuity of the Church, the one that must be stressed above everything else in our age obsessed with history. Just as the liturgy, in spite of all reinterpretation and all reductions, has remained that which it has always been: the passage of the Church from the *status viae* to the *status patriae*, and as such the source of all real life of the Church, prayer, i.e. the thirst and hunger of man for the living God and a living encounter with Him, is that which kept that life alive.

In themselves, liturgy and prayer are not renewal for they are above and beyond the category of renewal. But if, as we all feel and believe today, we need a renewal, then we must rediscover them as its source and condition.

VIII

TOWARDS A THEOLOGY
OF COUNCILS

> "There are diversities of gifts,
> but the same Spirit, and there are
> diversities of administrations, but
> the same Lord, and there are di-
> versities of operations, but it is the
> same God, who worketh all in all."
> —I Corinthians 12:4-6.

1.

A clarification of the idea of "council" (synod, *sobor*),
of its place and function in the life of the Church, is on the
theological agenda of our time. There is, on the one hand,
the challenge from outside: Rome and her council, the ecumenical movement and its progressive embodiment in the form
of "councils." There is, on the other hand, the internal situation of the Orthodox Church herself. On all levels of her life
a growing tendency towards a more "conciliar" form of church
government can be detected. For the first time in many centuries the various autocephalous churches seem to be overcoming their national isolation and self-sufficiency and to
acknowledge the need for coming together, as they have at
recent pan-Orthodox conferences. On the diocesan and parish
levels, councils, committees and commissions have become so
self-evident that a young Orthodox would probably not believe
that only fifty years ago they virtually did not exist. And yet,

---

* Originally published in *St. Vladimir's Theological Quarterly* 6.4 (1962),
pp. 170-184.

although there seems to exist a basic agreement that "conciliarity" (*sobornost'*) belongs to the very essence of the Orthodox concept of the Church, an obvious uneasiness appears when it comes to applying this general principle to life. Tensions, conflicts, controversies indicate a fundamental confusion as to the real meaning and practice of "conciliarity," a clash between opposing conceptions of councils, their constitution, rights and functions. We see this confusion in the constant tension between priests and parish councils, in the rising tide of various laymen's organizations, youth movements, etc., all claiming the right to take an active part in church government and to limit what seems to them an unjustified clerical monopoly. This confusion calls for a constructive rethinking of the very principle of conciliarity, for its truly Orthodox definition and interpretation. We need a theology of councils as a general foundation and framework for the practice of conciliarity. And although it will take much time and effort to elaborate it in all its details, the task cannot be postponed any longer. Distortions and heresies are creeping into the life of the Church, and silence means betrayal. We must begin—this essay being no more than a beginning—by an attempt to clarify some basic presuppositions, to indicate some possible directions for a constructive discussion.

2.

The Orthodox Church claims to be the church of councils. This claim is clear enough in its negative connotations when directed against Roman papalism or Protestant individualism. But what does it mean as a positive affirmation? To realize the difficulties implied in answering this question, we must remember, first, that no theological definition of a "council" has so far been commonly accepted,[1] and, second, that in her history the Orthodox Church has had not one, but several patterns of councils, which in many respects differed rather substantially one from another. Thus, for example, there is no

[1] Cf. Nicholas Afanassiev, "Le Concile dans la théologie orthodoxe russe," in *Irénikon* 35 (1952), pp. 316-339.

evidence of any "councils" in the modern meaning of this term for the hundred years between the so-called Apostolic Council in Jerusalem (Acts 15) and the "gatherings of the faithful" in Asia mentioned by Eusebius in connection with Montanism.[2] Does this mean, to quote a Russian historian of the early councils, that the "conciliar institution did not function for a whole century"?[3] But then how can this institution be an essential element of the Church's life? All early councils known to us are exclusively episcopal in their membership. But they differ considerably one from another as to their form and functions. The ecumenical councils cannot be isolated from the imperial context within which they operated. The provincial councils described in the various canonical collections of the fourth and fifth centuries are short conventions of bishops of all the churches, whereas the later patriarchal synods became a permanent organ of church government. I have analyzed elsewhere the ecclesiological implications of these differences,[4] and there is no need to repeat this analysis here. But there remains the significant fact that in Russia, for example, during the whole "synodal period" (eighteenth-nineteenth centuries) there were no councils of bishops, and the Russian episcopate as a whole met for the first time at the memorable Moscow Sobor of 1917-18; yet this time not as a bishops' council, but as a council of bishops, clergy and laity. This meant a radically new idea of church government and of the council itself, an idea which has provoked and still provokes controversies within the Church.

It is evident, therefore, that a purely external study of the councils, their constitution, membership and procedures cannot give us a clear-cut definition of what councils must be in our own time and situation. The "conciliar principle" firmly proclaimed by our whole Tradition cannot be simply identified with any of its multiple historical and empirical expressions. And thus, from the "phenomenology" of councils, we must

[2] Eusebius, *Eccles. Hist.*, V, 16, 10.

[3] A. I. Pokrovsky, *The Synods of the First Three Centuries* (Sergeiev Posad, 1914—in Russian), p. 14.

[4] Cf. my essay "The Idea of Primacy in Orthodox Ecclesiology," in *The Primacy of Peter* (The Faith Press, London, 1963), pp. 30-56.

go to their "ontology," i.e., to their relation to the totality of the Church's life, to their ecclesiological roots and foundations.

3.

To achieve this we must, first of all, overcome the one-sided, yet usual, tendency to approach the problem of councils exclusively from the point of view of church government. In our "westernizing" theological systems, ecclesiology was indeed reduced to the question of "church order," to the institutional aspect of the Church. It is as if theologians had tacitly admitted that "institution" has priority over "life," or, in other terms, that the Church as the new life of grace and communion with God, as the reality of redemption, is "generated" by the Church as institution. Within this approach the Church was studied as a set of "valid" institutions, and the whole ecclesiological interest was focused on the formal conditions of "validity" and not on the *reality* of the Church herself. In the Orthodox perspective, however, this *reality*—the Church as the new life in Christ and participation in the new aeon of the Kingdom, has priority over "institution." This does not mean that the institutional aspect of the Church is secondary, contingent and non-essential — such an assumption would lead us to a protestantizing deviation in ecclesiology. It means only that institution is not the "cause" of the Church, but the means of her expression and actualization in "this world," of her identity with, and participation in, the reality of the New Being. Elsewhere I proposed to define as *sacramental* the relationship between the Church as institution and the Church as the reality of the Body of Christ and the Temple of the Holy Spirit. Sacrament, in this connotation, primarily means the *passage* from the *old* into the *new*, for this passage constitutes the very essence of the Church's life.[5] There exists, therefore, an organic and essential link between "institution" and "reality" (grace, new life, new creation) but its definition in terms of

[5] Cf. my essay "Theology and Eucharist," in *St. Vladimir's Theological Quarterly* 5.4 (1961), p. 10 and following.

cause and effect is misleading because it replaces an ecclesiology of contents with an ecclesiology of form, centered almost exclusively on the question of validity; and validity is a purely juridical and formal concept which in itself and by itself neither reveals nor communicates any living content. To debate whether three drops of water are "sufficient" to make a baptism valid, or whether it requires "immersion," is perfectly meaningless as long as the institutional form of a sacrament is understood merely as a *causa efficiens* of a result, whose real meaning and "content" are not revealed in this form itself. Any form agreed upon as "necessary and sufficient," i.e. given a juridical sanction, can guarantee "validity." In the Orthodox perspective, however, the "validity" of the institution or "form" comes to it from its ontological adequacy to the reality which it truly "represents," makes present, and therefore can communicate and fulfill. The institution is *sacramental* because its whole purpose is constantly to transcend itself as institution, to fulfill and actualize itself as New Being; and it can be sacramental because as institution it *corresponds* to the reality it fulfills, is its real image.

These general remarks must now be applied to the problem of councils. As long as they are considered only in terms of "power" and "government" their understanding will remain hopelessly one-sided. The first question is not: "What is a *valid* council?" or: "Who are the members of a council?" or even: "How much power has a council?" The first question is: "*What* is a council and how does it reflect the *conciliar nature* of the Church herself?" Before we understand the place and the function of the council *in* the Church, we must, therefore, see the *Church herself as a council*. For she is indeed a council in the deepest meaning of this word because she is primarily the revelation of the Blessed Trinity, of God and of divine life as essentially a perfect council. The Trinitarian foundations of the Church have been badly neglected in the modern ecclesiological revival, which has been dominated heavily by the idea of organism and organic unity on the one hand, that of "institutionalism" on the other hand.[6] But the idea of organism isolated from a Trinitarian context (i.e.

[6] Ibidem, p. 14.

unity as unity of *persons*) may lead to a dangerously impersonal and almost "biological" concept of the Church. The
Church is Trinitarian in both "form" and "content" because
she is the restoration of man and his life as an image of God,
who is Trinity. She is an image of the Trinity and the gift
of Trinitarian life because life is redeemed and restored in her
as essentially *conciliar*. The new life given in Christ is unity
and oneness: "that they may be one *as we are*" (John 17:11).
Being council in "content," the divine gift of life, the Church
is, therefore, council in "form," as institution, for the purpose
of all her institutional aspects is to fulfill the Church as perfect
council, to grow into the fulness of "conciliar life." All her life,
and not only a "council" in the technical sense of this term, is
conciliar because "conciliarity" is her essential quality. Each
act of her self-edification—worship, prayer, teaching, preaching,
heaing—is conciliar for it is both founded in the *sobornost'*
of her new life in Christ and its fulfillment or actualization.
And it is this *conciliar ontology* of the Church in the totality
of her essence and life that constitutes the framework for the
function of the council in church government.

4.

The Church is *conciliar* and the Church is *hierarchical*.
There exists today a tendency to oppose these two qualifications
of the Church, or at least to emphasize one over the other.
On the "clerical" side, conciliarity is viewed as contained
within the hierarchical principle, as limited to hierarchy. A
council here is primarily a council of the hierarchy itself and,
ideally, the laity ought to be excluded from it. Many a priest
considers the participation of laity in various church councils
as a regrettable compromise with the spirit of our time, a
compromise to be disposed of when the clergy recovers sufficient "control" of the Church. On the "lay" side, we see the
opposite trend. Here it is the "hierarchy" that must ultimately
submit itself to "conciliarism," to become the executors of
decisions taken by councils of which the laity are an integral,
if not the leading, part.

It is indeed tragic that these two tendencies are accepted today as the only alternatives, for both are wrong. They are the result of a deviation from the truly Orthodox concept of conciliarity, which excludes the "clerical" as well as the purely "democratic" interpretations and which is neither opposed to the hierarchical principle nor diluted in it. The truth is that the hierarchical principle belongs to the very essence of the council, as the latter is revealed and understood in the Church. The perfect "council," the Blessed Trinity, is a hierarchy and not an impersonal equality of interchangeable "members." Orthodox theology has always stressed this hierarchical concept of Trinitarian life, so that the very oneness of God is ascribed precisely to the unique type of relationship between the persons of the Trinity. The Trinity is the perfect council *because* the Trinity is the perfect hierarchy. And the Church, since she is the gift and the manifestation of the true life, which is Trinitarian and conciliar, is hierarchical *because* she is conciliar, hierarchy being the essential quality of conciliarity. To oppose these two principles is to deviate from the Orthodox understanding of both hierarchy and council. For *sobornost'*, as revealed in the Church, is not a dissolution of persons in an impersonal unity which would then be unity only inasmuch as it rejects and ignores the distinction of persons, their unique and personal being. *Sobornost'* is *unity of persons,* who fulfill their personal being in "conciliarity" with other persons, who are *council* inasmuch as they are persons, so that *many are one* (and not merely "united") *without ceasing to be many.* And this true conciliarity, the oneness of many, is by its very nature *hierarchical,* for hierarchy is, above everything else, the total mutual recognition of persons in their unique, personal qualifications, of their unique place and function in relation to other persons, of their objective and unique vocation within the conciliar life. The principle of hierarchy implies the idea of *obedience* but not that of *subordination,* for obedience is based on a personal relationship whereas subordination is, in its very essence, an impersonal one. The Son is fully *obedient* to the Father, but He is not *subordinated* to Him. He is perfectly obedient because He perfectly and fully *knows* the Father as Father. But He is not subordinated to Him because subordination implies imperfect knowledge and relationship and, therefore, the necessity of "enforcement" . . . Hierarchy, thus, is not a relationship of "power" and "submission" but of a perfect obedience of all to all in Christ, obedience being the recognition and the knowledge of the personal gifts and charisms of each by all. Whatever is truly conciliar is truly personal and, therefore, truly hierarchical. And the Church is hierarchical simply because she is the restored life, the perfect society, the true council. To ordain someone to a hierarchical function does not mean his elevation *above* the others, his opposition to them as "power" to "submission." It means the recognition by the Church of his personal vocation within the *Ecclesia*, of his appointment by God, who *knows* the hearts of men and is, therefore, the source of all vocations and gifts. It is, thus, a truly conciliar act, for it reveals the obedience of all: the obedience of the one who is ordained, the obedience of those who ordain him, i.e. recognize in him the divine call to the ministry of government, the obedience of the whole Church to the will of God.

For this reason, all contemporary attempts to limit the "power" of the clergy or to give the laity a share in this power are based on an incredible confusion. "Clergy" are, by definition, those whose special ministry and "obedience" is to govern the Church and whom the Church has recognized as *called* to this ministry. This confusion can be explained only by a complete secularization of the very idea of church government and of the Church herself. The partisans of lay participation in church government do not seem to understand that the "spiritual power" which they acknowledge in the clergy—the power to perform the sacraments, to preach, to confess, etc. — not only is *not* different from the power to administer the Church, but that it is the *same* power. Those who edify the Church through Word and Sacrament are those who govern it, and vice versa, those who govern it are those whose ministry is to build it by Word and Sacrament. The real question concerning church government, and more specifically, its conciliar nature, is not whether laity should or should not be given a share in the power of the clergy. In this form the question is a nonsensical one, for it implies a confusion between clergy and laity, alien to the whole tradition of the Church, to the very foundations of Orthodox ecclesiology. The real question concerns the relation between the ministry of government and the conciliar nature of the Church. How does the hierarchical principle *fulfill* the Church as *council?* The unfortunate reduction of the whole problem of church government to a competition between clergy and laity obscures this real question, which, if it is properly understood and answered, solves at the same time the "clergy-laity" problem.

5.

The government of the Church operates on three distinct levels: the parish, the diocese, and supra-diocesan entities such as the metropolitan district, the autocephalous church and, ultimately, the Church Universal. But before we analyze each one of them from the "conciliar" point of view, we must briefly acknowledge a very important difference which exists between our present situation and the early Church, a difference which, although it is obvious to every one who has studied the canonical tradition of the Church, has nevertheless been the object of no serious ecclesiological study. In the early Church every "parish" was in fact a "diocese," if by parish we mean a local *ecclesia*—a concrete, visible community—and by "diocese" a church governed by one bishop. As is well known, there existed at the beginning no "parish priests," and each local community was normally headed by a bishop. All definitions and descriptions of church government in classical canonical collections are given, therefore, in reference to the normal bearer of ecclesiastical power, i.e., the bishop. This means that in order to elucidate the basic structure of church government, one must begin with the "local church" in its early and classical expression.

Several recent studies in early ecclesiology stress — and rightly so — the central and unique position of the bishop in the *ecclesia*. The trend is still to defend the "monarchical" episcopate, and to the old arguments several new ones have been added, especially since the rediscovery of the "eucharistic," sacramental ecclesiology of the early Church. And yet brought to its extreme this trend may lead to a distorted picture. In fact, the term "monarchical" is scarcely a happy one when applied to the early episcopate. All available evidence points to the very real importance of the *presbyterium* in the local church, the college of presbyters or elders being precisely the *council* of the bishop and an essential organ of church government. Long before their transformation into heads of separate communities the members of the "second order" existed as a necessary collective complement of the bishop's power, and early rites of ordination point to the "gift of government" as the principal charism of the presbyters. From the very beginning the government of the Church was truly *conciliar*, and it is precisely the relationship between the unique function and ministry of the bishop, on the one hand, and the government of the presbyters, on the other hand, that reveals to us the basic contents of what we described above as "hierarchical conciliarism" or "conciliar hierarchy," as the organic unity of the conciliar and the hierarchical principles within the Church.

This relationship reveals, first, the true nature of church government. Here again, the term "sacramental" may be used. On the one hand, the presbyters really *govern* the Church, i.e. take care of all the immediate needs of the community, both material and spiritual. But, on the other hand, it is the function of the bishop, his own and unique ministry or *leitourgia*, to *refer* all these acts of church life to the ultimate purpose of the Church, to *transform* them into acts of the Church's self-edification and self-fulfillment as the Body of Christ. And he does it primarily through his functions of *proistamenos*, the president of the eucharistic assembly, which is the sacrament of the Church in which all gifts, all ministries, all vocations are indeed united and sealed as acts of the "same God, who worketh all in all" (I Cor. 12:6). "Government," "administration" are thus revealed to be not just autonomous areas within the Church, but an integral part of the Church as the *sacrament* of the Kingdom. The gift of government is a charism, and the presbyters are not simple "advisors" of the bishop, but in ordination they truly receive this charism, as *their* charism. Their government is *real*, and yet they can do nothing without the bishop, i.e. without his *recognition* of all their acts as acts of the Church, for he alone has the "power" to unify and to express the life of the community as the "new life" of the Church of God. The government of the Church is thus truly hierarchical and truly conciliar. The presbyters, or "elders," are the leading members of the *ecclesia*, those in whom the whole Church has recognized the gifts of wisdom, justice, teaching, administration. They are not opposed to laity, but are its true *representatives*, for they express and manage all the real *needs* of the people, and this is why they *are presbyters*. Their government is conciliar because in their plurality they can express the whole reality of the concrete community, the variety of its needs and aspirations. But this plurality is transformed into, and sealed as, *oneness* by the bishop, whose specific charism is to "fulfill" the Church as one, holy, catholic and apostolic. If the presbyters were mere "subordinates" of the bishop, delegates of his power, executives of his orders, with no initiative, no "life," of their own, the bishop would have nothing to "transform," nothing to express, nothing to fulfill. The Church would cease to be a council, a body, a hierarchy and would become "power" and "subordination." She would no longer be the *sacrament* of the new life in Christ. But it is the real life of the Church as council, as family, as oneness that the bishop *fulfills*, and he does this because it is his very charism to have nothing of his own but rather to belong—truly and absolutely—to all, to have no other life, no other power, no other end than to unite all in Christ.

It is impossible to analyze here even briefly the process which transformed the original "episcopal" structure of the local church into what we know today as parish. This process, although it represents one of the most radical changes that ever took place in the Church, remained, strange as it may seem, virtually unnoticed by ecclesiologists and canonists. And this lack of ecclesiological reaction explains why it is on the parish level that the crisis of church government seems to have its focus today. It has not been sufficiently understood that the transformation of the presbyter-member of the bishop's coun-

cil into the hierarchical head of a separate community transformed in fact the very idea of church government and power.
The bishop, on the one hand, was deprived of his "council,"
and his power became indeed "monarchical." The priest, on
the other hand, became a simple subordinate of this monarchical power, and from "conciliar" the bishop-priest relationship
became a relationship of subordination and "delegation of
power." All this meant a deep transformation of the original
conciliar understanding of both hierarchy and *ecclesia*. The
concept of hierarchy was identified with that of subordination,
of greater and lesser degrees of power. As for the parish,
deprived of the conciliar government which the "episcopal"
Church had in the presbyterium, it lost for several centuries
even the rudimentary forms of conciliar life, ceased to be
"council" in any real meaning of this word. It was thus forced,
first, into a purely passive understanding of the *laos* as completely subordinated to the hierarchy, and then, the progress
of democratic ideas helping, into a lay rebellion *against* the
hierarchy. The "clericalization" of the Church was to provoke
inevitably its logical counterpart—a rebellion. And yet, this
rebellion should not be explained entirely by ignorance, evil
influences of the "modern world," etc. From the Orthodox
point of view, "clericalism" is also a deviation, an error. And
the attempts of today's laity to have a greater "share" in church
life, obscured and deficient as they are, are nourished by a
confused yet justified desire to recover the *sobornost'*, the true
conciliarity of the Church. To crush them by an excess of
clericalism would be as bad as to accept them in their secularistic, legalistic, democratic forms. What we must seek is the
restoration of the eternal truth of the Church.

6.

First of all, we must simply acknowledge the fact that
today the immediate, concrete expression of the Church is no
longer the visible gathering of the faithful under the bishop,
but the *parish*. A Christian knows the Church and lives in the
Church as a member of his parish, which to him is the only

visible *ecclesia.* The diocese is for him a more or less abstract administrative echelon, not a living reality. The parishioners see the bishop on certain solemn occasions or appeal to him when a crisis arises in their parish. Because of this *real* situation, all attempts simply to return to the "episcopal" experience of the Church in its second- or third-century forms (*episcopus in ecclesia et ecclesia in episocopo*) will remain the domain of academic wishful thinking as long as we ignore the reality of the parish and the position of the priest in it. We must admit that many of the characteristics of the early "episcopal" community have been assumed by the parish, just as the priest has been given many of the bishop's functions. Today, the priest is the normal celebrant, pastor and teacher of the Church, all functions which in the early Church were fulfilled by the bishop.

This transformation raises two important questions. A first one, which we cannot analyze here in all its applications, concerns the bishop-priest relationship. To explain the change in the priest's status only in terms of "delegated power," as is done by the supporters of "episcopalism" *à outrance,* to reduce, in other words, the priest to the position of a bishop's delegate, is simply impossible. The priest is ordained to the priesthood, and not to be a "delegate," and this means that he has the priesthood of the Church in his own right. One cannot be priest, teacher and pastor by "delegation," and there can be no "delegated charism." The very transformation of his status was possible because from the beginning the presbyter was a priest, shared in the priestly functions. But then if he is, in a real sense, the head of a community, if his ministry is to fulfill it as "Church," the second question, that of the *conciliar aspects* of his power, must of necessity be raised. It must be admitted that for a long time, the parish as community, as *ecclesia,* simply did not exist outside a common attendance at worship; and the absence of "conciliarity" transformed the very piety of the faithful into an individualistic and liturgical piety from which the very idea of "community" and oneness of life were excluded. From this point of view, the ideas of *parish council* and *parish meeting* emerge, not from a source alien to tradition, but, in spite of all possible and actual deviations, from the deep instinct of the Church. The only tragedy is that on both sides, the "clerical" and the "lay," this conciliarity is understood and formulated within a narrow juridical framework, is expressed in terms of "rights" and "duties," "voting" and "decision-making" and other purely secular categories. There exists the deeply un-Orthodox opposition of "spiritual" matters to "material" ones, an opposition which contradicts and destroys the sacramental nature of the Church, where all that is "material" is transformed and spiritualized, and all that is spiritual possesses a power of transformation.

The conciliar principle which has been "forced" on the parish need not be either rejected or "limited" by reinforcement of "clericalism." It must be *churched*. This means, on the one hand, the acceptance by the clergy of the true hierarchical principle, which is not naked "power" but a deeply spiritual and pastoral concern for the Church as family, as oneness of life and manifestation of spiritual gifts. Not only must the priest not be afraid of "conciliarity," he must encourage and seek it, he must help every member of the Church to discover his particular "gift" and "vocation" within the life of the Body and unite all these gifts in the unity of life and "edification" of the Church. This means, on the other hand, a slow process of lay education, the overcoming by the laity of their defensive reflexes and attitudes. And this will take place only when the laity understand that the priest really *needs* them, that he needs not their "votes," but their talents, their advice, their real "council" or, in other terms, their real participation in the life of the Church. True conciliarity is neither expressed nor achieved in the purely formal and abstract "right to vote." One must realize that there is in fact nothing to vote upon in the Church, for all the issues that may arise in the life of the Church are ultimately related to Truth itself, and Truth cannot be a matter of voting. Yet to reach this Truth, to "apply it to life," requires an effort of mind and heart, of conscience and will, and in this effort all can and must participate and help, all can have a "voice": this is true conciliarity. If indeed the "power of decision," the final responsibility, belongs to the priest, in the process of reaching that decision as truly ecclesial, he needs the help of all, for his power is to express the "mind of the Church." The mind of the Church is Christ's mind in us, our mind in Christ, it is the obedience of free children and not that of slaves, an obedience based on knowledge, understanding, participation and not on blind subordination. It is knowledge of Truth that makes us truly free and truly obedient. All this means that the *parish council* properly understood is not a committee of practical and business-minded men elected to "manage" the "material interests" of the parish, but the *council* of the priest in all aspects of church life. There should exist indeed a special *rite* of appointing the parish elders to the council, which would express and emphasize the spiritual dimensions of their ministry; and there is a real need for retreats and sessions at which active laypersons would be guided to understand the mystery of the Church... All this, however, will remain wishful thinking as long as clergy themselves contribute to the secularization of the laity by limiting their initiative in the life of the Church to "finances" and "fund-raising" and by ignoring the Orthodox concept of the *laos tou Theou*, the People of God. And if the *conciliar principle* is not restored on the parish level, its other expressions will remain meaningless and inoperative.

7.

Of all the levels of church government, the diocese is probably the most "nominal" today. It is somehow squeezed between the reality of the parish and that of the supra-diocesan power—the patriarch, the synod, etc. And yet it is on the diocesan level that the essential "power" in the Church—the bishop—is to be expressed and fulfilled. There exists, therefore, a double problem: that of the relationship between the diocese and the parish, and that of its place within a wider grouping of churches.

We have stated already that the "parish" has acquired many characteristics of the early "episcopal" church and is, in fact, the actual form of the local church. Yet it is highly significant that during the Christianization of the Roman

Empire, as Christian communities increased in number, the office of the bishop, which we know to have been the essential office of the local church, was not multiplied accordingly but remained attached only to principal churches. The attempt to introduce into the Church the so-called *chorepiscopoi*, or rural bishops, failed. This radical departure from the early structure of the local Church is usually explained as an acceptance by the Church of secular principles of government, i.e. as a certain "collapse" of the early ecclesiology. But this explanation is, to say the least, one-sided. The office of the bishop and his place in the whole life of the Church were too central, too essential to have been so easily "adjusted" to a non-ecclesial pattern of government. There must have been a reason within the Church herself, within her own "logic," which made her prefer the dislocation of the local church into parishes to the multiplication of bishops. To find this reason is essential for the proper understanding of the diocese-parish relationship in our own situation. It seems to us that virtually all historians who have dealt with the changes in ecclesiastical structure following the conversion of Constantine have overlooked one very important "sociological" factor. It is well known that during the first three centuries the Church remained almost exclusively an urban phenomenon, and the expansion of Christianity began with the great metropolitan centers of the Graeco-Roman world. This means that the local church, in its earliest form, did not correspond to, or express, a *natural* community as an organic and pre-existing society, but was the *ecclesia*, the gathering of people belonging to a great variety of backgrounds, social positions, etc. All early evidence, beginning with St. Paul's epistles, supports this affirmation. The Church was *in* Rome but it was not yet the Church *of* Rome. This means also that, not being identified with any class, group, district or "way of life," the early "local church" had a natural "catholicity," an all-embracing quality, so that being absolutely free from any "organic" connections with "this world," she could truly represent the whole of it, be *open* to all. The conversion of the empire meant, from this point of view, a progressive identification of each local church with a natural community, with an organic local "society" finding in the Church the religious expression and sanction of its existence. But a natural local community is never truly "catholic," for it is, by its very essence, self-centered and limited in its own interests and needs. It is ontologically "selfish," this being especially true of the rural communities, and it was this danger of "naturalization," i.e. of a complete identification with the natural community, that the Church faced beginning with the fourth century — the danger, in other terms, of loosing the catholicity of her life. The only way to counteract this danger was to keep the "local churches" within a wider ecclesiastical framework, thus preventing them from being completely identified with "local life" with all its inescapable limitations and self-centeredness. The acceptance by the Church of the diocesan structure —the bishop remaining in the "metropolis" and the priests becoming heads of parishes — was thus not a compromise with the imperial administrative structure, but, on the contrary, a reaction of the ecclesiastical organism to the danger of being "absorbed" by natural society.

What was true centuries ago remains true — *mutatis mutandis* — today. Sociological conditions and structures have changed, but a parish is still essentially conditioned by its environment and, therefore, naturally limited in its "catholicity." Its life, the very scope of its possibilities and resources depends, of necessity, on a given "situation" which the parish, if left to itself, cannot and probably must not fully *transcend*. It may be a "middle-class" or a "worker" or a "missionary" or a "suburban" parish, and although ideally none of these qualifications ought simply to determine its life, none of them can be ignored. Therefore, it is from the *diocese* that a parish receives its *catholicity*, i.e. the constant challenge to transcend itself as a self-centered and self-sufficient community, to identify itself not only with its own "people" and their "religious needs," but with the *Church* and her eternal "needs." Catholicity is the identity of each church with the one, holy, catholic and apostolic Church, and for each community to be "catholic" means to be "accorded with the whole," to live not only *together* with all other communities, but also *towards* an ultimate goal, which transcends all local needs, all local "situations" and limitations, for it is nothing else but the Kingdom of God. And the bearer, the organ and the minister of catholicity is the bishop. It is his charism and duty to give the Church *direction* and *purpose,* to call each parish and all of them together to fulfill themselves as movement, as pilgrimage towards the Kingdom, to *edify* the Church. The diocese, thus, is *parishes together,* united in the bishop, who by his "episcopacy" — supervision, guidance, teaching, organizing — transforms their separate existences into one life which is indeed the life of the Church. A parish has neither the resources nor the inner impetus for a full catholicity. It can have it only *together* with other similar communities, which all together *transcend* their natural limitations, and they have it within a "catholic structure" which transcends each one of them separately and yet is their life as oneness, communion and unity of purpose.

But here again the very nature of the diocese requires the full restoration of the conciliar principle. Just as the parish because of its lack of conciliarity was for a long time a mere "cultic" institution, the diocese, if understood only in terms of "central administration," becomes a mere bureaucracy with the bishop as head not so much of the Church but of various administrative organs. To be a living center for all parishes, the real organ of their unity and common life, the bishop must be in a conciliar relationship with all of them, and this must be achieved through the bishop's council, i.e. the *presbyterium.*

The priest is the organic link between the bishop and the parish, yet not only in terms of "subordination" and "delegation of powers" but precisely in those of "conciliar unity." The priests *together* with the bishop are the living image of the diocese as *Church,* for in each priest his whole parish is truly "re-presented," made present, just as in the unity of the bishop with his priests the catholicity of the Church is made present to all parishes. The *presbyterium,* i.e. a corporate unity of priests with a bishop, must be restored, complementing the actual individual relationship between the bishop and each priest. This is the only organic diocesan council, organic because rooted in the very nature of the Church. Here not only are all affairs of the diocese discussed but the very *direction* of the Church's life is shaped and acknowledged. The decisions of the bishop are then no longer "executive orders" but organic decisions of the Church herself. Modern means of communication, the whole modern "way of life" would make it indeed easy for the "presbyterium" to meet with the bishop regularly — three or four times a year. It would give the diocese a reality which it lacks today. The conciliarity of the parish would find its organic fulfillment in the conciliarity of the diocese.

8.

Finally, the conciliarity of the Church on any supradiocesan level — the metropolitan district or province, the autocephalous church and, ultimately, the Church Universal — is expressed and fulfilled in the *council of bishops.* The churches come together and fulfill themselves as One Church *in* and *through* the unity of bishops. *Episcopatus unus est*, and the supreme power in the Church belongs to the bishops. This truth needs no elaboration for the whole Tradition supports it. We have discussed elsewhere [7] the structure and the meaning of episcopal conciliarism, and there is no need to repeat this discussion here. The only point which indeed needs elucidation is the modern trend to include priests and laity in the "supreme authority" of the Church, to make not bishops' councils but the councils of bishops, priests and laity the organ of that authority. The fundamental danger of this trend is that, by undermining and confusing the hierarchial principle, it undermines at the same time the genuine conciliarity of the Church. If, as we tried to show, hierarchy is the very form and condition of conciliarity, it really *belongs* to the bishops to express the *whole* life of the Church, to be the true *representatives* of her fulness. The actual structure of our clergy-laity councils, however, creates the impression that each "order" of the Church has its specific "interests," so that the laity, for example, has needs and interests different from, if not

[7] Cf. "The Idea of Primacy in Orthodox Ecclesiology" quoted above.

opposed to, those of the clergy. Clergy become representatives of clergy, and laity those of the laity. But then the "conciliarity" of the Church simply ceases to exist and is replaced by a "balance of power" which results too often in constant frustration for both clergy and laity. In fact, however, it is the very essence and purpose of the *clergy* to express and to fulfill the real "interests" and needs not of "laity" as opposed to clergy, but of the *laos* — the People of God, the Church of Christ. No one in the Church has interests or needs different from those of the Church herself, for it is the very life of the Church to unite all of us in grace and truth. If the true conciliarity of which we speak here is restored on each level of the Church, if every member of the Church fully participates in her life according to his calling, gifts and position, if, in other words, the Church is fully and truly *council* in all her manifestations, there is simply *no need* for anything else as the ultimate expression of this council but the council of bishops — the very image and fulness of the one, holy, catholic and apostolic Church. This does not mean that the council of bishops has to be a secret, closed meeting of "executives." It can and must be open to the participation, advice, interest and comments of the whole Church. "Public opinion" in its truly Christian form — as concern for the Church, as an active interest in her life, as free discussion of her problems, as initiative — is another and most welcome form of "conciliarity," and the fear of it, the tendency of our hierarchy to act by means of *faits accomplis*, without any previous discussion of ecclesiastical matters with the body of the Church, is indeed a dangerous tendency, a misunderstanding of the true nature of power in the Church.

The Church is hierarchical because it is conciliar. It fulfills itself as "council" by being hierarchical. This fundamental truth is the starting point for a truly Orthodox theology of councils.

IX

FREEDOM IN THE CHURCH

1.

When the invitation was extended to me to prepare a paper on "Freedom in the Church," my first reaction was that of all possible subjects this particular one ought to be treated not by an Eastern Orthodox but by a Westerner. For the great debate on freedom and authority has been indeed a specifically Western debate, one can even say the very *crux* of Western spiritual and intellectual development. The Orthodox East took no active part in it, partly because at the time of its theological climax, during the Reformation and the Counter-Reformation, the separation between the East and the West was already complete, partly because, as we shall see, the very essence of this debate was alien to the whole spiritual and intellectual tradition of Orthodoxy. Why then, such was my thought, should I interfere with the discussion of a problem which is truly a Western "specialty"? On second thought, however, I decided to accept the invitation, and this precisely for the reason which at first seemed to justify my abstention. For perhaps it is the very freedom from certain Western thought-forms and positions that could help an Orthodox, if not to solve the problem, then at least to ask whether other approaches to it are open to the Christian mind. And it is the result of this questioning, of this attempt to look at the problem of freedom in the Church from a standpoint different from that moulded in the West, that I dare in all humility to summarize in this paper.

* A paper read at the St. Xavier Symposium, at St. Xavier College, Chicago, in 1966, and published in *The Word in History*, ed. T. Patrick Burke (New York, Sheed & Ward, 1966) pp. 120-132.

My first question concerns precisely the formulation of
the problem, as it is reflected even in the title given to this
paper: "Freedom in the Church." One is immediately struck
by the dichotomy implied in this formulation which the pre-
position *in* indicates, suggesting that *freedom* and *Church*
are two different concepts, which are, if possible, to be brought
together, but which even when coordinated and reconciled
remain distinct from one another. The ways and methods of
this "coordination" may, in turn, differ, depending on whether
one puts the emphasis on *freedom* or on *Church*. One may,
while asking for more freedom, still subordinate it to the
Church, and one may, while accepting the Church, still subordinate it to freedom. In both cases, however, *freedom* and
Church are thought of and remain two distinct concepts, and
the problem consists in finding the best mode of their "correlation" and "interplay." And such has been, up to now at
least, the Western formulation of the problem in its two
main religious expressions: the Catholic (emphasis on the
Church) and the Protestant (emphasis on freedom). But
perhaps the first task of a theological investigation of freedom
in the Church is precisely to challenge and to revise the very
presuppositions on which this formulation is based.

Are they not the result of a development — spiritual,
theological and ecclesiastical — in which *freedom* has come to
be understood and defined mainly, if not exclusively, in terms
of *authority*, in which, in other terms, freedom and authority
appear to "ground" each other as two necessary poles of an
essential dichotomy? Freedom here is the relation to an authority, and its definition and even experience depend ultimately on the definition of a corresponding authority, for
without this authority freedom becomes a meaningless vacuum. Given a specific "authority," how much "freedom" does
it allocate to those who are *under* it? — such, in an oversimpli-
fied form, seems to be the ultimate question. And whether this
freedom is defined as freedom *from* (power, control, guidance,
authoritative pronouncements) or as freedom *to* (express oneself, theologize, act, etc.) it still remains dependent on, and
ultimately subordinated to, the concept and the definition of
authority.

But it is this very subordination, this very dichotomy, that, in my opinion, must be questioned and rejected if we are to see the real problem of freedom and Church. And it must be rejected because in fact it is a self-destructive dichotomy. Pushed to its logical conclusions, it simply annihilates the two concepts which it claims to "ground" and to define. And if the institutional Church is slow to realize it, and is still dreaming of an optimistic compromise in which some reasonable freedom will not threaten and undermine some reasonable authority, provided the spheres of each are authoritatively defined, the tragic dialectic of freedom, which constitutes the real spiritual itinerary of the so-called Christian world and which is inescapably rooted in the tragedy of freedom within the Church, is here to denounce this dream and to doom it in advance. From Saint-Just with his theory of necessary regicide, through Nietzsche and Dostoievsky, to Berdiaev, Camus, Sartre and the "death of God" theologians, one and the same fundamental truth reveals itself: if freedom as concept and experience is posited and determined by the concept and experience of authority, such freedom can be satisfied and can fulfill itself with nothing short of the "murder," of the annihilation of that authority itself. "This man must either reign or die," claims Saint-Just pointing at the King, and Nietzsche with his followers, when they proclaim that God is to die if man is to be free, are only taking the next logical and final step. Once poisoned with freedom, man cannot stop halfway, as Joseph de Maistre saw every clearly; and as long as authority remains, there is no freedom. In absolute terms, the formula "more freedom, less authority" is not different from "more authority, less freedom." For it is the very principle of authority, and not the amount of it, that freedom negates, for whatever the amount of the authority, it ultimately negates and destroys freedom. And thus the benevolent king dies, and Nietzsche prefers the "night and more night coming" of a Godless world to this source and sanction of all authority.

And yet the inescapable logic of the whole "freedom-authority" dichotomy is that when freedom, in order to fulfill itself, annihilates authority, it also annihilates itself. For not only does it become meaningless, an empty form, without its opposition to and its revolt against authority but also, in fact, it is not fulfilled as long as the last "authority" remains, which is death. It is the eternal merit of Dostoievsky to have shown us in Kirillov of *The Possessed* this inescapable interdependence between supreme freedom and suicide: "He who dares kill himself is God." Yet in order to become God one must kill himself! And it seems to me rather significant that Thomas Altizer, one of the deeper and more consistent representatives of the "death of God" movement, enthusiastically accepts Kirillov as a positive hero and credits Dostoievsky with having created in him the "modern image of Christ." [1] "What a marvelous coincidence," he writes "that Dostoievsky . . . should have anticipated in his portrayal of Kirillov a radically modern understanding of Jesus Himself." [2] And it is with the same sympathy, almost enthusiasm, that the same Altizer quotes a writer for whom the ultimate victory of life will be manifested in its "willingness to die."

Such is, I repeat, the inescapable logic of freedom as long and inasmuch as it is defined in reference to authority, i.e., in terms of a limit. It would not be real freedom if it did not negate and ultimately annihilate that limit. Yet, because precisely of its ontological dependence on authority, by annihilating the latter, it annihilates itself. Is there a way out of this dead end? What are the presuppositions of a Christian theology of freedom?

2.

It is at this point, it seems to me, that the Eastern Orthodox tradition may be of some help. I do not pretend, of course, that the Orthodox East has been always and consistently free from a surrender to the freedom-authority dichotomy. Those who have glanced through the few things I have written about my Church know that I am not guilty of any romantic idealization of her past. But I speak here, not of historical sins

[1] T. Altizer, *Mircea Eliade and the Dialectic of the Sacred* (Philadelphia, Westminster Press, 1963), p. 112.

[2] Ibid., p. 111.

and deviations, but of the Orthodox Principle (in the way in which Paul Tillich spoke of the Protestant Principle), and it cannot be denied that one of its basic elements is precisely the rejection of freedom understood and defined in terms of authority. This rejection constitutes the very center of the Orthodox critique of the West, both Roman Catholic and Protestant, and if I mention this critique here it is not for reasons of confessional polemics, but because it may help us to understand the positive contents of the Orthodox doctrine of freedom in the Church.

In his essay "On the Western Confessions of Faith" the great Russian lay theologian A. S. Khomiakov wrote: "The Church is an authority, said Guizot in one of his remarkable works, while one of his adversaries, attacking him, simply repeated these words. Speaking in this way, neither one suspected how much untruth and blasphemy lay in the statement... *No — the Church is not an authority, just as God is not an authority and Christ is not an authority, since authority is something external to us.*" [3] For Khomiakov the initial tragedy of the West, transcending its internal schism, or rather provoking it, was the identification of the Church with something alien to her nature — an external and objective authority. It made inevitable a revolt against this authority, but the revolt remains necessarily within the framework of that which it negates — and resulted therefore in a simple replacement of one external authority with another. "The Church inspired by God," he writes, "became, for the Western Christian, something external, a kind of negative authority, a kind of material authority. It turned man into its slave, and as a result acquired, in him, a judge." [4] Once more, I quote these harsh words only because they can lead us into the real dialectic of freedom, and I am fully aware that the temptation of an external or material authority is indeed a universal temptation. The important point here is that, in the thought of Khomiakov (and it could be shown that he truly reflects

[3] In *Ultimate Questions: An Anthology of Modern Russian Religious Thought*, ed. by Alexander Schmemann (New York, Holt, Rinehart and Winston, 1965), p. 50.

[4] Ibid., p. 50.

and formulates a position common to the whole Orthodox East), this kind of authority is derived not from the Church, not from her theandric nature, not from her God-inspired life, but from that which in the New Testament and in Church Tradition is described as "this world," i.e. the fallen state of man. The very principle of authority as something external to man is thus the result of the fall, the fruit of man's alienation from true life. But then the freedom which that authority posits as its own point of application, as its necessary counterpart, is also a "fallen freedom," a negative freedom, a freedom of opposition and revolt and not the ontological freedom in which man was created and from which he alienated himself in his fall. It is in fact a *pseudo-freedom*, for in its fight against one external authority it is motivated and dominated by another authority to which it is sooner or later enslaved. And it cannot be otherwise, because it is a *negative* freedom, made up of revolt and protest and having no positive contents of its own. Whatever "contents" it may find in its revolt will again and inescapably become "authority" and provoke the same endless processs.

According to Khomiakov the central tragedy of Western Christianity consisted in this, that it accepted as its basis, as its formative principle, the principle of authority — which is the very principle of the fallen world; and this acceptance, of necessity, led to the opposite principle of "fallen freedom." A principle not only alien to the nature of the Church but radically opposed to it was introduced into the very texture of her life. The whole problem of freedom in the Church was thus vitiated in its very foundation, and became incapable of a right solution. For the Church is not a combination of authority *and* freedom, of limited authority and limited freedom, a combination which, if it is kept, preserves from abuses on both sides. The Church is *not* authority, and therefore there is no freedom *in* the Church, but the Church herself *is* freedom, and only the Church is freedom. There can be no continuity between the fallen freedom of man and the Church as freedom, because there is no real freedom outside the Church but only the meaningless fight of mutually annihilating "authorities." Therefore it is not by applying to the

Church the abstract and natural concept of "freedom" that one understands freedom in the Church. Rather it is by entering the *mysterion* of the Church that one understands it as the mystery of freedom. Ecclesiology is indeed the starting point of a theology of freedom.

3.

If ecclesiology, as a theological discipline, as a systematic treatise, has failed so far to reveal the life of the Church as the mystery and gift of freedom, it has been due to one of its greatest deficiencies: the neglect of the Holy Spirit in His relation to the Church. For reasons which it is impossible even briefly to analyze here (but of which some, at least, are directly connected with what we have said about the acceptance of "authority" into the concept of the Church), the doctrine of the Holy Spirit was in many ways cut off from the doctrine of the Church.

"And in the Holy Spirit, the Church," such is the earliest form of the third article of the Creed, and it unites—one could almost say it identifies — the Holy Spirit with the Church. But in the course of centuries this article was dislocated. If within systematic theology the Holy Spirit was given all honor and attention in the *De Deo uno et trino*, in the *De Ecclesia* He retained what could be termed without exaggeration a subordinate position. From being understood as the very life of the Church, He came to be seen as a *sanction* and a *guarantee*. Where authority was stressed as the formative principle of the Church, He was presented as the guarantee of that authority. Where individual freedom was stressed against authority, He became the *guarantee* of such freedom. And finally having acquired a clearly defined "function" in the Church, He began to be *measured*. "It is not by measure that God gives the Spirit" (John 3:34). Theology, however, spent its time measuring the Spirit. The wind of Pentecost was duly deposited as a capital of grace to be used with caution. No wonder that the Holy Spirit, not only as the source but indeed as the very content of that freedom which *is* the Church, as both the gift and the fulfillment of freedom, or better to say as Freedom itself, was forgotten.

The purpose of this essay is only to define, if possible, the future task of theology. And it is obviously impossible even to outline adequately in this short paper the various steps that would lead us from a fresh investigation of the doctrine of the Holy Spirit to a new vision of the Church as freedom. I can only state that in my opinion the first step here must be greater attention to the very Person of the Holy Spirit as has been revealed to us in the Holy Scriptures and in the spiritual tradition of the Church. We must recover the *vision* and the *experience* of the Holy Spirit. The biblical vision of Him, first of all, as the *ruah*, the wind "which blows where it wills, and you hear the sound of it, but you do not know whence it comes or whither it goes" (John 3:8), and also as the hypostatic Life of the Father and, thus, of the Blessed Trinity itself. Writes Professor Verhovskoy:

> To be the Spirit of something means to be the living expression of its content, its dynamic power. The Holy Spirit is often described in Scripture as Power, and the manifestations of the Spirit are always manifestations of a divine, living, creative power. We find the same idea in many names of the Holy Spirit. He is Light — as the living and creative manifestations of the Divine Wisdom. If the Son is Wisdom and Truth, the *Spirit* of that Wisdom is the Holy Spirit; in Him, or better — by Him, the whole Wisdom and the whole Truth of the Son is revealed as Life.[5]

Here is the fundamental intuition, common to the entire Eastern Orthodox tradition concerning the Holy Spirit: He is the Life of God, and this means, in terms of this paper—the hypostatic Freedom of God.

In the context of the problem which interests us here, this intuition can be formulated in the following way: without the manifestation of the Holy Spirit, without our communion

[5] S. Verhovskoy, *God and Man* (in Russian — New York, Chekhov, 1956), p. 367.

with Him, God would indeed be *authority*, the authority of all authorities, and there would be, therefore, no other freedom but that of *revolt*, the freedom of Kirillov. And without the Holy Spirit not only God but, in fact, the whole of reality, all being, would also be "authority" — an external, objective, compulsory order, Berdiaev's repulsive "world of objectivity." Truth would be Authority, as well as Justice, Order, Equality, etc., and, in fact, all these "values" *are* authorities in the fallen world, including ultimately freedom itself: an empty and meaningless principle of choice and dissent, a "right" leading nowhere. But it is the very "function" of the Holy Spirit to abolish authority, or rather to transcend it, and He does this by abolishing the *externality* which is the essence of authority and the essence of "this world" as the fallen world. The proper role of the Holy Spirit is to connect and to unite, not by a form of "objective" link, but by revealing and manifesting the *interiority* of all that exists, by restoring and transforming the "object" into the "subject" (the *it* into the *thou,* in the terms of Martin Buber). And He does it not from outside as "sanction" or "guarantee," not as "authority," but from "inside," for He Himself is the "interiority" of all that exists, the life of life, the gift of Being. He is the uniqueness, the "fragrance" of everyone and everything, the light of eternity in each moment of time, the reflection of divine beauty on the ugliest human face. He is both Freedom itself and the "content" of freedom, or rather in Him the tragic contradiction between freedom as an eternal possibility of an eternal choice and thus as an eternal, self-annihilating vacuum, and freedom as fullness of possession, as fulfillment of life — the contradiction which inescapably makes one freedom negate the other — is resolved. *Freedom is free.* It is free not only from enslavement to authority but also from enslavement to itself. And it is free because it is neither a negation nor an affirmation of something external, which both are inescapably "authority." It is the *Presence*, not of an abstract or formal principle, but of a Person who is the very meaning, the very joy, the very beauty, the very fullness, the very truth, the very *life* of all life — a Person whom we *possess* in knowledge, love and communion, who is not "external" to us, but is *in* us, as light, love and truth, as our *communion* with everything.

This *vision* of the Holy Spirit is also the experience of the Church. A certain approach to theology, although of course it does not negate that experience, denies it the status of a "source" of theology, that of a *locus theologicus*. It draws a line between theology as a rational structure, as a science, and "mysticism," and it relegates the latter to a special religious category or phenomenon, distinct from theology. But in the Eastern Tradition all genuine theology is, of necessity and by definition, *mystical*. This means not that theology is at the mercy of individual and irrational "visions" and "experiences," but that it is rooted in, made indeed *possible*, by the Church's experience of herself as *communion of the Holy Spirit*. The famous Palamite controversy about the "created" or "uncreated" nature of the light seen in the mystical experience of the "hesychasts" was, among other things, a controversy about the nature of theology, or rather of the object of theology, which is Truth. Is the truth of theology a rational deduction from the "data" and "propositions" of the sources? Is it, in other terms, based on an external "authority," *a priori* proclaimed as such, made an "authority"? Or is it, primarily, the description of an experience, of *the* experience of the Church without which all these "data" and "propositions," although they may be "objectively" true and consistent, are not yet the Truth. For the Truth, whose knowledge, according to the Gospel, makes us free, is certainly not an "objective truth," certainly not an "authority" — for in this case the whole dialectic of freedom would again and inescapably be set in its hopeless motion. It is the presence of the Holy Spirit, for it is this presence alone which creates the "organ" of Truth in us and thus transforms the Truth as "object" into "subject." The one who has no Spirit knows no Truth and is condemned to replace it with authority and guarantee. "Where will we find a guarantee against error," asks Khomiakov, and he answers: "Whoever seeks beyond hope and faith for any guarantee of the Spirit is already a rationalist. For him the Church, too is unthinkable, since he is already, in his whole spirit, plunged in doubt."⁶ And here, therefore, the experience of the saints, of the "seers of the Spirit," to quote a beautiful liturgical expression, is decisive. St. Seraphim of Sarov, a Russian saint of the nineteenth century and one of the last great representatives of the Eastern spiritual tradition, says: "When the Spirit of God descends to man and overshadows him with the fullness of His outpouring, then the human soul overflows with unspeakable joy, because the Spirit of God turns to joy all that He may touch."⁷ We have here a perfect, yet existential and not rational, summary of the doctrine of the Holy Spirit, of His relation to the Church, and of His very nature as freedom. And it is this doctrine which alone may free us from all false dichotomies and lead us into the proper understanding of the Church as freedom.

4.

We can come now to practical conclusions. "And I believe in the Holy Spirit, the Church." The Church is the presence and the action of the Holy Spirit. And this means that the Church *is* freedom. Freedom, in other words, is not a "part," an element within the Church coexisting with and related to another element — authority. The Church, being the presence, the Temple of the Holy Spirit, is that reality in which the very dichotomy of authority and freedom is abolished, or rather, is constantly transcended and overcome, and this constant victory *is* the very life of the Church, the victory of *communion* over alienation and externality. But — and this is very important — the Church is freedom precisely because she is total obedience to God. This obedience, however, is not the fruit of a surrender of freedom to an ultimate and ultimately "objective" Authority, acknowledged finally as invincible and unshakable, as indeed the "end" of freedom. It is, paradoxically as it may sound, the fulfillment of freedom. For the

---

⁶ *Ultimate Questions*, p. 54.

⁷ Quoted in *A Treasury of Russian Spirituality*, ed. G. Fedotov (New York, Harper Torchbooks, 1965), p. 275.

ultimate gift of the Holy Spirit is not a "state," not a "joy"
or "peace" in itself. It is again a Person: Jesus Christ. It is
the possession of Christ and my being possessed by Christ,
it is my love for Christ and His love for me, it is my faith in
Christ and His faith in me, it is "Christ in me" and "I in
Christ." And Christ is *obedience:* "obedient unto death, even
death on a Cross" (Phil. 2:8). His obedience is the expression
not of any subordination, of any surrender of freedom to
Authority, but precisely of His total unity with His Father, of
His divinity itself! For not only is His obedience free (for any
freedom can freely surrender itself), but it is the very manifestation, the very essence of His freedom. And if Christ is
the gift of the Holy Spirit, if Christ is the life of the Church,
then the essence of this life is obedience, not to Christ but
Christ's obedience. It is truly a divine obedience because it is
an obedience beyond the dichotomy of freedom and authority,
because it comes not from imperfection but from the perfection of life revealed in Christ.

All this means that in the Church freedom is manifested
as obedience of all to all in Christ, for Christ is the one who,
by the Holy Spirit, lives in all in communion with God. No
one is above and no one is beneath. The one who teaches has
no "authority," but a gift of the Holy Spirit. And the one
who receives the teaching receives it only if he has the gift of
the Holy Spirit, which reveals to him the teaching not as
"authority" but as Truth. And the prayer of the Church is
not for "sanctions" and "guarantees," but for the Spirit Himself — that He may come and abide in us, transforming us into
that living unity in which the obedience of all to all is un-
ceasingly revealing itself as the only freedom.

It is here, of course, that the study of the "phenomenology" of freedom in the Church could and should begin. My
task was only to outline — and even this in a very preliminary
way — a kind of "prolegomena" to such a study, to show, in
words obviously inadequate, that the mystery of the Church
as freedom is hidden in the mystery of God as the Blessed
Trinity — in the grace of our Lord Jesus Christ, the love of
God the Father, in the communion of the Holy Spirit. And
this mystery begins to be revealed and communicated to us

when the same man says of himself *"doulos Iesou Christou"* —
"The slave of Jesus Christ" — and then, to each one and to
all of us, "Stand fast in the freedom in which Christ has set
us free" (Gal. 5:1).

X

THE ECUMENICAL AGONY

PRELIMINARY NOTE: THE HARTFORD APPEAL

In January 1975 some seventeen American theologians belonging to, but not officially representing, a wide range of American churches met at the Hartford Seminary Foundation in Hartford, Connecticut, to discuss a common reaction to "Pervasive, false and debilitating notions" which, in the words of one of them, "they believed were undermining contemporary Christianity and its influence in society." A preliminary formulation of thirteen such "notions" or "themes" was prepared by Professor Peter L. Berger and Pastor Richard John Neuhaus, the two initiators and conveners of the meeting. After three days of discussions, during which the original draft was substantially altered and each of the denounced "notions" given an examination, the group agreed on the text of an "appeal for Theological Affirmation," better known as "The Hartford Appeal," "The response to the Appeal," writes Peter Berger, "far exceeded the expectations of the participants. Both here and elsewhere, notably in Europe, the Appeal has been greeted by acclaim, ridicule, anger, and, especially among lay-people, an enormous sense of relief that 'somebody finally said what needed to be said.' Whatever may or may not be the merits of the Appeal, the response to it unquestionably says something important about the current state of religion" (*Against the World for the World,* p. 9).

The group met once more in September 1975, to analyse and to evaluate response to the Appeal, and to clarify and elaborate its intentions. The essays prepared for and discussed at that meeting were published in 1976 in the book *Against the World for the World,* edited by Peter Berger and Richard Neuhaus (New York, The Seabury Press, 1976).

Three Orthodox signed the appeal — Dr. Ileana Marculescu, then Visiting Professor of Philosophy and Religion at Union Theological

* Originally published under the title "That East and West May Yet Meet," in *Against the World for the World: The Hartford Appeal and the Future of American Religion,* ed. by Peter L. Berger and Richard John Neuhaus (New York, The Seabury Press, 1976), pp. 126-137.

Seminary, Fr. Thomas Hopko, Professor of Dogmatics at St. Vladimir's Seminary, and myself. As the only Orthodox who attended both meetings (Fr. Hopko signed but did not attend and Dr. Marculescu was present only at the first meeting), I was asked to prepare an essay. It is this essay that is reprinted here, following the complete text of the Appeal itself.

AN APPEAL FOR THEOLOGICAL AFFIRMATION

The renewal of Christian witness and mission requires constant examination of the assumptions shaping the Church's life. Today an apparent loss of a sense of the transcendent is undermining the Church's ability to address with clarity and courage the urgent tasks to which God calls it in the world. This loss is manifest in a number of pervasive themes. Many are superficially attractive, but upon closer examination we find these themes false and debilitating to the Church's life and work. Among such themes are:

THEME 1: *Modern thought is superior to all past forms of understanding reality, and is therefore normative for Christian faith and life.*

In repudiating this theme we are protesting the captivity to the prevailing thought structures not only of the twentieth century but of any historical period. We favor using any helpful means of understanding, ancient or modern, and insist that the Christian proclamation must be related to the idiom of the culture. At the same time, we affirm the need for Christian thought to confront and be confronted by other world views, all of which are necessarily provisional.

THEME 2: *Religious statements are totally independent of reasonable discourse.*

The capitulation to the alleged primacy of modern thought takes two forms: one is the subordination of religious statements to the canons of scientific rationality; the other, equating reason with scientific rationality, would remove religious statements from the realm of reasonable discourse altogether. A religion of pure subjectivity and nonrationality results in treating faith statements as being, at best, statements about the believer. We repudiate both forms of capitulation.

THEME 3: *Religious language refers to human experience and nothing else, God being humanity's noblest creation.*

Religion is also a set of symbols and even of human projections. We repudiate the assumption that it is nothing but that. What is here at stake is nothing less than the reality of God: *We did not invent God; God invented us.*

THEME 4: *Jesus can only be understood in terms of contemporary models of humanity.*

This theme suggests a reversal of "the imitation of Christ"; that is, the image of Jesus is made to reflect cultural and countercultural notions of human excellence. We do not deny that all aspects of humanity are illumined by Jesus. Indeed, it is necessary to the universality of the Christ that he be perceived in relation to the particularities of the believers' world. We do repudiate the captivity to such metaphors, which are necessarily inadequate, relative, transitory, and frequently idolatrous. Jesus, together with the Scriptures and the whole of the Christian tradition, cannot be arbitrarily interpreted without reference to the history of which they are part. The danger is in the attempt to exploit the tradition without taking the tradition seriously.

THEME 5: *All religions are equally valid; the choice among them is not a matter of conviction about truth but only of personal preference or life style.*

We affirm our common humanity. We affirm the importance of exploring and confronting all manifestations of the religious quest and of learning from the riches of other religions. But we repudiate this theme because it flattens diversities and ignores contradictions. In doing so, it not only obscures the meaning of Christian faith, but also fails to respect the integrity of other faiths. Truth matters; therefore differences among religions are deeply significant.

THEME 6: *To realize one's potential and to be true to oneself is the whole meaning of salvation.*

Salvation contains a promise of human fulfillment, but to identify salvation with human fulfillment can trivialize the promise. We affirm that salvation cannot be found apart from God.

THEME 7: *Since what is human is good, evil can adequately be understood as failure to realize potential.*

This theme invites false understanding of the ambivalence of human existence and underestimates the pervasiveness of sin. Paradoxically, by minimizing the enormity of evil, it undermines serious and sustained attacks on particular social or individual evils.

THEME 8: *The sole purpose of worship is to promote individual self-realization and human community.*

Worship promotes individual and communal values, but it is above all a response to the reality of God and arises out of the fundamental need and desire to know, love, and adore God. We worship God because God is to be worshiped.

THEME 9: *Institutions and historical traditions are oppressive and inimical to our being truly human; liberation from them is required for authentic existence and authentic religion.*

Institutions and traditions are often oppressive. For this reason they must be subjected to relentless criticism. But human community inescapably requires institutions and traditions. Without them life would degenerate into chaos and new forms of bondage. The modern pursuit of liberation from all social and historical restraints is finally dehumanizing.

THEME 10: *The world must set the agenda for the Church. Social, political, and economic programs to improve the quality of life are ultimately normative for the Church's mission in the world.*

This theme cuts across the political and ideological spectrum. Its form remains the same, no matter whether the content is defined as upholding the values of the American way of life, promoting socialism, or raising human consciousness. The Church must denounce oppressors, help liberate the oppressed, and seek to heal human misery. Sometimes the Church's mission coincides with the world's programs. But the norms for the Church's activity derive from its own perception of God's will for the world.

THEME 11: *An emphasis on God's transcendence is at least a hindrance to, and perhaps incompatible with, Christian social concern and action.*

This supposition leads some to denigrate God's transcendence. Others, holding to a false transcendence, withdraw into religious privatism or individualism and neglect the personal and communal responsibility of Christians for the earthly city. From a biblical perspective, it is precisely because of confidence in God's reign over all aspects of life that Christians must participate fully in the struggle against oppressive and dehumanizing structures and their manifestations in racism, war, and economic exploitation.

THEME 12: *The struggle for a better humanity will bring about the Kingdom of God.*

The struggle for a better humanity is essential to Christian faith and can be informed and inspired by the biblical promise of the Kingdom of God. But imperfect human beings cannot create a perfect society. The Kingdom of God surpasses any conceivable utopia. God has his own designs which confront ours, surprising us with judgment and redemption.

THEME 13: *The question of hope beyond death is irrelevant or at best marginal to the Christian understanding of human fulfillment.*

This is the final capitulation to modern thought. If death is the last word, then Christianity has nothing to say to the final questions of life. We believe that God raised Jesus from the dead and are "... convinced that there is nothing in death or life, in the realm of spirits or superhuman powers, in the world as it is or in the world as it shall be, in the forces of the universe, in heights or depths — nothing in all creation that can separate us from the love of God in Christ Jesus our Lord" (Romans 8:38 f.).

[*Against the World for the World*, pp. 3-5; a complete list of the signatories follows, pp. 5-7.]

When the editors of this volume of reflections on Hartford asked me to write a chapter on Orthodoxy, I was tempted to decline the assignment, and for a very simple reason. It was clear to me that the Hartford Appeal would not generate among the Orthodox any significant reaction comparable to the one it has already provoked among the Roman Catholics and the Protestants. This proved to be true. Here and there a few "triumphalist" remarks were made in which the document was greeted as a welcome and timely sign of *their* (Westerners') recovery and return: recovery from what the Orthodox always knew to be wrong, return to what they always knew to be right.

But, on the whole, the statement itself, as well as the controversy which it inaugurated within the American theological community, remained and is likely to remain extrinsic to the Orthodox Church. The reason for this is clear: convinced that the trends, ideas and thought-forms denounced at Hartford as "false and debilitating" have had no impact on Orthodox theology, the Orthodox see in the Hartford phenomenon a purely Western development. While sincerely applauding it, they are not involved with it and they bear no responsibility for the outcome. Hence, my first reaction was that whatever the future of Orthodoxy here or elsewhere might be, I did not see how I could relate it to Hartford or write an article about a nonexistent relationship.

On second thought, however, I realized I was wrong. I saw that this absence of reaction — or rather the reason for it — is in itself a very significant fact with implications not only for Orthodoxy and its future but also for the Hartford event and its own ultimate future. I realized finally that as one of only two Orthodox participants in the Hartford meeting I have a double duty: to try to explain to my Western brothers the true meaning of the Orthodox "silence," and to my fellow Orthodox why, in spite of its Western character and context, the Hartford Appeal concerns them, not less but perhaps even more than other American Christians. Such then is the double purpose of this essay, rooted in my own double and somewhat ambiguous experience: that of an Orthodox within the Hartford group, that of a "Hartford man" within the Orthodox Church.

1.

I said that the Orthodox reaction to Hartford — that is, its absence of reaction — is to be explained primarily by the Western origin and orientation of the Appeal. Because of this, the Orthodox do not consider that they have anything to do with it. It seems to me quite important to acknowledge the truth of at least the first of these affirmations — its Western origin. It is absolutely true that the Hartford Appeal is indeed a Western document, the term "Western" referring here not only to that particular — and clearly Western — religious situation from which the Appeal stems and at which it is aimed, but also to its basic theological presuppositions, conceptual language, and, in general, the entire spiritual tradition to which it unmistakably belongs.

While participating in the Hartford meeting, I could not help feeling within myself a certain inner *dedoublement*. On the one hand, having spent all my life in the West and having lived a quarter of a century in America, I had no difficulty in understanding what it was all about, in identifying myself with the concerns of the group, and, finally, in signing, in full conscience and conviction, the Appeal. Yet, on the other hand, as an Orthodox, I also very strongly felt a certain malaise, a kind of "inner distance" separating me from my non-Orthodox colleagues. Clearly there was nothing personal in it, for seldom have I attended friendlier meetings. It was not a formal disagreement either, for, as I have said, I wholeheartedly shared the group's "negations" as well as its "affirmations." It was the experience, familiar to me since my first contacts with the ecumenical movement, of the Orthodox transplanted as it were into a spiritual and mental world radically different from his own; forced to use a theological language which, although he understands it, is not his language; and who, therefore, while agreeing on one level, experiences and realizes on another level the frustrating discrepancy between that formal agreement and the totality of the Orthodox *vision*.

If I begin by referring to that experience, it is because I am convinced that it would be useless to discuss the problem of Hartford and Orthodoxy without at first understanding the real meaning and the true scope of that discrepancy, and without realizing that it constitutes the main cause of that "failure" which characterizes the ecumenical encounter between Orthodoxy and the West — a failure which cannot be concealed by the massive presence of Orthodox officials at all ecumenical gatherings, and which is not less real and profound even if the majority of the Orthodox are unaware of it.

Thus, a few words about that failure are in order, and here again a personal recollection may be of some help. My own "ecumenical baptism" took place in 1948 at the first assembly of the World Council of Churches, which was held in Amsterdam. And I remember very vividly how, upon my arrival and while going through the registration routine, I met a high ecumenical dignitary who in a very friendly fashion, obviously with the intention to please me, informed me that the Orthodox delegates would be seated at the extreme right of the assembly hall together with the representatives of the Western "high churches" — such as the Swedish Lutherans ("who, as you may know, *do* have the apostolic succession . . ."), the Old Catholics and the Polish Nationals. From sheer curiosity — for certainly I had nothing against sitting with those excellent people — I asked him who made that decision? His answer was that it simply reflected the "ecclesiological" makeup of the conference, one of whose main themes would be precisely the dichotomy of the "horizontal" and "vertical" ideas of the Church. And obviously the Orthodox belong (don't they?) to the "horizontal" type. To this I half jokingly remarked that in my studies of Orthodox theology I had never heard of such distinctions, and that without this information, had the choice been left to me, I might have selected a seat at the extreme "left" with the Quakers, whose emphasis on the Holy Spirit we Orthodox certainly share.

I hope that the point of this reminiscence is clear. The important fact of Orthodox participation in the ecumenical movement and in the encounter — after so many centuries of almost total separation — between the Orthodox and the West is precisely that the Orthodox *were not given a choice;* that from the very beginning they were assigned, not only seats but a certain place, role and function within the ecumenical movement. These "assignments" were based on Western theological and ecclesiological presuppositions and categories, and they reflected the purely Western origin of the ecumenical idea itself. We joined a movement, entered a debate, took part in a search whose basic terms of reference were already defined and taken for granted. Thus, even before we could realize it, we were caught in the essentially Western dichotomies — Catholic versus Protestant, horizontal versus vertical, authority versus freedom, hierarchical versus congregational — and were made into representatives and bearers of attitudes and positions which we hardly recognized as ours and which were deeply alien to our tradition. All this, however, was due not to any Machiavellian conspiracy or ill will, but precisely to the main and all-embracing Western presupposition that the Western experience, theological categories and thought forms are universal and therefore constitute the self-evident framework and terms of reference for the entire ecumenical endeavor.

Hence the initial misunderstanding that has never been fully cleared, and hence the ultimate failure of that encounter in spite of the presence and efforts of many brilliant Orthodox theologians and spokesmen, and, in the last years, of the massive participation by virtually all Orthodox churches.[1] What the Western architects of the ecumenical movement never fully understood is that for the Orthodox the ecumenical encounter, first of all and above all, means the first free and therefore truly meaningful encounter with the *West as a totality*, the West as the other "half" of the initially one Christian world, separated from Orthodoxy not by a limited number of doctrinal disagreements but primarily by a deep difference in the fundamental Christian *vision* itself. It is this Western vision and experience, inasmuch as the Orthodox saw in them a deviation from and a mutilation of the once common faith and tradition, that they were anxious to discuss, believing such discussion to be the self-evident and essential condition for any further step.

Such, however, was not at all the Western presupposition. First of all, the West had long ago lost almost completely any awareness of being just the half of the initial *Christianitas*. Its own historical and theological "blooming" began at the time when the Christian East, which dominated the first Christian millennium, was entering its prolonged "dark age," was becoming voiceless and silent. Quite rapidly the West identified itself with *Christianitas*, the East slipping into a corner of its memory, mainly, alas, as the object of conversion to Rome or to Protestantism. Existentially, the West remembered not its separation from the East but its own tragic fragmentation into Catholic and Protestant camps and the dialectics of

---

[1] Cf. my essay "Moment of Truth for Orthodoxy" in *Unity in Mid-Career: An Ecumenical Critique*, eds. Keith R. Bridston and Walter D. Wagoner (New York, Macmillan, 1963), pp. 47-56.

Reformation and Counterreformation. And it was then that, at first negatively and then positively, the ecumenical categories began to be elaborated and that the Western mind was shaped. Thus, shortly after World War I when Orthodoxy emerged on the ecumenical horizon, the shape of the Western mind was already there, clearly determined by Western self-sufficiency.

This does not mean that the Orthodox were not greeted with sincere joy and genuine Christian love. One can say that for a certain period they were even quite popular. On the one hand, their very presence — especially in the absence of Roman Catholicism in those early days — made the movement truly ecumenical and not merely pan-Protestant. On the other hand, these representatives of "ancient" and "venerable" churches were welcomed as suppliers of that "mysticism" and "spirituality," of those "rich" liturgical traditions which the West periodically requires as useful spiritual vitamins. There was, by all means, a "honeymoon." But to every serious student of the ecumenical movement it must be clear that at no time has the Orthodox "witness" (presented mainly, if not exclusively, in separate Orthodox statements attached to the minutes of all major ecumenical conferences) had any significant impact on the orientations and theological development of the movement itself.

2.

But how and why is all this related to Hartford in general, and to its eventual meaning for Orthodoxy in particular? My answer is that sooner or later, in a new way and in a different context, the Hartford debate is bound to face the same question that Orthodoxy tried unsuccessfully to raise within the ecumenical movement: the question of the spiritual destiny of the West, of that Western culture which has truly become today *the* culture. And if that question is not raised and faced, Hartford will, of necessity, lead to another spiritual dead end.

Indeed, the only consensus reached at Hartford concerns the alarming surrender of religion to culture, to the pervasive secularism of the modern world, and, as a consequence of that surrender, to the "loss of transcendence." But if that consensus is to become the starting point of a reconstruction, a re-thinking of our situation, then the next question concerns that culture itself or, more exactly, its own roots in the religion which today deplores "cultural captivity." It is precisely this question, however, that Orthodoxy addressed — although perhaps not very *claire et distincte* — to the Christian West; and it is this question that the West has neither heard nor understood.[2] It has not understood that beneath all divergences and disagreements, theological and nontheological, between the East and the West, there always existed the essential difference in the experience and understanding of *transcendence* itself, or rather of the essentially and uniquely Christian affirmation of both the absolute transcendence of God and of His *real presence* — that is, His immanence to the world and to man, to the totality of His creation. That which the Orthodox East rejected in the West, rather than clearly denounced, was ultimately the breakdown of that transcendence-immanence antinomy, of the basic cosmological, ecclesiological intuition of Christianity, an intuition which alone founds the Christian approach toward world, history and culture.

This, and ultimately only this, stood at the heart of the debates and controversies which seem so hopelessly archaic and irrelevant to so many ecumenically minded people: created versus uncreated grace, the Palamite distinction between the divine essence and the divine energies, the essence of the mystical experience (the "nature" of the light *seen* and experienced by the saints), the essence of sanctification. None of these themes can, for obvious reasons, be elaborated here, and I can only declare and affirm that they are relevant and essential because they ultimately concern not only religion and theology but precisely *culture*, as man's self-understanding

[2] The reader who wants to understand the difficulties of the East-West encounter in the twentieth century should read the essays of Fr. Georges Florovsky, who was for three decades the main Orthodox spokesman in the ecumenical movement. These essays have been collected in three volumes: *Bible, Church, Tradition: An Eastern Orthodox View* (Nordland, 1972), *Christianity and Culture* (Nordland, 1974), and *Aspects of Church History* (Nordland, 1975).

and self-determination in relation to God, nature, history and action.

What Orthodoxy implies is that virtually none of the "errors" denounced in the Hartford Appeal would have been possible without, first of all, a dislocation and a breakdown of the transcendence-immanence antinomy itself, of the fundamental Christian *theologia*, just as all affirmations contained in the Appeal, which before being accepted and implemented must simply be *heard*, also imply and presuppose a radical reconversion to that vision. In a way, the Appeal sounds as if the cultural captivity and dissolution of religion, the loss by the latter of transcendence, were almost accidental, and that all it would take to improve the situation is a new balancing of our man-centered culture by a God-centered religion. Then, we are told, the Church will again be able to "address with clarity and courage the urgent tasks to which God calls it in the world." The whole point of the Orthodox argument, however, is that such balancing is impossible, would be abortive, without a radical re-examination of the process which, two thousand years after the incarnation and Pentecost, and after the call to *deification* addressed to man by Christ and the Holy Spirit, resulted in the triumph of man-centered culture and the secularistic rebellion against transcendence.

It is at this point that the Orthodox question — aimed at the West since the very beginning of the separation — acquires its whole meaning. Thus, if the Orthodox are silent about the Hartford Appeal, it is not because of indifference or ignorance or some combination (typical, alas, of many Orthodox reactions to the West) of superiority and inferiority complexes. It is because *rebus sic standibus* they have nothing to say as long as the *preliminary* question, at which I tried to hint here, is not raised. Only then will Orthodoxy find its proper place in the debate on which ultimately depends the destinies of "modern man." Only then will Orthodoxy cease to be what it still is for the West today: a marginal supplier of valuable but unessential "mystical" and "liturgical" contributions, but which, when it comes to serious matters ("the task of the Church in the world"), is expected to express itself in a

theological "idiom" whose very adequacy to that task Orthodoxy has always questioned.

In this sense Hartford may be a new beginning, may supply
us with a new opportunity and new possibilities — the possibility, for example, of that genuine encounter which did *not*
take place within the by now aging ecumenical movement.
Such an encounter, as I hope I have shown, is needed for
Hartford and that which it represents. But it is also needed,
and badly, by Orthodoxy.

3.

I began this essay by affirming that the Orthodox nonre-
action to the Hartford Appeal is rooted primarily in their
conviction that the Orthodox Church was neither touched nor
contaminated by the pervasive themes denounced at Hartford
as false and debilitating. And in a way this is true. Orthodox
theology, or better, the Orthodox confession of faith, remains
not only conservative but, on a deeper level, entirely shaped
by its essential dependence on the classical, patristic tradition.
Thus, formally, the Orthodox can justify their *de facto* non-
involvement in Western theological debate.

But only "formally." For the paradox of the Orthodox
situation is that it is precisely this theological conservatism,
this adamant faithfulness not only to the content but also to
the very form of their doctrinal tradition, that conceals from
the Orthodox their own, and I dare say tragic, surrender to
that very "culture" from which they claim their Orthodox
faith immunizes them. And the truly tragic aspect of that
surrender is that they are unaware of it, naively ignorant of
the evergrowing schizophrenia in which they live.[3]

There is no need to prove that today Orthodoxy is no
longer confined to the East. The single most important fact
in the history of Orthodoxy in this twentieth century is the

---

[3] Cf. my articles on "Problems of Orthodoxy in America": "The Canonical
Problem," *St. Vladimir's Theological Quarterly*, vol. 8.2 (1964), pp. 67-85;
"The Liturgical Problem," vol. 8.4 (1964), pp. 164-85; "The Spiritual
Problem," vol. 9.4 (1965), pp. 171-93.

growth of the Orthodox *diaspora*, the implantation of Orthodox communities in virtually all parts of the world. In America alone the Orthodox outnumber the Episcopalians and,
what is more significant, their churches progressively lose
their "immigrant" character and acquire those of the "native"
religion. One of the signs of the irreversibility of this trend
is the recent transformation of the former Russian Diocese,
whose origins go back to Russian Alaska, into the Orthodox
Church in America, an independent (autocephalous) church
with no national or ethnic reference in its name (It is still
opposed, however, by many other Orthodox churches abroad.)
Clearly, Orthodoxy is here to stay and to become an organic
part of the Western religious landscape.

But — and it is here that what I termed schizophrenia
begins — the Orthodox seem totally unaware of the tremendous spiritual implications and the challenge of that new
situation. They do not seem to be aware of the fact that *cul-
turally* the entire Orthodox Church (and not only the Orthodox
diaspora) lives today in the West, exposed to the Western
way of life and to the Western vision and experience of the
world. They are naively convinced that as long as they perform their Byzantine liturgical services, and on each first Sunday of Lent (the "Triumph of Orthodoxy") solemnly proclaim their indefectible attachment to the "Faith of the
Fathers, the Faith that affirms the universe," they preserve
Orthodoxy. And if, in addition to this, they cover the whole
world with more or less successful replicas of Byzantine, Russian, Serbian and other Orthodox churches; if they fight for
the recognition of Orthodoxy as the "fourth major faith",
and if they remain attached to a few of their "ancient" and
"colorful" customs, Orthodoxy is safe and they have fulfilled
their duty. What they are not aware of is that the Byzantine
liturgy — which they dutifully and in faithfulness to their
Orthodox heritage attend on Sunday — by its every word and
rite challenges the culture in which they live and which they
enthusiastically adopt as their "way of life" Monday through
Saturday; that the Orthodox faith which they so proudly
confess on the Sunday of Orthodoxy contains and posits a
vision of man, world, nature, matter, entirely different from

the one which in fact shapes not only their lives but their mental and psychological makeup as well.

Hence, the schizophrenia. The same priest who on Sunday morning celebrates again and again the "epiphany" of that Orthodox vision will later — in the hall downstairs, in his counseling, in his leadership — apply in fact all the "pervasive themes" of the American civil religion. For all practical purposes the Orthodox have enthusiastically adopted the basic principle of American religion: that it is very good to have many religions (each one "enriching" the other with its own "contributions," usually in the form of culinary recipes and colorful yet innocent customs) as long as deep down they are in fact the same religion with the same basic hierarchy of values. And since it is difficult to beat the Orthodox on the level of customs and all kinds of exciting ancient ceremonies, Orthodoxy enjoys a certain success and begins to attract more and more those who, disenchanted or even disgusted with the West, seek in things "oriental" the satisfaction of their religious emotions.

It is, then, this schizophrenia that, in my opinion at least, makes or ought to make Hartford relevant for the Orthodox: a question; a challenge addressed to them also; a mirror in which, if they are honest, they should recognize themselves and their own situation.

I know there are those Orthodox who affirm and preach that the Orthodox can and must live in the West without any "reference" to the Western culture except that of a total negation, to live in fact as if the West did not exist, for it is totally corrupt, heretical and sick beyond repair. To achieve this, one must create artificial islands of Greek or Russian or any other Orthodox culture, shut all doors and windows, and cultivate the certitude of belonging to the sacred remnant. What these "super-Orthodox" do not know, of course, is that their attitude reflects precisely the ultimate surrender to that West which they abhor: that in their ideology Orthodoxy is being transformed for the first time into that which it has never been — a *sect*, which is by definition the refusal of the *catholic* vocation of the Church.

And there are those who maintain, as I have tried to say,

a peaceful coexistence of Orthodoxy with a culture which, in reality, claims the whole man: his soul, his life and his religion.

Both attitudes are ultimately self-destructive. Thus, what I mean by the "relevance" of Hartford for the Orthodox is contained in the question it addresses to us: if ours is, as we always claim, the *true faith*, has not the time come to show — to ourselves in the first place — how it works in life, in that eternal tension between the total, absolute and truly apophatic transcendence of God and His real and wonderful presence in this created, fallen and redeemed world?

XI

THE MISSIONARY IMPERATIVE

1.

Until quite recently the Eastern Orthodox Church was regarded in the West as a *nonmissionary* church. It was an opinion commonly held that the great missionary movement which marked so deeply the Christian West during the last centuries somehow by-passed the "static" Christianity of the East. Today this view seems to have lost some of its strength: new historical research has made it quite clear that the Orthodox achievements in the field of mission, although somewhat different from those of the West, are nonetheless important and impressive.[1] Our purpose in this brief essay, however, is not to present a historical or statistical survey of the Orthodox missionary expansion. It is much more important to try to understand and to analyze, be it only tentatively and partially, the missionary *imperative* in the Orthodox tradition, or, in other terms, the relation in it between mission, on the one hand, and the faith, the life and the whole spiritual "vision" of Orthodoxy, on the other hand. A theology of mission is always the fruit of the total "being" of the Church and not a mere specialty for those who receive a particular missionary calling. But for the Orthodox Church there is a special need to

---

* Originally published in *The Theology of Christian Mission*, ed. by Gerald H. Anderson (McGraw Hill, New York, 1961), pp. 250-257.

[1] Josef Glazik, *Die Russisch-Orthodoxe Heidenmission seit Peter dem Grossen: Ein missionsgeschichtlicher Versuch nach russischen Quellen und Darstellungen* (Münster, Aschendorffsche Verlagsbuchhandlung, 1954). By the same author: *Die Islammission der Russisch-Orthodoxen Kirche* (Münster, Aschendorffsche Verlagsbuchhandlung, 1959).

reflect upon its basic missionary motivations, because its presumably nonmissionary character has been too often explained by, and ascribed to, the very essence, the "holy of holies" of Orthodoxy: its sacramental, liturgical, mystical ethos. Even now, as the study of Orthodox missions seems to correct the traditional view, there remains the temptation to explain these missions as a marginal "epiphenomenon" in the history of Orthodoxy, as something that happened in spite of its general tendencies and trends. This is why a *theological* clarification is necessary. Can a church whose life is centered almost exclusively on the liturgy and the sacraments, whose spirituality is primarily mystical and ascetical, be truly missionary? And if it is, where in its faith are the deepest motivations of the missionary zeal to be found? In somewhat simplified terms this is the question addressed, explicitly or implicitly, to the Orthodox Church by all those for whom "ecumenical" means necessarily and unescapably "missionary."

2.

It is without any doubt in Orthodox ecclesiology, i.e. in the doctrine and experience of the Church, that we find the basic elements of an answer. To formulate them, however, is not an easy task. It must be kept in mind that the Orthodox Church has never been challenged by an ecclesiological or doctrinal crisis comparable to the Reformation or Counter-Reformation. And because of this it had no compelling reason to reflect upon itself, upon the traditional structures of its life and doctrine. There was no theological elaboration of the doctrine of the Church, this doctrine never having been questioned or opposed. It was in the ecumenical encounter with the West, an encounter whose beginnings must be traced back to the early 'twenties (Stockholm, 1925, and Lausanne, 1927), that for the first time the Orthodox were requested not only to *state* their ecclesiological beliefs, but also to *explain* them, i.e. to express them in consistent theological terms, But at this point there appeared an additional difficulty which has remained ever since as the major difficulty of Orthodox

participation in the ecumenical movement. A dialogue necessarily presupposes an agreement on the terms that are being
used, a common language. Yet from the Orthodox point of
view, it was precisely the rupture in theological understanding,
the theological alienation of the West from the East, that first
made the "schism" so deep and then made all attempts to
heal it — from 1054 to the Council of Florence in 1438-1439 —
so hopelessly inadequate. Therefore, in the ecumenical encounter, the Orthodox Church had to face a Christian world
with several centuries of "autonomous" theological and spiritual development behind it, with a mind and thought-forms
radically different from those of the East. The questions it
asked of the Orthodox were formulated in Western terms,
were conditioned very often by specifically Western experience
and developments. The Orthodox answers were classified according to Western patterns, "reduced" to categories familiar
to the West but hardly adequate to Orthodoxy. This situation,
although years of contacts and conversations have no doubt
improved it, is still far from being overcome completely. The
"catholic language" has not yet been recovered. All this, in
addition to basic dogmatical differences, explains the "agony"
of Orthodox participation in the ecumenical movement and
constitutes a very real obstacle not only to agreement, but to
simple understanding. One must remember this when trying
to grasp the Orthodox approach to missions.

3.

"Heaven on earth": this formula familiar to every Orthodox expresses rather well the fundamental Orthodox experience of the Church. The Church is first of all and before
everything else a God-created and God-given reality, the
presence of Christ's new life, the manifestation of the new
"aeon" of the Holy Spirit. An Orthodox in his contemplation
of the Church sees it as the divine gift before he thinks of the
Church as human response to this gift. One can rightly describe
the Church as an eschatological reality, for its essential function is to manifest and to actualize in this world the *eschaton,*

the ultimate reality of salvation and redemption. In and through the Church the Kingdom of God is made already present, is communicated to men. And it is this eschatological, God-given fullness of Church (not any juridical theory of mediation) that constitutes the root of the ecclesiological "absolutism" of Eastern Orthodoxy — an absolutism which is so often misunderstood and misinterpreted by the Protestants. The Church as a whole is means of grace, the sacrament of the Kingdom. Therefore its structure — hierarchical, sacramental, liturgical — has no other function than to make the Church ever capable of fulfilling itself as the Body of Christ, as the Temple of the Holy Spirit, to actualize its very nature as grace. For the God-given fullness of the Church, or rather the Church as fullness — and this is an essential aspect of Orthodox ecclesiology — cannot be manifested outside these ecclesiastical structures. There is no separation, no division, between the Church invisible (*in statu patriae*) and the visible Church (*in statu viae*), the latter being the expression and the actualization of the former, the sacramental sign of its reality. Hence the unique, the central, ecclesiological significance of the Eucharist, which is the all-embracing sacrament of the Church. In the Eucharist "the Church becomes what it is," fulfills itself as the Body of Christ, as the divine *parousia* — the presence and the communication of Christ and of His Kingdom. Orthodox ecclesiology is indeed eucharistic ecclesiology. For in the Eucharist the Church accomplishes the *passage* from this world into the world to come, into the *eschaton*; participates in the ascension of its Lord and in His messianic banquet, tastes of the "joy and peace" of the Kingdom. "And Thou didst not cease to do all things until Thou hadst brought us back to heaven, and hadst endowed us with Thy kingdom...." (eucharistic prayer in the Liturgy of St. John Chrysostom). Thus the whole life of the Church is rooted in the Eucharist, is the fruition of this eucharistic fullness in the time of this world whose "image passeth by...." This is indeed the *mission* of the Church.

The Church is also *human response* to the divine gift, its acceptance and appropriation by man and humanity. If the order of the Church is shaped and conditioned by the eschatological fullness of the gift, is its sacramental sign, it is the acceptance of the gift and the growth into its fullness that is the purpose of the Christian community. The Church is fullness, and the Church is also increase and growth in faith and love, knowledge and *koinônia*. This response has two aspects, neither of which can be separated from the other, because they condition each other and together constitute the dynamics of Christian life and action. The first one is *God-centered:* it is the sanctification, the growth in holiness, of both the Christian individual and the Christian community, the "acquisition by them of the Holy Spirit," as the ultimate goal of Christian life as defined by one of the last and greatest of Orthodox saints, St. Seraphim of Sarov (d. 1836). It is the slow transformation of the old Adam in us into the new one, the restoration of the pristine beauty which was lost in sin, the illumination with the uncreated light of Mount Tabor. It is also the slow victory over the demonic powers of the cosmos, the "joy and peace" which *hinc et nunc* make us partakers of the Kingdom and of life eternal. The Orthodox spiritual tradition has always stressed the mystical nature of Christian life, as life "hidden with Christ in God." And the great monastic movement, which started in the fourth century after the Church was officially recognized by the Roman Empire, given a "status" in this world, was nothing else but a new expression of the early Christian eschatologism, the affirmation of Christianity as belonging ontologically to the life of the "world to come," the negation of any permanent home and identification in this world.

The second aspect of the Church as *response* is *man- or world-centered.* It is the understanding of the Church as being left in this world, in its time, space and history, with a specific task or mission: "to walk in the same way in which He walked" (I John 2:6). The Church is fullness and its home is in heaven. But this fullness is given to the world, sent into the world as its salvation and redemption. The eschatological nature of the Church is not the negation of the world, but, on the contrary, its affirmation and acceptance as the object of divine love. Or, in other terms, the entire "other-worldliness" of the Church is nothing but the sign and the reality of the love of God for this world, the very condition of the Church's mission to the world. The Church thus is not a "self-centered" community but precisely a missionary community, whose purpose is salvation not from, but of, the world. In the Orthodox experience and faith it is the Church-sacrament that makes possible the Church-mission.

4.

We can try now to formulate with more precision the various aspects of the "missionary imperative" as it is implied in the Orthodox experience of the Church. This imperative is the essential expression of the Church as gift and fullness, its projection in the time and space of this world. For if, on the one hand, nothing can be *added* to the Church — its fullness is that of Christ Himself — the manifestation and the communication of this fullness constitute, on the other hand, the very life of the Church in this "aeon." On the day of Pentecost, when the fullness of the Church was realized once for all, the *time of the Church* began, the last and the crucial segment of the history of salvation. Ontologically the only *newness* and, therefore, the only *soteriological content* of this segment is precisely *mission:* the proclamation and the communication of the *eschaton*, which is already the being of the Church and indeed its only being. It is the Church as mission that gives to this time its real significance and to history its meaning. And it is mission that gives to the human response in the Church its validity, makes us real co-workers in the work of Christ.

Nothing reveals better the relation between the Church as fullness and the Church as mission than the Eucharist, the central act of the Church's *leitourgia*, the sacrament of the Church itself. There are two complementary movements in the eucharistic rite: *the movement of ascension* and the *movement of return*. The Eucharist begins as an ascension toward the throne of God, toward the Kingdom. "Let us now lay aside all earthly cares," says the offertory hymn, and we prepare ourselves to ascend into heaven with Christ and in Christ, and to offer in Him — His Eucharist. This first movement, which finds its fulfillment in the consecration of the elements, the sign of the acceptance by God of our Eucharist, is, to be sure, already an act of mission. The Eucharist is offered "on behalf of all and for all," it is the fulfillment by the Church of its priestly function: the reconciliation of the whole creation with God, the sacrifice of the whole world to God, the intercession for the whole world before God. All this *in Christ*, the God-man, the unique priest of the new creation, the "one who offers and the one who is offered. . . ." But this is accomplished by a total separation of the Church from the world ("The doors, the doors!" proclaims the deacon as the eucharistic prayer begins), by its ascension to heaven, its entrance into the new "aeon." And then, precisely at the moment when this state of fullness has been reached and consummated at the table of the Lord in His Kingdom, when "we have seen the true light and partaken of the heavenly Spirit," the second movement begins — that of *return into the world.* "Let us depart in peace," says the celebrant as he leaves the altar and leads the congregation outside the temple — and this is the last, the ultimate, commandment. The Eucharist is always the End, the sacrament of the *parousia*, and yet it is always the *beginning*, the *starting point:* now mission begins. "We have seen the true light, we have enjoyed life eternal," but this life, this light, are given to us in order to "transform" us into Christ's witnesses in this world. Without this ascension into the Kingdom we would have had nothing to witness to. Now, having once more become "His people and His inheritance," we can do what Christ wants us to do: "You are witnesses of these things" (Luke 24:48). The Eucharist, transforming "the Church into what it is," transforms it into mission.

5.

What are the objects, the goals, of mission? The Orthodox Church answers without hesitation: these objects are *man* and *world* — not man alone, in an artificially "religious" isolation from the world, and not "world" as an entity of which man would be nothing but "part." Man not only comes first but is indeed the essential object of mission. And yet the Orthodox

idea of evangelism is free from individualistic and spiritualistic connotations. The Church, the sacrament of Christ, is
not a "religious" society of converts, an organization to satisfy
the "religious" needs of man. It is *new life* and redeems therefore the whole life, the total being of man. And this whole
life of man is precisely the world in which and by which he
lives. Through man the Church saves and redeems the world.
One can say that "this world" is saved and redeemed every
time a man responds to the divine gift, accepts it and lives by
it. This does not transform the world into the Kingdom or
the society into the Church. The ontological abyss between
the *old* and the *new* remains unchanged and cannot be filled
in this "aeon." The Kingdom is yet *to come*, and the Church
is not *of* this world. And yet this Kingdom to come is already
present, and the Church is fulfilled *in* this world. They are
present not only as "proclamation" but in their very reality,
and through the divine *agape*, which is their fruit, they *perform* all the time the same sacramental transformation of the
old into the *new*, they make possible real action, real "doing"
in this world.

All this gives the mission of the Church a *cosmical* and a
historical dimension that in the Orthodox tradition and experience are essential. State, society, culture, nature itself,
are real *objects* of mission and not a neutral "milieu" in which
the only task of the Church is to preserve its own inner freedom, to maintain its "religious life." It would require a whole
volume to tell the story of the Orthodox Church from this
point of view: of its concrete *participation* in the societies
and cultures of which Orthodoxy became the total expression
of their whole existence; of its *identification* with nations
and peoples, yet without betrayal of its "other-worldliness,"
of the eschatological communion with the heavenly Jerusalem.
It would require a long theological analysis to express adequately the Orthodox idea of the *sanctification of matter*, or
precisely the cosmical aspect of its sacramental vision. Here
we can only state that all this is the object of Christian mission, because all this is assumed and offered to God in the
sacrament. In the world of the incarnation, nothing "neutral"
remains, nothing can be taken away from the Son of Man.

XII

THE WORLD AS SACRAMENT

Let me insist, first of all, upon the tentative nature of this essay. Our subject here is one that is only now beginning to be studied, and I am in no position to offer any kind of final thesis; rather, I see myself as taking part in our common search for the light — a search that will one day, perhaps, lead us to concrete and consistent conclusions, but not yet. I am weary of those speeches and articles that propose to solve all problems once and for all with neat ready-made answers: we find them even in connection with the liturgical movement, even when a subject like this comes up for discussion — "The World as Sacrament" — a subject that surely ought to make us move very cautiously and tentatively indeed. My own thoughts have achieved neither certainty nor finality. I only feel sure that this kind of subject has enormous importance for Christian theology.

Although I use the word "theology," this is not going to be a theological essay — at least not if by theology we imply "definitions." It seems to me a great tragedy that in the past, sacramental reality should so often have been made the object of clear definitions after the juridical model — definitions so lucid and thin that they tended to obscure and even to diminish the things defined. We are concerned with that reality itself, newly rediscovered. My own approach to it is by way of my own tradition — the liturgical experience, the living tradition of the Eastern Orthodox Church — and only in a secondary way through the formal theology derived from that tradition.

* A paper read at the meeting of the Catholic Art Society, Georgetown University, June 1964, and originally published in *The Cosmic Piety: Modern Man and the Meaning of the Universe*, ed. by Christopher Derrick (P. J. Kennedy and Sons, New York, 1965), pp. 119-130.

And I am raising questions, not proclaiming answers.

Let me begin with my title: a rich phrase, drawing together the two great preoccupations of Christian thought and activity today. "World" and "sacrament": here we have two great concerns, the two objects that outstandingly engage our thinking and acting as Christians in the world of today.

It hardly needs to be stressed that our time is marked by a new degree of concern for the world; this is at the forefront of our modern consciousness. I find it, for example, explicit in Pope Paul VI's encyclical *Ecclesiam Suam*, and in the very idea of "dialogue" as well. This point of view has been gaining ground for decades: the idea that the Church exists to save the whole world, not merely to satisfy the religious needs of the individual, narrowly conceived. This hardly needs saying today.

On the other hand, and of equal importance, we are experiencing something in the nature of a complete rediscovery of the sacramental nature of Christian life. This is not merely a renewed insistence upon the importance of particular sacramental acts in the life of the individual. That is most necessary, but we are going further, to reassert a sacramental character in the whole of life.

Thus when we bring together the two words "world" and "sacrament," we can see in sharp focus two basic tendencies of our time — two aspects, perhaps, of a single tendency; and this is an exercise not wholly original, perhaps, but still worth attempting. A perspective is needed, a frame of vision to help the thought and work of the future. What *is* the relationship between these two concepts, these two realities, world and sacrament? If we gain some new insight into the sacramental nature of Christian life, will that help us to understand the world? If we develop a greater degree of concern for the world, will that deepen our experience and understanding of the sacraments?

But before attempting a synthesis along these lines, we should perhaps focus our attention on each of the terms separately. In the long history of Christian theology and spirituality, people have spoken of "the world" in two ways, both of them well rooted in the Gospel. On the one hand, we say that "God so loved the world that He gave His only-begotten Son"; that the eucharistic sacrifice is an act of giving for the sake of the world; that the world is an object of divine love, divine creation, divine care; that it is to be saved, transfigured, transformed. But in another sense, and with equal authority in Scriptures and church Tradition, we speak of the world negatively: it is the thing we must leave, a prison from which we must be free, God's rival, deceptively claiming our love with its pride and its lust.

No doubt I am oversimplifying here, but it seems to me that the true Christian experience involves some kind of synthesis between these two visions of "the world." The negative vision is very positive in a spiritual sense; that is to say, it is genuinely necessary to leave the world, to cultivate detachment and freedom from it. But this detachment develops too easily into a kind of indifference, a lack of regard for God's creation; gradually the Church becomes aware of this tendency and corrects it by a renewed emphasis upon concern for the world and its goodness.

Today, we are very plainly at the second stage of this cycle, increasingly involved in the world and its affairs. Perhaps we go too far; there is certainly this danger. We find it suggested in certain quarters that we should drop the ideas of God and religion completely, so as to devote ourselves more wholly to the world and to others, living as men in the world of men. In "honesty to God," we are asked to dismiss Him: so far has the pendulum swung from self-centered pietism.

That is where we find ourselves today — and we must insist again that both views of the matter are rooted in revelation and the experience of the Church. If we chose one of them and pushed it to its logical extreme, ignoring the other, we would end up in heresy: the original Greek sense of that word refers to error based on false choice, to mistaken selectivity. If we insist upon choosing where we ought to effect a synthesis or reconciliation, we shall tend toward heresy.

Here, then, we must reconcile and synthesize. Acceptance of the world is more than justifiable, it is necessary. There can be no Christianity where the world is not seen as an object of divine love. On the other hand, there is every justification for that detachment, that abandonment of the world so heavily stressed in the ascetical tradition. To effect a living synthesis between these two principles is, precisely, to define the Christian attitude to the world; and one of my chief purposes in this essay is to suggest that we cannot effect this synthesis or see this wholeness, we cannot do full justice to both Christian visions of the world, unless we come to see the world as sacrament, and ourselves and our whole created environment in sacramental terms.

Where the sacramental itself is concerned, we can make a similar approach, and we shall discover a similar need for synthesis. In all our various Christian traditions, we are taught to think of the sacramental as existing first and primarily in the form of a particular and fixed number of *sacraments,* these being conceived as more or less isolated acts of the Church, and concerned principally with the personal needs of the individual Christian. In some traditions there are seven of these acts, in others two; but theology and piety alike have always tended to concentrate upon one thing — the grace which these acts offer to individuals.

Unfortunately, this kind of concern with the sacraments, valid and indeed necessary though it has been, has tended to be self-defeating. Theorizing about isolated sacramental acts, we lost the sacramental sense in general. The number of these acts, their institution, the conditions of their validity and so on — we asked those questions in too narrow and concentrated a fashion, so that everything else became nonsacramental in our minds.

Consider baptism, for example. We all agree that water is necessary for ordinary baptism: but how often does one feel that a classical theologian really likes water, has ever really noticed what it is? There is a real question here. Why should *water* be chosen as the matter for this sacrament? What is so special about water? — or (in the case of another sacrament) about bread and wine? Such questions have been pushed to one side: in considering the matter of the sacraments, the theologians have tended to display a minimizing and reluctant frame of mind, concerning themselves too anxiously with the minimal requirements of mere validity, with the smallest possible trickle of water, with wine measured in drops, with the faintest possible smear of oil. We seem to have wandered very far from the holy materialism ("God so loved the world . . .") upon which Christian spirituality ought to be based.

Certainly there has been concentration upon grace instead. But in this situation, the idea of grace itself suffered loss. We stopped thinking of the coming of the Spirit, of the huge wind from heaven. We thought instead of something small, something attenuated and weak, something to be defined legally and measured out in small doses. God gives His grace in a great torrent, not to be measured by men; and yet, down the centuries, theology seems to have concentrated upon measuring it, and — inevitably — upon reducing it to something that men might hope to measure. What kind of grace was it? Was it preventing grace, sanctifying grace, efficacious grace? Where was it to be found in the official, numbered list?

This frame of mind, this approach has had its day. It can hardly survive in the new atmosphere generated by the liturgical movement and the recovered theological insights of our time. A new vision of these matters is necessary. It may not come immediately in any final form, but we must work toward it, relating faith and theology once again to worship, claiming the *lex orandi* back from the dry hands of the antiquarians and reestablishing it as the fertile soil in which (and nowhere else) the *lex credendi* can fruitfully grow.

Think of the eve of the Epiphany in some Orthodox church in a Greek or Russian village, a simple, unsophisticated place. After Vespers, water is blessed: this makes the climax of the feast, and the people rush for that water, clamor for it. Why? Not for any dry, theoretical reason. Surely they see here some possibility of communion with the sacramental world, some healing of man's estrangement from the good creation. An experience of that kind lies close to the center of what I am trying to say.

Let me try to come closer, by way of the greatest of the sacraments, by asking how the world is related to the Eucharist. This is a small particular part of a very large subject; if in this context I ignore other aspects of eucharistic theology,

it is not because I am ignorant of them or consider them unimportant. Classical theology — scholastic theology in particular — has had much to say about the Eucharist, and very
fruitfully; but this question of the world in the Eucharist has
been neglected.

Under an impulse theological rather than liturgical, we
have tended to concentrate on the great moment of change:
when, how is the bread changed into Christ's body, the wine
into His blood? And our attention has been deflected, therefore, from what was there before that moment.

Only bread and wine: very ordinary things. And in all
liturgies, ancient and modern, a brief great moment comes
when those very ordinary things are being offered to God
while still retaining their ordinary and natural character. We
take two things out of our daily and secular world, and place
them apart on the altar.

Consider the bread and wine at that moment. What are
they there for? We can, of course, look on them as mere raw
material, mere instruments for the coming of grace. In that
case, their particular character and origin will be unimportant.
But we shall miss the point if we think along those lines.
The Church insists that the bread must be bread and the wine
must be wine. Why?

These things placed upon the altar acquire thereby a
separate and sacred character. They stand close to the veil
that separates our world, our daily experience from God's
life, and soon they pass through that veil. But it is bread and
wine that make that transition, and they do so not merely as
fruits of this world — of this cornfield, that vineyard — but as
symbols and even as vehicles of the whole world itself in its
entirety.

One could quote widely from Christian sources to illus-
trate this point, that according to the mind of the Church our
initial offering in the Eucharist is not merely of two things
but also of our whole world, our whole life in all its dimensions. A great Russian poet — not a church-goer — once said:
"Every time the priest celebrates the Eucharist, he holds in
his hands the whole world, like an apple."

This is not only symbolic, it is hard rational fact. Our

world breeds life; by the chemistry of growth, bread is nourished up out of dead minerals; our own life depends upon
that bread; the "dead" world becomes our body, our life. If
we are to consider the whole world as something sacramental,
it must be initially because of this transformation which is
happening all the time. When we offer bread and wine and
place them on the altar, not only is our act relevant to Christ's
offering two thousand years ago, but we are also relating that
offering to the facts, the physical basis of our human condition
as it has existed from the very beginning.

Any such thought of our first beginning takes us back at
once to Genesis, to Adam and Eve, to creation, to God. Let
us not be sidetracked into worries about historicity. The real
point here concerns the human condition as God has revealed
it. And here, in the first chapters of Genesis, we find a clear
statement of this sacramental character in the world. God
made the world, and then man; and he gave the world to man
to eat and drink. The world was God's gift to us, existing
not for its own sake but in order to be transformed, to become
life, and so to be offered back as man's gift to God.

In our ecclesiastical training, much stress is always laid
on the priest's difference from ordinary men, on the supernatural character of his function. True; but in such matters,
we should perhaps understand the "supernatural" as being the
natural in an extraordinary degree. Man was created as a
priest: the world was created as the matter of a sacrament.
But sin came, breaking this unity: this was no mere issue of
broken rules alone, but rather the loss of a vision, the abandonment of a sacrament. Fallen man saw the world as one
thing, secular and profane, and religion as something entirely
separate, private, remote and "spiritual." The sacramental
sense of the world was lost. Man forgot the priesthood which
was the purpose and meaning of his life. He came to see himself as a dying organism in a cold, alien universe.

Turning again to the Eucharist with this picture in mind,
we see it as the simple original act, the human act which man
failed to perform, now restored however by the new Adam,
the perfect man. It is not simply an arbitrary means toward a

private and limited relationship with God. It is a new creation in Christ of the whole world.

We are in a position now to see the duality in the Christian idea of sacrament, corresponding to the duality — discussed earlier — in the Christian idea of the world. On the one hand, sacrament is rooted in the nature of the world as created by God: it is always a restoration of the original pattern of things. On the other hand, it is rooted in Christ personally. Only through the perfect man can the broken priesthood of humanity be restored. Only through Him can the dark, primordial ocean become the living waters of baptism. Only by way of His cross can the dead world come to new life. Our task remains, but He has gone before, doing the hard work for us. If we kneel to pray, to adore, to offer our lives, we are only attaching ourselves and assenting to His own similar but all-embracing act.

Why can there be no new sacrifice in the Christian dispensation? Not merely because Christ's sacrifice was (as juridical theologians say) perfect. Perfect, in many senses, it certainly was — not least, in embracing all things. After that particular act, there was simply nothing left in the universe that could be offered to God in any first and original fashion. It had all been done.

If, therefore, we remember our nature and our origins, we shall see in that bread and wine placed upon the altar not merely our individual selves but the whole world, and we shall then see them — immediately — in their final point and consummation. We place ourselves and the world upon the altar, then take a second look at them, and see there Christ: He stands at the center and offers all to the Father.

That moment of change deserves a kind of attention that it seldom gets. What *happens* at the consecration? Theology has much to say here: I am not rejecting it or criticizing it, but we sometimes overlook some implications of the Preface and the Sanctus, even of the word "Eucharist" itself.

The Preface is always an act of thanksgiving, reaching its climax in that old biblical doxology: "Holy, holy, holy, Lord God of Sabaoth: heaven and earth are full of Thy glory." There might appear to be some incongruity here. We are at the moment of tragedy, of sacrifice: the moment of the broken body and the spilt blood. And we choose that moment, of all moments, to sing a happy song of triumph and delight and gratitude — perhaps with a great choir to prolong and emphasize the joy of the moment.

There is no incongruity here, nor inadvertence. Here again there is a need for reconciliation and synthesis: only thus, and only at that moment, do we rediscover and see the whole truth about the world. It is a world of sin and suffering and grief; Christian optimism cannot deny this, seeing rather the bloodstained cross as its essential and characteristic representation. But it is also a holy and happy world, something freely given to us by divine love, and the synthesis is effected in Christ's offering, in his suffering and final victory.

And so the Eucharist is not simply a way of discharging our duty of thanks to God, although it is that as well. It is not merely one possible relationship to God. It is rather the only possible holding together — in one moment, in one act — of the *whole* truth about God and man. It is the sacrament of the world sinful and suffering, the sky darkened, the tortured Man dying: but it is also the sacrament of the change, His transfiguration, His rising, His Kingdom. In one sense we look back, giving thanks for the simple goodness of God's original gift to us. In another sense we look forward, eschatologically, to the ultimate repair and transfiguration of that gift, to its last consummation in Christ.

With such an exploration of the Eucharist in depth, liturgical theology is very emphatically concerned; and it does involve a new kind of attention to the materials involved, to water and bread and wine and the whole world, the whole of created reality. God orders a kind of materialism, not as a concession to our weakness, but in order to teach us something about the world given to us, and therefore about His own love for us.

It may be a mistake for us to dwell too seriously upon nature and supernature in sharp distinction, as though our natural life were something ignoble, apart from occasional visitations from above. Christ never spoke of the natural and the supernatural. He spoke rather of the old and the new,

and especially of the renovation of the old. Sacrament is movement, transition, passage, Pascha: Christ knows the way and
guides us, going before. The world, condemned in its old
nature, revealed as life eternal in its new nature, is still the
same world, God's good work. Christ came to save it, not to
allow us means of thankful escape before it was discarded as
rubbish. Thoughts of "the life to come" can be misleading.
In a sense, we have no other world to live in but this, although
the mode of our occupying it, our whole relationship to space
and time (*tota ac simul possessio*) will be very different when
we are risen again in Christ.

If, then, our attention is to be given more seriously —
and even, in a carefully defined sense, wholly — to this world,
that does not mean that we are committed to "worldliness"
in the other sense of that twofold idea. We are not to suppose
that when jets can fly faster, when doctors can save more lives,
Congress will be able to certify that the Kingdom of God has
begun. Rather the reverse. The more deeply we think in
eucharistic and therefore in eschatological terms, the more
acutely we shall be aware that the fashion of this world passeth away, that things only acquire point and meaning and
reality in their relationship to Christ's coming in glory. In this
context, the unworldliness and detachment preached by so
many moralists return to their full importance.

Our lives are congested and noisy. It is easy to think of the
Church and the sacraments as competing for our attention
with the other world of daily life, leading us off into some
other life — secret, rarefied and remote. We might do better
to think of that practical daily world as something incompre-
hensible and unmanageable unless and until we can approach
it sacramentally through Christ. Nature and the world are
otherwise beyond our grasp; time also, time that carries all
things away in a meaningless flux, causing men to despair
unless they see in it the pattern of God's action, reflected in
the liturgical year, the necessary road to the New Jerusalem.

We have a simple task, and a happy one. Some say that
we should concentrate upon this world as though God did not
exist. We say rather that we should concentrate upon this
world lovingly because it is full of God, because by way of the

Eucharist we find Him everywhere — in hideous disasters as well as in little flowers. In a way, it is not supernatural at all; we return to our original nature, to the garden where Adam met God in the cool of the evening. No, we do not meet Him wholly and consciously: we are still fallen, still estranged, and our fallen nature could not at present survive that.

A sacramental correspondence is not an identification. It always points beyond. But it creates also a present unity, making us contemporary witnesses not only of Christ's death but also of His coming again, and of the fulfillment of all things in Him. Thankfully we accept from God's hands His lovely garden, the world. We eat its fruits, transform its substance into life, offer that life to God on Christ's cross and our daily altars, and look forward to the possession of it, as a risen body, in the Kingdom.

But it will be the *same* world, the *same* life. "Behold, I make all things new." These were God's last words to us, and they only say at the end, and eternally, what was in His mind at the very beginning, when He looked on the sacramental world of His creation and saw that it was good.